Voices of the New Feminism

VOICES OF THE NEW FEMINISM

Edited by Mary Lou Thompson

Beacon Press   Boston

First published by Beacon Press in 1970

Second printing, April 1971 (casebound)

First published as a Beacon paperback in 1971

Beacon Press books are published under the auspices of the Unitarian
Universalist Association
Published simultaneously in Canada by Saunders of Toronto, Ltd.
All rights reserved
Printed in the United States of America

Grateful acknowledgment is made to the following for permission to reprint material in this book:

to the *International Socialist Review* for "Pioneers of Women's Liberation," by Joyce Cowley. Reprinted with permission of *International Socialist Review*, 873 Broadway, New York, N.Y. 10003.

to *The Humanist* for "Sex Equality: The Beginnings of Ideology," by
Alice S. Rossi. This article first appeared in *The Humanist*, September/
October, 1969, and is reprinted by permission.

to Harper & Row, Publishers, Inc., for pp. 150–166, *The Church and the
Second Sex*, by Mary Daly. Copyright © 1968 by Mary Daly. Reprinted
by permission of Harper & Row, Publishers, Inc.

to the Swedish Institute for permission to reprint parts of the "Report
to the United Nations, 1968: The Status of Women in Sweden."

to David McKay Company, Inc., for "The Androgynous Life," from
Born Female, by Carolyn Bird. Copyright © 1968 by Carolyn Bird. Used
by permission of David McKay Company, Inc.

Contents

Foreword

Though the media have been much absorbed with what has been called "the new feminist movement," it is still possible to meet both men and women who question whether women have any legitimate complaints of discrimination in employment, education, under law, and in family roles. In this book some strong voices speak out on the inequities confronting women. The writers not only build a case of flagrant injustice to girls and women, but most of them propose a number of remedies which seem reasonably available under our present system, if concerned women—and men—demand them.

The Unitarian Universalist Women's Federation, made up of 18,000 women in the United States and Canada, seeks in this book to provide an educational tool for all women who wish to examine the situation of women in the world today. The book explores the alternatives available in a society that by its very changing nature is providing a far wider choice of life styles than was available even five years ago. One of many factors to be considered is that population pressures and the resulting pollution of the environment cannot be dealt with unless society provides other roles than motherhood for women.

While these authors do not always agree in their theories on the new feminism, each contributes to the general discussion of the changing position of women—and men—in the social revolution of our day.

This is the second book promoted by the UUWF dealing with the condition of women in our time. A first, *American Women: The Changing Image*, edited by Beverly Benner Cassara (1962) was sponsored by the Alliance of Unitarian Women, which in 1963 merged with the Association of Universalist Women to form the UUWF.

My thanks go to the Board and Executive Committee of the UUWF for their encouragement and sponsorship of this book, and to Constance H. Burgess, UUWF Executive Director, for her constructive suggestions. I also wish to acknowledge my debt to an untiring advocate of the civil rights of women, Catherine East, Executive Secretary of the Citizens Commission on the Status of Women of the United States Department of Labor, who has kept me informed on many matters affecting the situation of women. Thanks also to Laura Rasmussen, a UUWF member whose critical advice on the preparation of the book has been helpful; and to Sylvia Berkowitz of the UUWF staff.

Mary Lou Thompson

History

Pioneers of women's liberation

JOYCE COWLEY

The history of earlier feminist movements is relevant to today's New Feminism. At the start of earlier drives for women's rights, only a few strong voices were heard The antislavery movement was a catalyst in helping women realize their own oppression, and it is ironical that this realization came from being excluded from abolitionist meetings controlled by men.

Chance happenings of history affected the drive for women's rights. In the United States the pioneer experience hastened the day when some states extended suffrage for women, with Wyoming the first to grant the vote. After the Civil War, the extension of suffrage to the black male seemed to be an adequate concession, the white American man decided, as he left disfranchised at least one-half of the Negroes in America.

The violence that attended the suffrage movement in England perhaps tells us that frustration and anger are explosive qualities in the women's movement, as in all revolutions.

The push in both countries was primarily for legal rights— the right to vote, the right to custody of children, the right to control their own property. The drive for equal opportunities in employment is largely a twentieth-century phenomenon, now that nearly 40 per cent of the labor force is made up of women.

The story of the women's rights movement should be a part of history books and curriculum from grade school through college. This introduction will hopefully make that clear, and may lead to further reading.

Joyce Cowley has worked for labor unions and written extensively on the history of the women's rights movement. Her article appeared in The International Socialist Review *and was written in 1955.*

Women got the vote in the United States in 1920. The amendment to the Constitution granting women that right was the climax of a struggle that began almost a hundred years earlier. Suffrage leaders were ridiculed and persecuted while they were alive. Today they are either forgotten or contemptuously referred to as disappointed old maids who hated men. This concept of the women's rights movement as a war against men by sexually frustrated women is even accepted by some modern psychiatrists. But it is historically inaccurate and a great injustice to a number of truly remarkable women.

The status of women in society began to change with the breakdown of feudalism and the rise of capitalism. In the sixteenth and seventeenth centuries in England, women first entered trades. They were frequently partners in the husband's business; widows and daughters carried on the family business. There are records of women pawnbrokers, stationers, booksellers, contractors, and even shipowners. In the seventeenth century there were three women to every man in the woolen industry and many women were employed in the silk industry. They also worked in the fields, and the agricultural labor of women was an important factor in the new American colonies.

The "woman question" was discussed as early as the Elizabethan period, but this talk did not develop into an organized movement. It was in 1792 that Mary Wollstonecraft wrote the *Vindication of the Rights of Woman* which, historically, marks the conscious beginning of the struggle for women's rights. This book was a direct reflection of Mary Wollstonecraft's sympathies with the French and American revolutions, a demand that women's rights be included in the rights of man for which the revolutionists were fighting.

It was in America, not England, that the woman question first developed into an organized movement rather than a subject of discussion in literary circles. This reflects the more advanced position of women in the American colonies, which was strikingly different from that of women in Europe. The laws of the colonies, modeled on those of England, gave women few legal rights. But the realities of pioneer life, particularly the scarcity of women and the appreciation of their skills, meant that they actually had a great deal of responsibility, engaged in numerous occupations that were supposedly "masculine" and consequently enjoyed rights and privileges, and a degree of freedom, unknown to women in England.

The Puritan concept of work further influenced the general attitude toward women's activities. In their moral code, work was something you could never get too much of and they did not disapprove of women working; on the contrary, they encouraged it. It made no difference whether the woman was married or not; the more she worked the better, and the less likely she was to succumb to the temptations of the devil.

In the colonial period women could vote, and sometimes did vote, as the right to vote was based on ownership of property and not on sex. They were gradually disfranchised by laws prohibiting women from voting—in Virginia in 1699, New York, 1777, Massachusetts, 1780, New Hampshire, 1784, and New Jersey, 1807.

At that time men engaged in agriculture and women in home manufacture. Women made most of the products used by the colonists that were not imported. The preponderance of women in the earliest factories in the United States is due largely to the fact that their work was transferred from the home to the factory. This was particularly true of the first major industry, the spinning and weaving of cotton, and accounts for the prominent role of women in early labor struggles, especially the fight of cotton-mill workers for the ten-hour day.

The women's rights movement, however, did not grow out of the trade-union struggles of women. It was never closely associated with trade-union activities nor particularly interested in the problems of working women. This may seem contradictory unless you keep in mind that the women's movement was primarily a fight for legal, not economic, rights. The legal battle of the suffragists has been won, but in the twentieth century women still face severe discrimination in wages and job opportunities.

ANTISLAVERY AND WOMEN'S RIGHTS

The women's rights movement *did* spring directly from the abolitionist movement. Every prominent fighter for women's rights was *first* an abolitionist; and the two movements were closely allied for fifty years, although the "woman question" frequently caused division in the abolitionist ranks, as the Negro cause became more respectable and more popular than that of women.

Just how did the antislavery movement give birth to the struggle for women's rights? There is a simple explanation for what may seem at first a surprising evolution. Women who started out to plead for the slave found they were not allowed to plead. They were ridiculed when they appeared on a speakers' platform, they were not accepted as delegates when they attended antislavery conventions. Within a short time, most of the women prominent in abolitionist circles spoke up for their own rights, too, although a formal organization advocating complete legal equality and suffrage was not formed for another twenty years.

A number of misconceptions about the pioneers for women's rights are prevalent. In the first place, it is assumed that they were all women—women united in a war against men. The truth is *men* were in the forefront of the struggle for women's rights, notably such spokesmen as William Lloyd Garrison, Frederick Douglass, and Wendell Phillips. They were attacked even more viciously than the women and labelled "hermaphrodites" and "Aunt Nancy men."

Furthermore, none of the women in this movement was exclusively preoccupied with sex equality and women's problems. They were, as I said, invariably abolitionists and frequently advocated a great many other reforms—the Utopian variety of socialism, trade unions, atheism, temperance, free love, birth control, and easier divorce. Many of these causes were not too popular in the early part of the last century, and this accounts to some extent for the common opinion that these women were freaks and probably immoral.

It is not true that most of the feminist leaders were either libertines or embittered virgins. With the exception of Susan B. Anthony, the best known—Lucretia Mott, Elizabeth Cady Stanton, Lucy Stone, Carrie Chapman Catt—were happily married. Mrs. Mott and Mrs. Stanton, founders of the movement, were mothers of large families. They did *not* marry weak husbands who were dominated by their crusading wives. The husbands were generally men of outstanding ability and achievement, enthusiastic supporters of the women's cause. The only reason they were to some extent overshadowed by their wives was that the unusual activities of the wives attracted a good deal of attention.

Frances Wright was probably the first woman to speak publicly in this country and to advocate women's rights. She was Scottish, coming to America in 1818. Brilliant and courageous, she was also one of the extremists, exactly the type who was slandered and laughed at, but never ignored. Among numerous other activities, she founded a colony primarily intended to set an example of how to free slaves and give them economic independence. But she was an opponent of marriage and her colony became more famous for its open repudiation of this institution than for any service to the Negro cause.

Opposition to marriage was common among the early advocates of freedom for women. They saw in it—quite correctly, in my opinion—an institution designed for the subjugation of their sex. In those days a married woman had no right to own property; her wages belonged to her husband and so did her children. The simplest way to avoid these evils was to stay single.

In spite of their audacity, these women frequently surrendered to local pressure. Mary Wollstonecraft gave birth to one illegitimate child; but when she became pregnant a second time by another lover, she found the struggle too difficult and married him. Frances Wright and her sister both married for the same reason—they were pregnant.

The sex question explains a lot about the notoriety associated

with the first feminist leaders. As the movement grew and became more respectable, it attempted to dissociate itself from ad-
vocacy of "free love," but was never completely successful.

About the same time that Frances Wright founded her well-
publicized colony, Lucretia Mott became a Quaker minister.
She is one of the most striking personalities in the women's
rights movement. Of unusual intellect and breadth of vision, she
studied intensively and was an active lecturer and organizer for
fifty years. She supported trade unions when they were almost
unknown and generally illegal, which was rare among abolitionist leaders, who seemed to think there was some kind of conflict
between the two movements. She also raised six children and
apparently enjoyed domestic activities like cooking and sewing,
although you wonder as you read her biography how she found
time for them.

She was at the meeting held in Philadelphia in 1833 where the
first antislavery group was organized and from which the
American Anti-Slavery Society developed. Although she spoke
several times during the convention and played an influential
role, it did not occur to her to sign the Declaration that was
adopted. Samuel May, in his reminiscences, wrote: "Men were
so blind, so obtuse, they did not recognize the women guests as
members of the convention."

Lucretia's next step was to form a Women's Anti-Slavery Society, but the women were so ignorant of parliamentary procedure that they found it necessary to get a man to chair the
meeting—James McCrummel, an educated Negro. The brazen
conduct of women in forming this society was attacked by clergymen as an "act of flagrant sedition against God." While
women were clothing and feeding the Negro on his way to
Canada, "clergymen huddled in churches and wrung their
hands, forecasting the doom of the American home and the
good old traditions."

Five years after the Women's Anti-Slavery Society was organized, it held a convention in Pennsylvania Hall, a public
building recently dedicated_to "liberty and the rights of man."
While the delegates conducted their business, a mob surrounded
the hall. Stones were thrown at the windows, breaking pane

after pane, and vitriol was hurled through the gaping holes, while a cry rose, "Burn the hall!" Two or three hours after the women vacated the hall, it went up in flames.

That night Philadelphia was in an uproar. The mayor wanted to stop abolitionist activities and police protection was nonexistent. The mob headed for the home of James and Lucretia Mott. There was a period of tense waiting inside the house while the yells and turmoil in the street grew closer. But as the minutes passed, the noise seemed to recede and gradually fade into the distance. The next day they learned that a friend had joined the mob and when they were within a block of the house, he flourished a stick and cried, "On to the Motts!" then led them up a succession of wrong streets. This was one of many similar incidents for Lucretia Mott, and her calm composure in a riot became legendary.

Sarah and Angelina Grimke, aristocratic women from the South, were among the earliest speakers and organizers of the abolitionist movement. I came across an interesting quotation from a speech by Angelina Grimke delivered before a Massachusetts legislative committee in 1832:

> As a moral being I feel I owe it to the slave and the
> master, to my countrymen and to the world, to do all
> that I can to overturn a system of complicated crimes
> built upon the broken hearts and prostrate bodies of
> my countrymen in chains and cemented by the blood,
> sweat and tears of my sisters in bond.

Evidently Churchill knew a good phrase when he saw it.

Factional struggles inside the abolitionist movement led Lucretia Mott and Elizabeth Cady Stanton to call a convention for women's rights in 1848.

Eight years earlier, a fight had taken place over the election of a woman to a business committee of the American Anti-Slavery Society. The vote was favorable to the candidate, Abby Kelly; and the antiwoman group seceded from the organization and formed their own antislavery society. A world-wide antislavery convention had been called in London. Purged of its reac-

tionary elements, the American Anti-Slavery Society elected
Lucretia and two other women to their executive committee
and chose her and Charles Remond, a Negro, as delegates to the
London convention. Lucretia also headed the delegation from
the Women's Anti-Slavery Society.

Another delegation—100 per cent male, of course—was sent
by the newly formed organization. In London every effort was
made to keep peace by persuading the women delegates to
withhold their credentials, but Lucretia insisted that the responsibility for rejection must rest with the convention.

Wendell Phillips opened the fight on the convention floor by
proposing that all persons with credentials be seated. He pointed
out that the convention's invitation had been addressed to all
friends of the slave, and Massachusetts had interpreted this to
mean men *and* women. Clergymen at the convention were
particularly eloquent in their opposition to seating women.
"Learned Doctors of Divinity raced about the convention hall
Bible in hand, quoting words of scripture and waving their fists
beneath the noses of disputing brethren who did not know
woman's place."

The reactionaries won. Women were admitted as guests only
and seated behind a curtain which screened them from public
gaze. Garrison, the greatest figure in the abolitionist world, was
scheduled to be the main speaker. On his arrival he climbed the
stairs to the women's balcony, sat beside Lucretia behind the
curtain, and remained there until the close of the convention.

It was on this trip to England that Lucretia met Elizabeth
Cady Stanton, a young bride of one of the delegates. It was here
that they decided to start a crusade for women's rights on their
return to America, although eight years passed before they
were able to carry out their plans and call the Seneca Falls Convention of 1848.

WOMEN ORGANIZE

This Equal Rights Convention, the first ever held in any
country, was the official beginning of the suffrage struggle. The
first day of the convention had been advertised as open to

women only. When the women arrived at the Unitarian church they found they were locked out. A young professor climbed through a window and opened the door for them. On the spot, they decided to admit men, which turned out to be a fortunate decision for the suffrage cause.

James Mott was chairman of the meeting, as the women were still timid and did not know too much about parliamentary procedure. The Declaration of Sentiments adopted by the convention was signed by sixty-eight women and thirty-two men. The resolutions called for complete equality in marriage, equal rights in property, wages, and custody of children, the right to make contracts, to sue and be sued, to testify in court—and to vote.

Elizabeth Cady Stanton introduced the suffrage amendment. It was opposed by Lucretia Mott because she considered it too radical and thought it would arouse public antagonism and ridicule. Frederick Douglass seconded Mrs. Stanton's motion and made one of the most eloquent speeches in history for woman's equality and her right to vote. His speech inspired the women to overcome their hesitation and pass the suffrage resolution. Within a year a National Woman's Rights Association was organized and state and national conventions were held regularly.

The women's movement was met with a storm of abuse, particularly from the clergy, although a great many men just considered it funny. Within a few years, as it gained momentum, it met more serious opposition. Opponents of suffrage were divided as to whether the population would decrease because women were unsexed or illegitimately increase because of the practice of free love.

A typical example of the antisuffrage point of view appears in a book by Dr. L. P. Brockett, quoted at some length in Hare's biography of Lucretia Mott. It gives a picture of just what would happen if women were allowed to vote and declares it will be a gala day for the prostitutes, as "modest refined-Christian women" would refuse to go to the polls in such company. Hare paraphrases the book:

> What a lesson of evil would be taught children on that day. Imagine the innocent offspring, clutching its

mother as it stands in the presence of "poor wretches, bedizened in gaudy finery, with bold, brazen faces, many of them half or wholly drunk and uttering with loud laughter, horrible oaths and ribald and obscene jests! What an impression the child would receive! And if the mother attemped to tell her daughter that these were bad women, the child might query: 'But mother, they are going to vote. If they were so very bad, would they have the same right to vote that you and other ladies have?' Unable to answer so precocious a question, the 'modest, refined Christian mother' would scurry home, leaving the polls to her male representatives and the women of the underworld."

To drive home the lesson, [says Hare] the book is illustrated with a picture showing the refined woman at the polls completely surrounded by a vicious group of derelicts of both sexes. The picture vividly warns any woman who is on the verge of becoming a follower of Lucretia Mott, the type of men and women with whom she must associate if she votes. It also discloses the unintentional fact that the voting male is the uncouth immigrant, the bowery heeler, and the pimp; the same male hailed by opponents of female rights as woman's natural representative in affairs of government. One glance at the men in the picture convinces the reader that woman's benign influence in the home had gone awry, despite this best chosen argument of the anti-suffragettes.

Dr. Brockett also predicts that some disastrous changes will occur in the appearance of women:

The blush of innocence, the timid, half-frightened expression which is, to all right-thinking men a higher charm than the most perfect self-conscious beauty, will disappear and in place of it we shall have hard, self-reliant bold faces, and in which all the loveliness will have faded, and naught remain save the look of power and talent.

The suffrage workers encountered additional ridicule at this time due to the introduction of the Bloomer costume. It was rather strange in appearance, consisting of trousers partly concealed by a full skirt that fell six inches below the knees. Elizabeth Cady Stanton, Lucy Stone, and Susan B. Anthony probably suffered greater martyrdom because of this costume than for any other phase of their crusade, and after a few years they discontinued wearing it, feeling that it did more harm than good. Nevertheless, the outfit did give much greater freedom of action and was adopted by many farm women of the period and recommended by doctors for use in sanitariums. It was the first step toward the freedom of the modern dress.

Mrs. Stanton became one of the most active suffrage leaders and it was in this period that her life-long collaboration with Susan B. Anthony began. She was the mother of five boys and two girls, and whenever her schedule of lectures, conventions, and meetings became too heavy, she would threaten to interrupt it by having another baby. Lucy Stone, now best known as the woman who insisted on keeping her maiden name, also became prominent in the 1850's. Lucy's use of her own name grew out of her original opposition to marriage. When she did marry, the unusual ceremony attracted considerable comment, none of it favorable. She and Henry Blackwell opened the wedding with a statement:

> While we acknowledge our mutual affection by publicly assuming the relation of man and wife, yet in justice to ourselves and a great principle, we deem it a duty to declare that this act on our part implies no sanction of, nor promise of voluntary obedience to, such of the present laws of marriage as refuse to recognize the wife as an independent, rational being while they confer upon the husband an injurious and unnatural superiority, investing him with legal powers which no honorable man would exercise and no man should possess. We protest especially against the laws which give the husband:
>
> 1. The custody of the wife's person.

2. The exclusive control and guardianship of their children.

3. The sole ownership of her personal property and use of her real estate, unless previously settled upon her, or placed in the hands of trustees as in the case of minors, lunatics and idiots.

4. The absolute right to the product of her industry.

They continued with the regular marriage ceremony, omitting the word "obey," but there was a popular feeling, especially since Lucy kept her own name, that they were not really married.

Many Negro women like Harriet Tubman, the extraordinary leader of the underground railway, and Sojourner Truth, also played an active role in the women's rights movement. Tubman is reported to have been an amazingly eloquent speaker, but for reasons of personal safety the speeches were rarely recorded.

Even a bare outline of the lives of these early women leaders arouses admiration. Lecturing for women's rights was not exactly a soft occupation. Traveling was pretty rough then and the reception was likely to be rough, too. These women kept going at a remarkable pace in spite of large families and heavy domestic responsibilities.

Mrs. Stanton wrote most of her speeches after midnight while the children were sleeping—I don't know when she slept. Most of the women continued their work without let-up even when they were in their sixties and seventies. Lucretia Mott was eighty-three when she spoke at the twenty-fifth anniversary of the suffrage association. They were middle-class women but many of them faced economic hardships. Lucy Stone went to Oberlin College—the first to admit women—and worked her way through, sweeping and washing dishes at three cents an hour. Her life as an abolitionist and women's rights speaker was not exactly a cinch either. She lived in a garret in Boston, sleeping three in a bed with the landlady's daughters for six and one-fourth cents a night. Constance Burnett in *Five for Freedom* describes a fairly typical meeting at which she spoke. (She

was the outstanding orator of the women's movement, a real
spellbinder.)

Lucy posted her own meetings, hammering her signs
on trees with tacks carried in her reticule and stones
from the road. The first poster usually drew an army
of young hoodlums who followed her up and down
streets, taunting, flinging small missiles and pulling
down her notices as soon as her back was turned . . .
For her ability to remain unperturbed through
hoots, jeers and murderous assault, she had few equals.
It was a common thing for her to face a rain of spitballs
as soon as she stepped before an audience. Once a hymn
book was flung at her head with such force it almost
stunned her. On another night, in midwinter, icy
water was trained on her from a hose thrust through
a window. Lucy calmly reached for her shawl, wrapped
it around her shoulders and went on talking.
At an open air anti-slavery meeting on Cape Cod,
the temper of the crowd seemed so dangerous that
all the speakers, one after the other, vanished hastily
from the platform. The only two left were Lucy and
Abby Kelly's husband, Stephen Foster, a firebrand
abolitionist of the same mettle from New Hampshire.
Before either of them could get to speak, Lucy
saw the mob begin its advance. "They're coming,
Stephen. You'd better run for it," she warned him
hurriedly.
Stephen no more than Lucy ever ran from danger.
"What about you?" he protested, and with that the
surging, yelling mass was upon them. Overpowered,
Foster disappeared in the melee, and Lucy, suddenly
deserted, looked up into the face of a towering ruffian
with a club.
"This gentleman will take care of me," she suggested
sweetly, taking his arm, and too astonished for words,
he complied. Reasoning calmly with him as he

steered her out of the violence, she won his reluctant admiration and his consent to let her finish her speech. The platform was demolished by then, but he conducted her to a tree stump, rounded up the rest of the "gentlemen" and preserved order with raised club until she was through talking. Lucy gave the whole gang a piece of her mind, not neglecting to collect twenty dollars from them to replace Stephen Foster's coat, which in their gentlemanly exuberance they had split in two.

During the Civil War there was little activity in the women's movement. All of the women were devoted to the abolitionist cause and enthusiastically entered into various types of war work. But the end of the war brought the end of the fifty-year alliance between the woman's cause and the Negro movement.

The split took place when Negro men got the vote. The Republican Party and the Negro leaders were both pressing for passage of the Fourteenth and Fifteenth Amendments to the Constitution to enfranchise Negro men. The Republicans were not particularly interested in Negro rights but they wanted votes. The Democrats, who opposed the Negro vote, now gave lip service to woman suffrage in order to annoy the Republicans and hypocritically charge them with hypocrisy.

Negro leaders argued that this was the "Negro's hour" and it was a matter of practical politics to push through the vote for Negro men while it had a chance of ratification. Adding woman suffrage to the amendment would inevitably result in its defeat. Negro and abolitionist leaders insisted that they were devoted to the woman's cause and would continue to fight for universal suffrage after Negro men got the vote.

Many of the women were embittered by what they considered a sell-out. Elizabeth Cady Stanton, in an argument with Wendell Phillips, said: "May I ask just one question, based on the apparent opposition in which you place the Negro and woman? Do you believe the African race is composed entirely of males?"

For fifty years these women had fought for the abolitionist

cause and they felt that they had won the right to be included in the suffrage amendment. They would not agree to being left out on grounds of political expediency. They got little support and the Fifteenth Amendment was passed, giving the vote to Negro men only.

At the American Equal Rights Association convention in 1869, a formal split occurred, with the majority, the more conservative grouping, supporting the Boston abolitionist wing. Among the majority were Julia Ward Howe and Lucy Stone, who formed the American Woman Suffrage Association. The radical minority, led by Susan B. Anthony and Elizabeth Cady Stanton, organized the National Woman Suffrage Association. For twenty years these two groups remained separate.

As I have indicated, the principal cause of the split was the division of opinion over supporting Negro suffrage while the question of woman suffrage was postponed. I've read some eloquent statements on both sides of this argument. Negro leaders like Frederick Douglass, the first man to speak up for woman suffrage in this country, felt that the Negro cause was jeopardized by the women who selfishly advanced their own demands instead of waiting until it was more "practical" to advocate suffrage for women, too. Women felt this attitude was a great injustice on the part of the abolitionists, showing ingratitude to the women who had fought so long and so courageously for the Negro cause.

In Lucretia Mott's biography there is a description of the Centennial Anniversary of the Declaration of Independence:

> The newly enfranchised citizens appreciated what had been done for them—by *their* sex. Women on the sidewalks watched them carry banner after banner emblazoned with the names of Garrison or Phillips or Douglass. They searched in vain for a tribute to Lucretia Mott, or the author of *Uncle Tom's Cabin*, or any other woman of the anti-slavery conflict.

Both the Negro and the woman's movement were greatly weakened by the split in their ranks and it was another fifty years before women got the vote. In several accounts of this split written by men in sympathy with the Negro side of the argument, the women were held responsible for the delay because extremists in their ranks insisted prematurely on suffrage.

Historically there is not much point in speculating about what would have happened if the Negroes and women had stuck together—how long this would have delayed Negro suffrage (if at all)—and whether or not woman suffrage would have been won at an earlier date. Most Negro men were enfranchised in name only, and even to this day [1955] millions have not been able to exercise their constitutional right to vote. Personally I can't help sympathizing with the women who felt they had been deserted and betrayed. It's unfortunate that the reform movement was split as a result, but I'm not sure this was entirely the fault of a few women "radicals." There were heterogeneous elements in the Equal Rights Association, many of whom felt that their cause, Negro emancipation and enfranchisement, had been won, and it is probable that this conservative element would have broken away in any case.

The history of the woman's movement from this point on, divorced from the other reform struggles for which the women originally fought, becomes a bit dull. It is more bourgeois in character, exclusively concerned as it is with the vote.

Immediately after the passage of the Fifteenth Amendment, Susan B. Anthony decided to test the new law, which was worded in such a way that it might possibly be construed to include women. In Rochester, New York, she and twelve other women armed with a copy of the Constitution demanded the right to vote. The election inspectors were so startled by this move that the women were allowed to cast ballots. They were promptly arrested for voting illegally. Susan was fined $100. She refused to pay the fine, hoping that she would be imprisoned and the case could be carried to the Supreme Court. But the judge was a shrewd politician and did not order her arrest. The fine has not yet been paid.

In the twenty-five years following the Equal Rights Convention of 1848, women achieved many of their original demands.

More and more states passed laws giving married women the right to custody of their children, to disposal of their wages and their property.

Curiously enough, the first and most successful advocates of these laws were men whose interests were threatened. In upstate New York wealthy Dutch fathers-in-law became indignant when their daughters' property was squandered by spendthrift husbands. The Married Women's Property Bill was passed largely through their influence. In one of the Southern states a similar bill was introduced by a man who wanted to marry a wealthy widow. Heavily in debt himself, he knew her property could be attached to pay his debts if they got married. When the bill passed she could keep her property and they could both live comfortably on her income.

The Territory of Wyoming was the first to give women the vote in 1869; Utah followed the next year; Colorado and Idaho a little later. Pioneers in the West, accustomed to women who could load a gun, ride a horse, and run a homestead as competently as a man, were more easily persuaded than Eastern men that women are not frail or feeble-minded. Twenty years later when Wyoming applied for statehood, the fact that women voted there became a political issue. Wyoming declared: "We will remain out of the union one hundred years rather than come in without woman suffrage."

Susan B. Anthony continued to campaign for another thirty years. Her final speech to a Woman's Rights Convention was made in 1904 when she was eighty-six years old. An incident reported in *Five for Freedom* gives some idea of her remarkable energy:

> During this year[1] Susan delivered 171 lectures, besides
> hundreds of impromptu talks. She traveled ceaselessly.
> The journey home through the Rockies in January
> became rugged when her train ran into mountainous
> drifts. Tracks had been recently laid, breakdowns
> were frequent and waits interminable. Passengers
> had nothing to eat but the cold food they had the

[1] Describing a year at the height of her career—Ed.

foresight to bring. Many nights were spent sitting bolt upright.

Susan did get back finally, in time for the annual convention of her National Woman Suffrage Association in the capital.

"You must be tired," they greeted her in Washington. "Why, what should make me tired?" asked Susan. "I haven't been doing anything for two weeks."

The restfulness of transcontinental rail trips in the 1870's was not apparent to others.

By 1900, the suffrage movement had become more powerful, but so had the opposition. The liquor interests, afraid that women would vote for prohibition, poured millions of dollars into campaigns to defeat woman suffrage. In state after state women lost out when the suffrage question came to a popular vote. The following circular published in Portland, Oregon, is an example of how the liquor crowd worked:

It will take 50,000 votes to defeat woman suffrage. There are 2,000 retailers in Oregon. That means that every retailer must himself bring in twenty-five votes on election day.

Every retailer can get twenty-five votes. Besides his employees, he has his grocer, his butcher, his landlord, his laundryman and every person he does business with. If every man in the business will do this, we will win.

We enclose twenty-five ballot tickets showing how to vote.

We also enclose a postal card addressed to this Association. If you will personally take twenty-five friendly voters to the polls on election day and give each one a ticket showing how to vote, please mail the postal card back to us at once. You need not sign the card. Every card has a number and we will know who sent it in.

Let us all pull together and let us all work. Let us each get twenty-five votes.

This was signed by the Brewers and Wholesale Liquor Dealers Association. In this case the liquor interests were successful and woman suffrage was defeated. In spite of such defeats, the suffrage cause won more and more mass support. Jesse Lynch Williams gives a description of a suffrage parade which he watched from the window of a Fifth Avenue club:

It was Saturday afternoon and the members had crowded behind the windows to witness the show. They were laughing and exchanging the kind of jokes you would expect. When the head of the procession came opposite them, they burst into laughing and as the procession swept past, laughed long and loud. But the women continued to pour by. The laughter began to weaken, became spasmodic. The parade went on and on. Finally there was only the occasional sound of the clink of ice in the glasses. Hours passed. Then someone broke the silence. "Well boys," he said, "I guess they mean it!"

In Albany, a representative from New York City said that not five women in his district endorsed woman suffrage. He was handed a petition signed by 189 women in his own block.

TURN TO MILITANT TACTICS

The split following the Civil War lasted twenty years. In 1890 the two suffrage organizations united as the National American Woman Suffrage Association. But in 1913 the movement split again, this time over the question of militant tactics imported from Great Britain.

The British suffragists started later than the American, but once they got going, they really went to town. The militant suffragist movement in England, organized by Emmeline Pankhurst and her daughters in 1905, battled cops and hounded public officials. They chained themselves to posts or iron grillwork of public buildings and went on talking while the police sawed them loose. They climbed on rafters above Parliament and lay there for hours so that they could speak out at any opportune moment. Hundreds were arrested. In jail they continued to battle prison officials, went on hunger strikes, were subjected to forcible feeding.

A book written by one of Mrs. Pankhurst's daughters gives a colorful glimpse of the lively character of their protest. A poster, reproduced in the book, reads: "*Votes for Women*—Men and women, help the Suffragettes to rush the House of Commons, on Tuesday evening, the 13th of October." (In the subsequent trial there was a good deal of debate as to just what the word "rush" meant.)

The title of Chapter 20, "June and July 1909," is followed by a brief summary: "Attempt to insist on the constitutional right of petition as secured by the Bill of Rights, arrest of Mrs. Pankhurst and the Hon. Mrs. Haverfield, Miss Wallace Dunlop and the hunger strike, 14 hunger strikers in punishment cells. Mr. Gladstone charges Miss Garnett with having bitten a wardress."

Chapter 21, "July to September 1909," gives this summary: "Mr. Lloyd George at Lime House, 12 women sent to prison, another strike, hunger strikers at Exeter Gaol, Mrs. Leigh on the roof at Liverpool, Liverpool hunger strikers," etc. Some of the pictures have captions like "Lady Constance Lytton before she threw the stone at New Castle." "Jessie Kenny as she tried to gain admittance to Mr. Asquith's meeting disguised as telegraph boy."

Two American women, Alice Paul and Lucy Burns, took part in the English demonstrations, were imprisoned and went on hunger strikes. They returned to this country determined to introduce some new methods into the now rather conventional woman's movement.

In 1913, Miss Paul organized a suffrage parade in Washington, D.C. Some 8,000 women marched down Pennsylvania Avenue. As the procession approached the White House, it was blocked by hostile crowds. "Women were spit upon, slapped in the face, tripped up, pelted with burning cigar stubs, insulted by jeers and obscene language." Troops had to be brought from Fort Meyer. Afterwards the suffragists forced a Congressional inquiry and the chief of police lost his job.

Alice Paul concentrated on passing a federal amendment which the older suffragists had more or less shelved while they fought local battles from state to state. Miss Paul followed the political tactics of the English movement. This was to hold the party in power responsible for the delay in granting woman suffrage and to campaign against *all* candidates of that party regardless of whether or not they supported suffrage as individuals. By that time women had the vote in a number of states and Miss Paul systematically campaigned against all candidates of the Democratic Party, in power at the time.

Conservative elements in the suffrage movement did not accept this tactic and Miss Paul and others were expelled in 1913. They formed a new organization which took the name National Woman's Party in 1916. This organization also followed the British policy of putting a lot of pressure on top officials. (It got so that the British Prime Minister and cabinet officials were afraid to speak in public and only appeared at bazaars and social affairs.) To get favorable action from Wilson, who saw numerous delegations but kept stalling, a picket line was thrown around the White House in January 1917. It continued day after day. On Inauguration Day, in a heavy rain, 1,000 pickets circled the White House four times.

In April, war was declared but the picketing continued. In June patriotic mobs began to tear down their banners and maul the pickets. On June 22 police started arresting the women, who refused to pay their fines. Hundreds were sent to prison, including Lucy Burns and Alice Paul. A history of the National Woman's Party gives some details as to how they were treated:

> Instantly the room was in havoc. The guards from
> the male prison fell upon us. I saw Miss Lincoln, a
> slight young girl, thrown to the floor. Mrs. Nolan, a
> delicate old lady of seventy-three, was mastered by

two men . . . Whittaker (the Superintendent) in the
center of the room directed the whole attack, inciting
the guards to every brutality. Two men brought in
Dorothy Day, twisting her arms above her head.
Suddenly they lifted her and brought her body down
twice over the back of an iron bench . . . The bed
broke Mrs. Nolan's fall, but Mrs. Cosu hit the wall.
They had been there a few minutes when Mrs. Lewis,
all doubled over like a sack of flour, was thrown in.
Her head struck the iron bed and she fell to the floor
senseless. [As for Lucy Burns, they] handcuffed her
wrists and fastened the handcuffs over her head to the
cell door.

Alice Paul's hunger strike lasted twenty-two days. The authorities insisted on an examination of her mental condition.
The doctor reported: "This is a spirit like Joan of Arc and it's
useless to try to change it. She will die but she will never give
up."

In the meantime, speakers of the National Woman's Party
were arousing the whole country against the treatment of the
prisoners. Suddenly, on March 3, they were released. They
were promised action on the suffrage amendment; but the
following June, when Congress continued to stall, they started
picketing again. Soon they were back in jail and on their hunger
strikes.

The Senate finally voted on the amendment. It lost by two
votes. The women transferred their pickets to the Senate.

Alice Paul started a "watch fire" in an urn in front of the
White House. Every time President Wilson made a speech
abroad that referred to freedom even in a passing phrase, a copy
of the speech was burned in the "watch fire." Invariably, police
arrested the women who burned the speech. Evidently reports
reaching Europe of the "watch fire" embarrassed the President,
for he cabled two Senators asking them to support the suffrage
amendment.

In February 1919, the Senate voted again and the amendment
lost by one vote. In June it was finally passed. It still had to be

ratified by the states and this meant a state-to-state struggle lasting another year. The women of the United States voted in the presidential elections of 1920.

I seem to have given most of the credit for final passage of this law to the National Woman's Party. The older suffrage organization continued its work during these seven years. It had a membership of almost two million as compared with a top membership of fifty thousand in the National Woman's Party. But it was this militant minority that gave the final push to the suffrage drive.

Since I have limited myself to the struggle of American women for legal equality, I have not attempted to describe their economic development in this hundred-year period, their entry into industries, office work, trades and professions, or their role in the trade-union movement. That story would require another article, but its close relationship to the growth of the woman's movement is obvious. As women achieved economic independence, their demand for the vote was taken more seriously. Laws change slowly and are generally a reflection of changes that have already occurred on the economic and social level.

Almost thirty-five years have passed since women got the vote. We are in position now to appraise what women achieved when they won the suffrage and what they did *not* achieve.

Many people are disappointed over the results of woman suffrage—for example, all those who believed that politics would be "purified" by the participation of women. Reactionaries insist that suffrage and the entry of women into industry have actually achieved nothing, that modern women are miserably unhappy, frustrated and hysterical, and go insane at a faster rate than ever before. (All this because women are allegedly emotionally passive and have been forced against their true nature into competition with men.) The solution, if we are to believe them, seems to be to hurry back to what's left of the home, which is something like going all out for the horse as a means of modern transportation. *Modern Woman—the Lost Sex* by a woman psychiatrist, Marya Farnham, is a good example of this reactionary trend.

Even people who approve of modern woman are disappointed

at the results of the woman's rights struggle. Purdy in his biography of Mary Wollstonecraft says:

> All that has been done for women in the last century and a half has not saved them from the tragedies that afflicted Mary Wollstonecraft, Eliza Bishop and Fanny Blood. Inherited poverty, brutal or indifferent parents, disease following overwork and neglect, reluctant or faithless lovers, incompatible husbands, the struggle to wring a living from an apathetic world —has not been ended by female suffrage or any other abstract benefits women have recently achieved.

I can't help wondering just how many problems they thought woman suffrage could solve. The vote was a simple question of democratic rights and not a magic formula that could dissolve all the bitterness and frustrations of women's daily lives. Men have been voting a hundred years longer than women and they've still got problems. That doesn't mean they should give up voting. If Negroes suddenly achieved complete equality with whites, they would still face unemployment, the threat of war, reaction and all the other difficulties that confront every worker, regardless of race or sex. That doesn't mean they should give up the fight for full equality.

I don't doubt that women are unhappy. The legal equality and other democratic rights for which they fought so heroically are meaningless as long as their position in economic and family life remains basically unaltered.

The economic status of women is undergoing change. This is bringing about the first fundamental difference in women's lives. Women now constitute one-third of the labor force[2] and 25 per cent of all married women are working. This is a revolutionary development that in the long run will mean a great deal more than the vote.

But the majority of women still face discrimination in wages and jobs. The average income of women workers is less than half that of men. They are also doubly exploited, as wage earn-

[2] 40 per cent in 1968—Ed.

ers and as wives. A survey by General Electric revealed that the average work week of employed wives is 79 hours—40 on the job and 39 at home.

This explains why women are not too enthusiastic about their so-called "emancipation." Women workers are obviously *not* emancipated, any more than male workers, Negro workers, or any other section of the working class.

The structure of the family is also undergoing change, partly as a result of women's changing economic position. Women are not as restricted in their sex and family relationships as they were when Mary Wollstonecraft first rebelled against marriage.

I believe it is significant that the first women who fought for equality and women's rights directed a large part of their protest against bourgeois family relationships. Only at a later date did they center their attention on issues like the vote. It may be that in our re-examination of women's problems we will return to their starting point. In the light of modern psychological and anthropological knowledge, we should study the relations of husbands and wives, parents and children, in a society that is founded upon the institution of private property and where marriage laws and customs reflect this basic concept of private ownership.

Both the economic and sex status of women is changing, but these changes are only the first steps toward a revolution in human relationships which will take place in the future. The fight for freedom is indivisible and no basic change can be achieved in a society where men, as well as women, are not free.

When women are really emancipated from the economic exploitation and emotional restrictions of our society, men too will be freed from the frustrations and unhappiness which the same system inflicts upon them. But this can only be achieved in the cooperative atmosphere of a socialist commonwealth where our personal relationships will not be an expression of the property forms of a competitive society.

Ideology

Our revolution is unique

BETTY FRIEDAN

The organized feminist drive seemed to taper off after women received the vote in 1920. Indeed, the League of Women Voters, organized by some of the former feminists, made a point of divorcing itself from strictly female issues.

During World War II, many women entered the working force. Though many left after the war, they returned later in order to make contributions to the economic goals of their families. Meanwhile, well-to-do middle class women tended to turn to volunteerism in service to their communities or churches.

Betty Friedan's The Feminine Mystique, *published in 1963, gave voice to the simmering frustrations of many women and caused others to question some of their accepted values and roles. With the formation in 1966 of the National Organization for Women (NOW), which also admits males, the modern liberation movement officially began. Mrs. Friedan here articulates some of the tenets of the NOW philosophy.*

Betty Friedan is a graduate of Smith College, where she majored in psychology. She was a founder and first president of NOW from 1966 to 1970, and is currently chairman of the NOW Advisory Committee. She is widely heard as spokesman and lecturer on the reformist approach to the liberation of women.

31

We new feminists have begun to define ourselves—existentially —through action. We have learned that while we had much to learn from the black civil rights movement and their revolution against economic and racial oppression, our own revolution is unique: it must define its own ideology.

We can cut no corners; we are, in effect, where the black revolution was perhaps fifty years ago; but the speed with which our revolution is moving now is our unearned historical benefit from what has happened in that revolution. Yet there can be no illusion on our part that a separatist ideology copied from black power will work for us. Our tactics and strategy and, above all, our ideology must be firmly based in the historical, biological, economic, and psychological reality of our two-sexed world, which is not the same as the black reality and different also from the reality of the first feminist wave.

Thanks to the early feminists, we who have mounted this second stage of the feminist revolution have grown up with the right to vote, little as we may have used it for our own purposes. We have grown up with the right to higher education and to employment, and with some, not all, of the legal rights of equality. Insofar as we have moved on the periphery of the mainstream of society, with the skills and the knowledge to command its paychecks, even if insufficient; and to make decisions, even if not consulted beyond housework; we begin to have a self-respecting image of ourselves, as women, not just in sexual relation to men, but as full human beings in society. We are able, at least some of us, to see men, in general or in particular, without blind rancor or hostility, and to face oppression as it reveals itself in our concrete experience with politicians, bosses, priests, or husbands. We do not need to suppress our just grievances. We now have enough courage to express them. And yet we are able to conceive the possibility of full affirmation for man. Man is not the enemy, but the fellow victim of the present half-equality. As we speak, act, demonstrate, testify, and appear on television on matters such as sex discrimination in employment, public accommodations, education, divorce-marriage reform, or abortion repeal, we hear from men who feel they can be freed to greater self-fulfillment to the degree that women are released from the binds that now constrain them.

This sense of freeing men as the other half of freeing women has always been there, even in the early writings of Mary Wollstonecraft, Elizabeth Stanton, and the rest; our action-created new awareness has confirmed this.

Another point we are conscious of in the new feminism is that we are a revolution for all, not for an exceptional few. This, above all, distinguishes us from those token spokeswomen of the period since women won the vote, the Aunt Toms who managed to get a place for themselves in society, and who were, I think, inevitably seduced into an accommodating stance, helping to keep the others quiet. We are beginning to know that no woman can achieve a real breakthrough alone, as long as sex discrimination exists in employment, under the law, in education, in mores, and in denigration of the image of women.

Even those of us who have managed to achieve a precarious success in a given field still walk as freaks in "man's world" since every profession—politics, the church, teaching—is still structured as man's world. Walking as a freak makes one continually self-conscious, apologetic, if not defiant, about being a woman. One is made to feel there are three sexes—men, other women, and myself. The successful woman may think, "I am the exception, the 'brilliant' one with the rare ability to be an anthropologist, author, actress, broker, account executive, or television commentator; but you drones out there, you watch the television set. And what better use can you make of your life than doing the dishes for your loved ones?"

We cannot say that all American women want equality, because we know that women, like all oppressed people, have accepted the traditional denigration by society. Some women have been too much hurt by denigration from others, by self-denigration, by lack of the experiences, education, and training needed to move in society as equal human beings, to have the confidence that they can so move in a competitive society. They say they don't want equality—they have to be happy, adjust to things as they are. Such women find us threatening.

They find equality so frightening that they must wish the new feminists did not exist. And yet we see so clearly from younger women and students that to the degree that we push ahead and create opportunities for movement in society, in the process creating the "new women" who are *people first*, to that degree the threat will disappear.

We do not speak for every woman in America, but we speak for the *right* of every woman in America to become all she is capable of becoming—on her own and/or in partnership with a man. And we already know that we speak not for a few, not for hundreds, not for thousands, but for millions—especially for millions in the younger generation who have tasted more equality than their elders. We know this simply from the resonance, if you will, that our actions have aroused in society.

That wave of resonance is world wide. In Canada, they want to have an affiliate of our National Organization for Women, and propose that, ultimately, there will be a World Organization for Women. From Great Britain, France, Italy, the Scandinavian countries, Germany, Japan, New Zealand, women—young, vital new feminists—have asked for guidance.

WOMEN AND SEX

As an example of the new feminism in action, consider the matter of abortion law repeal. NOW was the first organization to speak on the basic rights of women on the question of abortion. We said that it is the inalienable human right of every woman to control her own reproductive process. To establish that right would require that all laws penalizing abortion be repealed, removed from the penal code; the state would not be empowered either to force or prevent a woman from having an abortion. Now many groups are working on abortion law repeal, while at the same time California and Washington, D.C., court decisions have spelled out the right of a woman to control her own reproduction.

What right has any man to say to any woman, "You must bear this child"? What right has any state to say it? The child-bearing decision is a woman's right and not a technical question needing the sanction of the state, nor should the state control access to birth control devices.

This question can only really be confronted in terms of the basic personhood and dignity of woman, which is violated forever if she does not have the right to control her own reproductive process. And the heart of this idea goes far beyond abortion and birth control.

Women, almost too visible as sex objects in this country today, are at the same time invisible people. As the Negro was the invisible man, so women are the invisible people in America today. To be taken seriously as people, women have to share in the decisions of government, of politics, of the church—not just to cook the church supper, but to preach the sermon; not just to look up the zip codes and address the envelopes, but to make the political decisions; not just to do the housework of industry, but to make some of the executive decisions. Women, above all, want to say what their own lives are going to be, what their own personalities are going to be, not permitting male experts to define what is "feminine" or isn't or should be.

The essence of the denigration of women is their definition as sex objects. And to confront our inequality, we must confront our own self-denigration and our denigration by society in these terms.

Am I saying therefore, that women must be liberated from sex? No. I am saying that sex will only be liberated, will only cease to be a sniggering dirty joke and an obsession in this society, when women are liberated, self-determining people, liberated to a creativity beyond motherhood, to a full human creativity.

Nor am I saying that women must be liberated from motherhood. I am saying that motherhood will only be liberated to be a joyous and responsible human act, when women are free to make, with full conscious choice and full human responsibility, the decision to be mothers. Then and only then, will they be able to embrace motherhood without conflict. When they are able to define themselves as people, not just as somebody's mother, not just as servants of children, not just as breeding receptacles, but as people for whom motherhood is a freely chosen part of life, and for whom creativity has many dimensions, as it has for men.

The hostility between the sexes has never been worse. The image of woman in avant-garde plays, novels, in the movies, and in the mass image that you can detect behind the family situation comedies on television is that mothers are man-devouring cannibalistic monsters, or else Lolitas, thing-like sex objects: objects not even of heterosexual impulse, objects of a sadistic or masochistic impulse. That impulse is much more a factor in the abortion question than anybody ever admits: the punishment of women.

I maintain that motherhood is a bane and a curse, or at least partly that, as long as women are forced to be mothers—and only mothers—against their will. Women today are forced to live too much through their children and husband—too dependent on them, and, therefore, forced to take too much varied resentment, vindictiveness, inexpressible resentment, and rage out on their husbands and their children.

Perhaps the least understood fact of American political life is the enormous buried violence of women in this country today. Like all oppressed people, women have been taking their violence out on their own bodies, in all the maladies with which they plague the doctors' offices and the psychoanalysts. They have been taking out their violence inadvertently and in subtle and in insidious ways on their children and on their husbands. And sometimes, they are not so subtle, for the battered child syndrome that we are hearing more and more about in our hospitals is almost always to be found in the instance of unwanted children, and women are doing the battering, as much or more than men.

Man, we have said, is not the enemy. Men will only be truly liberated, to love women and to be fully themselves, when women are liberated to be full people. Until that happens, men are going to bear the burden and the guilt of the destiny they have forced upon women, the suppressed resentment of that passive stage—the sterility of love, when love is not between two fully active, fully participant, fully joyous people, but has in it the element of exploitation. And men will also not be fully free to be all they can be as long as they must live up to an image of masculinity that denies to a man all the tenderness and sensitivity that might be considered feminine. Men have in them enormous capacities that they have to repress and fear in themselves, in living up to this obsolete and brutal man-eating, lion-killing, Ernest Hemingway image of masculinity—the image of all-powerful masculine superiority. All the burdens and responsibilities that men are supposed to shoulder alone, make them, I think, resent women's pedestal, while the burden to women is enforced passivity.

So the real sexual revolution is not the cheap headlines in the papers—at what age boys and girls go to bed with each other and whether they do it with or without the benefit of marriage. That's the least of it. The real sexual revolution is the emergence of women from passivity, from thingness, to full self-determination, to full dignity. And insofar as they can do this, men are also emerging from the stage of identification with brutality and masters to full and sensitive complete humanity.

A revolutionary theory that's adequate to the current demand of the sexual revolution must also address itself to the concrete realities of our society. We can only transcend the reality of the institutions that oppress us by confronting them in our actions now; confronting reality, we change it; we begin to create alternatives, not in abstract discussion, but here and now.

Some women who call themselves revolutionaries get into abstractions. They say, "What's really wrong is marriage altogether. What's wrong is having babies altogether; let's have them in test tubes. Man is the oppressor, and women are enslaved. We don't want jobs because who wants to be equal to men who aren't free. All jobs today are just a rat race anyway."

Now we are rationalizing in radical terms of the extremists of the women's liberation ideology. This is a rationalization for inaction, because in the end we're going to weep and go home and yell at our husbands and make life miserable for a while, but we'll eventually conclude that it's hopeless, that nothing can be done.

If we are going to address ourselves to the need for changing the social institutions that will permit women to be free and equal individuals, participating actively in their society and changing that society—with men—then we must talk in terms of what is possible, and not accept what is as what must be. In other words, don't talk to me about test tubes because I am interested in leading a revolution for the foreseeable future of my society. And I have a certain sense of optimism that things can be changed.

Twenty-five years from now test-tube babies may be a reality. But it is my educated guess as an observer of the scene—both from what I know of psychology and what I've observed of actual women and men, old and young, conservative and radical, in this country and other countries—that for the foreseeable future people are going to want to enjoy sexual relationships and control the procreative act and make more responsible, human decisions whether and when to have babies.

We need not accept marriage as it's currently structured with the implicit idea of man, the breadwinner, and woman, the housewife. There are many different ways we could posit marriage. But there seems to be a reasonable guess that men and women are going to want relationships of long-term intimacy tied in with sexual relationship, although we can certainly posit a larger variety of sex relationships than now seem conventional. And it's not possible, much less conducive to health, happiness, or self-fulfillment, for women or men to completely suppress their sexual needs.

We can change institutions, but it is a fantasy deviation from a really revolutionary approach to say that we want a world in which there will be no sex, no marriage, that in order for women to be free they must have a manless revolution. We have to deal with the world of reality if we are going to have a real revolution.

I don't happen to think that women and men are so completely different that it is impossible for us to see each other as human beings. I think that it is as possible for men to put themselves finally in woman's place by an act of empathy or by guilt or by awareness of human rights as it has been possible for some whites to do for blacks. But it's perhaps not much more possible than that, though there are more bonds between men and women, and really men's stake in this revolution is greater, because a woman can make a man's life hell if it isn't solved. But I think it would be as much of a mistake to expect men to hand this to women as to consider all men as the enemy, all men as oppressors. This revolution can have the support of men, but women must take the lead in fighting it as any other oppressed group has had to.

I think that it is possible in education to create and disseminate the radical ideology that is needed to influence the great change in expectations and institutions for the revolution of women. In the education of women, I think it is nonsense to keep talking about optional life styles and the freedom of choice that American women have. They do not have them, and we should face this right away. You cannot tell a woman aged eighteen to twenty that she can make a choice to just stay home all her life with her children, her friends, and her husband. This girl is going to live close to a hundred years. There won't be children home to occupy her all her life. If she has intelligence and the opportunity for education it is telling her simply, "Put yourself in a garbage can, except for the years when you have a few little children at home."

The so-called second choice and option—go to school, then have children, stay out for twenty years and then get a job or go back to school—is not satisfactory either. I am not denying the need for occupational therapy for women of my generation who've had to do it this way, but any woman who has run the continuing education gamut knows the limitations of occupational therapy. Women have to do what they can, but they have enormous problems trying to get back after ten or fifteen years. They are mainly just a pool of semi-employable labor and have to be grateful for whatever they can get. Actually only a token few have been involved in these programs.

Some have the idea that there is another choice—and it is immediately implicit that this is a very freakish and exceptional choice—which is to be single-minded about a career like a man. The idea is, don't marry, don't have children, if you really want a demanding profession. Of course, if you do it this way, forget equality for women. I don't want to forget equality for women.

I don't accept for most women the necessity of making a choice
that no man has to make. This is not to say that women are not
to have a free choice to have children or not to have children, to
marry or not to marry; but the idea that this choice has to be influenced by professional or political pursuits, that you are going
to be sexually frustrated by choosing to be a scientist, is nonsense.

It is a perversion of the new feminism for some to exhort
those who would join this revolution to cleanse themselves of
sex and the need for love or to refuse to have children. This not
only means a revolution with very few followers—but is a
cop-out from the problem of moving in society for the *majority*
of women, who do want love and children. To enable *all*
women, not just the exceptional few, to participate in society we
must confront the fact of life—as a temporary fact of most
women's lives today—that women do give birth to children. But
we must challenge the idea that a woman is primarily responsible for raising children. Man and society have to be educated to
accept their responsibility for that role as well. And this is first
of all a challenge to education.

In Sweden I was impressed that these expectations are considered absolutely normal. The need for child-care centers is accepted as so important by all the fathers as well as the mothers
of the younger generation that every major young politician has
it high on his agenda. The equivalent of the Sunday editor of
The New York Times in Sweden, or a rising state senator,
would each tell me how both he and his wife have part-time
schedules so that they can both go on with their professions, and
how this is fine but they realize it's only makeshift because
what's really needed is more child-care centers. And the editor
would pick up the baby and say proudly that she relates to him
more than to his wife. And in the Volvo factory, even the public relations man with a crew cut says the same thing.

I couldn't believe it! I asked, "How do you explain this? Why
do so many have these attitudes?" And they said, "Education."
Eight years ago they decided that they were going to have absolute equality, and the only way to achieve this was to challenge the sex-role idea. The sex-role debate is not considered a

woman question, not even an individual woman question or a societal woman question, but a question for men and women alike. In the elementary schools boys and girls take cooking and child care, and boys and girls take shop. Boys and girls take higher mathematics. In the universities the dormitories are sexually integrated. They all have kitchens and boys and girls learn to live together, to cook and study as equals. The kitchens are very important—a boy will boast how good a cook he is, and the idea that this is woman's work is gone. This has been done in the course of one generation, and if Sweden can do it, the United States can do it.

Tokenism is worse than nothing. Tokenism is pretending that something is happening, to divert effort from the things that could really make something happen. It is terribly interesting to watch the experiments in continuing education at colleges like Radcliffe and Sarah Lawrence, but they have involved only a limited number of women. *This revolution has got to be for everybody.* Most women who want to get into graduate school simply can't get in at all because many universities won't accept women for part-time study when they've got enough men applying for full-time study.

Let's talk about what could be done that isn't just tinkering or tokenism. Every university should have a child-care center. A child development department in any university that doesn't address itself to this need is not confronting its own professional challenge. Another thing we could do, which NOW is trying to do, is to tackle sex discrimination in the universities in the broadest sense. If we get sex into Title VI as well as Title VII of the Civil Rights Act, so that sex discrimination in education is outlawed as well as race discrimination, we could then demand the removal of government contracts from any university that discriminated against women in assigning fellowships. We could then establish, by going to the Supreme Court, that it was discrimination against women not to give them maternity leave rather than requiring them to drop out of medical school. It is as much discrimination against women not to give them a maternity leave as it would be unconscionable to make a boy who has to go into military service lose his chance to get back into graduate school. And it is discrimination against a woman for the graduate school not to have a child-care center, much less not to give her a scholarship or fellowship. If more than a very few women are to enjoy equality, we have an absolute responsibility to get serious political priority for child-care centers, to make it possible for women not to have to bow out of society for ten or fifteen years when they have children. Or else we are only going to be talking of equal opportunities for a few.

Professional schools, and architecture especially, should change their approach. In Sweden, the more sophisticated young architects and planners are professionally confronting the problems of using technology to create new kinds of living places that don't require the slave work on the part of women that makes such a misuse of women's time. These architects do not accept the status quo of "woman as the servant of the house."

WOMEN AS A POLITICAL POWER

On the question of self-determination, we became painfully aware, in our attempts to get a bill of rights for women into the platforms of both political parties at the last presidential election and as a major issue in the election for all candidates for national office, that we need *political power*. Our only success then was getting the word "sex" added to a rather vague antidiscrimination sentence in the Republican platform.

We must overcome our diversity of varied political beliefs. Our common commitment is to equality for women. And we are not single-issue people; we want a voice for all women, to raise our voices in decision making on all matters from war and peace to the kinds of cities we're going to inhabit. Many large issues concern all of us; on these things we may differ. We will surmount this. Political power is necessary to change the situation of the oppressed 51 per cent, to realize the power potential in the fact that women *are* 51 per cent.

We will do it by getting into city hall ourselves, or by getting into Congress ourselves, regardless of whether our political party is Republican or Democratic or Peace and Freedom.

We're only going to do it by getting there ourselves; that's the nitty-gritty of self-determination for us—not to rely on Richard Nixon or a Senate with only one female or a House with only a few women to do it for us.

In this we can be united. We had notable successes, in spite of a general political failure on our part in respect to the platforms in the presidential election. In California through the initiative of one member of NOW, the NOW Bill of Rights for Women was incorporated into the state platform of the California Democratic Party. In other cities (Pittsburgh, Syracuse, New York) and states where we had active chapters and where those chapters took advantage of hearings that were held on platforms to raise these issues, we began to get *an awareness* of woman's existence from politicians to whom previously women were simply invisible people. Though it's not going to be easy, by 1972 I think we must be determined that we will have our own Julian Bonds, that we will find some way to confront and break through the travesty of women's visibility in American political conventions only as mini-skirted greeters or at ladies' luncheons.

We must begin to use the power of our actions: to make women finally *visible* as people in America, as conscious political and social power; to change our society *now*, so all women can move freely, as people, in it.

Female liberation as the basis

for social revolution

ROXANNE DUNBAR

The NOW organization has a definite reform program involving changes in legislation, employment practices, educational discrimination, repeal of abortion laws, organization of child-care centers, and combatting other sexist practices. The many radical women's liberation groups might or might not join in specific action programs in these areas. They would probably tend to demonstrate against particular discriminations, but many despair of curing most situations under the existing system. Such women, many of whom have participated in campus and anti-war demonstrations, call for a political revolution in which women are full participants.

They make it clear that they are not content to be silent operators of typewriters and mimeographs in the radical movement. Nor do they chose to function mainly as morale builders in a sexual role. If indeed Stokely Carmichael once said that the only place for a woman in SNCC was prone, he must by now regret this oft-quoted remark.

The female liberationists believe that women must know themselves as a first step in their emancipation. They meet in small groups to "rap"—sharing experiences, feelings, and ideas— or to discuss literature related to their movement. Ultimately some organize their theories in an ideology, often published in

44

one of their colorfully named newsletters or journals (No More Fun and Games, Off Our Backs, *etc.*).

Roxanne Dunbar, a theorist of female liberation who was active in liberation groups in Boston, has read widely in Marx and Engels, and on the caste system of India. She has discussed her ideas from the platform of women's meetings, in high schools and colleges, and in other groups. Most recently as a resident of Louisiana, she has brought many Southern women into the movement. Here she develops theories relating the women's liberation movement to "a world-wide struggle for human liberation in just societies."

1

The present female liberation movement must be viewed within the context of international social revolution and also within the context of the long struggle by women for nominal legal rights. The knowledge that is now available, gained in past struggles, makes the current women's movement more scientific and potent. Black people in America and the Vietnamese people have exposed the basic weakness of the system of white, western dominance under which we live. They have also developed means of fighting which continually strengthen themselves and weaken the enemy. The dialectics of liberation have revealed that the weak, the oppressed, can struggle against and defeat a larger enemy. Revolutionary dialectics teaches that nothing is immutable. Our enemy today may not be our enemy next year, or the same enemy might be fighting us in a different way tomorrow. Our tactics must be fitted to the immediate situation and open to change; our strategy must be formed in relation to overall revolutionary goals. From the blacks and the Vietnamese, most importantly, we have learned that there is a distinction between the consciousness of the oppressed and the consciousness of the oppressor.

Women have not just recently begun to struggle against their suppression and oppression. Women have fought in a million ways in their daily, private lives to survive and to overcome existing conditions. Many times those "personal" struggles have taken a self-destructive form. Almost always women have had to use sex as a tool, and have thereby sunk further in oppression. Many women still believe in the efficacy of fighting a lone battle. But more and more women are realizing that only collective strength and action will allow us to be free to build the kind of society that meets basic human needs. Collective activity has already had an enormous effect on our thinking. We are learning not to dissipate our strength by using traditional methods of exerting power—tears, manipulation, appeals to guilt and benevolence. We do not ignore what seem to be the "petty" forms of our oppression, such as total identification with housework and sexuality as well as physical helplessness. Rather we understand that our oppression and suppression are institutionalized, that all women suffer the "petty" forms of oppression. Therefore they are not petty or personal, but rather constitute a widespread, deeply rooted social disease. They are the things that keep us tied down day to day, and do not allow us to act. Further, we understand that all men are our policemen, and no organized police force is necessary to keep us in our places. All men enjoy male supremacy and take advantage of it to a greater or lesser degree, according to their own hierarchy of power.

It is not enough that we take collective action. We must know where we have come from and how we can be most effective in breaking the bonds. We have identified a system of oppression—sexism. To understand how sexism has developed and the variety of its forms of suppression, female liberation, as Betsy Warrior puts it, "must re-examine the foundations of civilization."

What we find in re-examining history is that women have had a separate historical development from men. Within each society, women experience the particular culture, but on a larger scale of human history, women have developed separately as a caste. The original division of labor in all societies was probably by sex. The female capacity for reproduction led to this division. The division of labor by sex has not put a lighter physical burden on women, as we might believe, if we look only at the mythology of chivalry in Western ruling-class history. Quite the contrary. What was restricted for women was not physical labor, but mobility.

Because woman's reproductive capacity led to her being forced into a sedentary (immobile, not inactive) life, the female developed community life. Men were alien to the female community. Their job was to roam, to do the hunting and war-making, entering the community only to leave again. Their entrances and exits probably caused disruptions. At some point, when women had developed food production and animal domestication to the point of subsistence, males began settling down. However, they brought to the community a very different set of values and behavioral patterns which upset the primitive communism of the female communities.

In a very real sense, the male was less "civilized" than the female. He had little political (governing) experience. The experience of the male had led him to value dominance; he had become unsuited for living as equals in the community, because he knew only how to overpower and conquer the prey. Other masculine values, formed in the transient existence as hunters, included competition (with the prey) and violence (to kill the prey). Gradually in some cases, but often through violent upheaval, males took over female communities, suppressing the female through domination and even enslavement. The political base for the taking of power came from the secret male societies formed by the men in reaction to female control of community institutions.

As societies became more affluent and complex, life was rationalized and ordered by introducing territoriality, or private property, and inheritance. Patrilineal descent required the male control of a female or a number of females to identify the rightful heirs. The offspring served as labor as well as fulfilling the function of transcendence for the father (the son taking over), and females were used for barter. This then led to the dominance of the male over a wife or wives and her (his) offspring. The female, like the land, became private property under masculine dominance. Man, in conquering nature, conquered the female, who had worked with nature, not against it, to produce food and to reproduce the human race.

II

In competing among themselves for dominance over females (and thereby the offspring) and for land, a few males came to dominate the rest of the male population, not just the female population. A peasant laboring class developed. Within that laboring class, males oppressed females, though the peasant male had no ultimate property rights over females (or land). The landlord could take any young girl or woman he wanted for whatever purpose.

The pattern of masculine dominance exists almost universally now, since those societies where the pattern developed have dominated preliterate societies through imperialism, and have passed those patterns on. The Western nation-states which have perfected imperialism were developed as an extension of male dominance over females and the land. Other races and cultures as well could be bought and sold, possessed, dominated through contract (and ultimately through physical violence and the threat of destruction, of the world if necessary). We live under an international caste system, at the top of which is the western white male ruling class, and at the very bottom of which is the female of the nonwhite colonized world. There is no simple order of "oppressions" within this caste system. Within each society, the female is dominated by the male. The female is classed with the very old and very young of both sexes ("women, children, and old men"). White dominates black and brown. The caste system, in all its various forms, is always based on identifiable physical characteristics—sex, color, age.

Why is it important to say that females constitute a lower caste?[1] Many people would say that the term caste can only properly be used in reference to India or Hindu society. If we think that caste can only be applied to Hindu society, we will simply have to find some other term for the kind of social category to which one is assigned at birth and from which one can-

[1] Caste: "One of the hereditary social classes . . . that restrict the occupation of their members and their intercourse with other castes (Webster's Seventh New Collegiate Dictionary).

not escape by any action of one's own; and, at the same time, we must distinguish such social categories from economic classes or ranked groups.

A caste system establishes a definite place into which certain members of a society have no choice but to fit (because of their race, sex, or other easily identifiable physical characteristics or occupations). A caste system, however, need not at all be based on a prohibition of physical contact between different castes. It only means that this physical contact will be severely regulated, or will take place outside the bounds deemed acceptable by the society; it means that the mobility of the lower castes will be limited.

Under the caste system in the Southern states, physical contact between the races is extensive. In the South under slavery, there was frequent contact between black "mammy" and white child, between black and white preadolescent children, and between white master and black slave women. It was after the end of legal slavery that contact between the races was restricted; yet contact still exists.

Between male and female, thousands of taboos control their contact in every society. Within each, there is a "woman's world" and a "man's world." Men initiate contact with women, often for the purpose of exploitation; women have little freedom to initiate contact with adult males.

The clearest historical analogy of the caste status of females is African slavery in the United States. When slaves were freed during the Civil War, the female slaves were included, but when the right to vote was in question, female blacks were excluded. They took a place beside disfranchised white females. To many, comparing the female's situation in general with that of a slave in particular seems farfetched. Actually, the reason the analogy is indicated has to do with the caste status of the African in America, not with slavery as such.

Slave status does not necessarily imply caste status. The restriction of slavery to Africans in the British colonies rested on the caste principle that it was a status rightly belonging to Africans as innately (racially) inferior beings. If a person was black, he was presumed to be a slave unless he could prove otherwise.

Caste was inclusive of the slave and free status, just as the caste status of women is inclusive of all economic classes, age, and marital status.

Caste, then, is not analogous to slavery. In Rome, where slaves were not conceived of as innately inferior, and did not differ racially from the enslaving group, slaves did not form a separate caste when they were freed. While they were slaves, however, they had no rights to property nor any legal rights. The master had the power of life and death over his slaves, just as in the slave South. As far as the legal category of the slave as property goes, Rome and America had a common social form. It was caste which produced the contrast between the effects of the two systems of slavery. It was the system of caste which gave African slavery in America its peculiarly oppressive character. That caste oppression is analogous to the situation of females both legally and traditionally. (When jurists were seeking a legal category for the position of African slaves in Virginia, they settled on the code of laws which governed wives and children under the power of the patriarch, the head of the family.)

In order to fully understand the power relations of black and white in American society and of male and female in all human societies, we must understand the caste system which structures power, and within which caste roles we are conditioned to remain.

Often, in trying to describe the way a white person oppresses or exploits a black person, or a man oppresses or exploits a woman, we say that the oppressor treats the other person as a "thing" or as an "object." Men treat women as "sex objects," we say; slavery reduced black human beings to "mere property," no different from horses or cattle. This interpretation of caste oppression overlooks the crucial importance of the fact that it is human beings, not objects, which the person in the higher caste has the power to dominate. Imagine a society becoming as dependent upon cattle as Southern plantation society was upon black people, or as men are upon women. The idea is ludicrous; the value of a slave as property lay precisely in his being a person, rather than just another piece of property. The value of a woman for a man is much greater than the value of a machine or hired person to satisfy his sexual urges and fantasies, do his housework, breed and tend his offspring. It is convenient for a man to have these satisfactions from "his woman," but his relation to her *as a person*, his position of being of a higher caste, is the central aspect of his power and dominance over her.

(A further example of the importance to the higher castes of dominating *human beings*, not mere objects, is the way men view their sexual exploitation of women. It is not merely the satisfaction of a man's private, individual, sexual urge which he fantasizes he will get from some women on the street. In addition, and more central to his view of women, he visualizes himself taking her, dominating her through the sexual act; he sees her as the *human* evidence of his own power and prowess. Prostitution, however exploitative, can never serve this same purpose, just as wage labor, however exploitative to the wage slave, could not have served the same purpose in Southern society that black slaves served.)

Black people fell under two patterns of dominance and subservience which emerged under slavery, and which are analogous to patterns of male-female relations in industrial societies. One pattern is the paternalistic one (houseservants, livery men, entertainers, etc.). The second pattern is the exploitative pattern of the fieldhands. Among females today, housewives and women on welfare are subject to the paternalistic pattern. The exploitative pattern rules the lives of more than a third of the population of females (those who work for wages, including paid domestic work) in the United States. But it is important to remember that females form a caste within the labor force, that their exploitation is not simply double or multiple, but is *qualitatively* different from the exploitation of workers of the higher castes—of males, particularly white males.

Though the paternalistic pattern may seem less oppressive or exploitative for females, it is actually only more insidious. The housewife remains tied by emotional bonds to a man, cut off from the more public world of work; she is able to experience the outside world only through the man or her children. If she were working in public industry, however exploitative, she could potentially do something about her situation through collective effort with other workers.

However, even for women who hold jobs outside the home, their caste conditioning usually prevails, preventing them from knowing even that they have the *right* to work, much less to ask for something more. Also, the jobs women are allowed are most often "service" (domestic) ones, demanding constant contact with men or children. Females and blacks, even under the alienating capitalist system, are subject to the paternalistic pattern of caste domination every minute of their lives.

A caste system provides rewards that are not entirely economic in the narrow sense. Caste is a way of making human relations "work," a way of freezing relationships, so that conflicts are minimal. A caste system is a *social system* which is economically based. It is not just some mistaken ideas which must be understood and dispensed with because they are not *really* in men's interest. No mere change in *ideas* will alter the caste system under which we live. The caste system does not exist just in the mind. Caste is deeply rooted in human history, and is the very basis of the present social system in the United States.

III

The present female liberation movement, like the movements for black liberation and national liberation in the past century, has begun to identify strongly with Marxist class analysis. And like other movements, we have taken the basic tools of Marxist analysis (dialectical materialism) and used them to expand the understanding of class analysis. Our analysis of women as an oppressed and suppressed group is not new. Marx and Engels as well as other nineteenth-century socialist and communist theoriticians analyzed the position of the female sex in just such a way. Engels identified the family as the basic unit of capitalist society, and of female oppression. "The modern individual family is founded on the open or concealed domestic slavery of the wife, and modern society is a mass composed of these individual families as its molecules." And "within the family, he [the man] is the bourgeois and the wife represents the proletariat."[2]

Marx and Engels thought that the large-scale entrance of women into the work force (women and children were the first factory workers) would work to destroy the family unit. However, in the West (Europe and the United States where proletarian revolutions have not succeeded, the family ideology has gained a whole new lease on life, and the lower-caste position of women has continued to be enforced. Even now when 40 per cent of the adult female population is in the work force, woman is still defined completely within the family, and the male is seen as "protector" and "breadwinner."

In reality, nearly half of all marriages end in divorce, and the family unit is a decadent, energy-absorbing, destructive, wasteful institution, against which children (young people), women, and some men are revolting. The powers that be, through government action and their propaganda force, the news media, are desperately trying to hold the family together. Daniel Moynihan and other government sociologists have correctly surmised that the absence of the patriarchal head among blacks has been instrumental in the development of "antisocial" black consciousness. Actually, in the absence of the patriarchal family, which this society has systematically denied black people, a sense of community life has developed. Among white Westerners, individualism and competitiveness prevail in social relations, chiefly because of the propagation of the ideology of the patriarchal family. The new sense of collective action among women is fast destroying the decadent family ideology along with its ugly individualism and competitiveness. Our demand for collective public child care is throwing into question the private family ownership of children.

Yet without the family unit and without the tie with a male, the female falls from whatever middle-class status she had gained by association with a man of that class. She quickly falls into the work force or has to go on welfare. Such was the case

[2] Friedrich Engels, *The Origin of the Family, Private Property, and the State*, 1884.

for African slaves when a master voluntarily freed them, and when slavery was ended as an institution. Lower-caste status almost always means potential or actual lower-class status as well. For women who are supported by and gain the status of their husbands, working-class status is always a potential threat, if she does not perform her wifely duties well. However, many of these supported women have chosen to enter the work force in the vast pool of female clerical workers, in order to gain the economic independence that is necessary to maintain self-respect and sanity. On these jobs, the women are still subjected to patterns of masculine dominance. But often on the less personal ground of work, a woman can begin throwing off the bonds of servitude.

IV

How will the family unit be destroyed? After all, women must take care of the children, and there will continue to be children. Our demand for full-time child care in the public schools will be met to some degree all over, and perhaps fully in places. The alleviation of the duty of full-time child care in private situations will free women to make decisions they could not before. But more than that, the demand alone will throw the whole ideology of the family into question, so that women can begin establishing a community of work with each other as we never before have in a political context. Women will feel freer to leave their husbands and become economically independent, either through a job or welfare.

Where will this leave white men and "their" families? The patriarchal family is economically and historically tied to private property, and under western capitalism with the development of the national state. The masculine ideology most strongly asserts home and country as primary values, with wealth and power an individual's greatest goal. The same upper class of men who created private property and founded nation-states also created the family. It is an expensive institution, and only the upper classes have been able to maintain it properly. However, American "democracy" has spread the ideology to the working class. The greatest pride of a working man is that he can support "his" wife and children and maintain a home (even though this is an impossibility for most). The very definition of a bum or derelict is that he does not maintain a wife, children, and home. Consequently, he is an outcast. It is absurd to consider the possibility of women sharing the privilege of owning a family. Even though women quite often do support families including their husbands, they gain no prestige from doing so. In fact, the family without a male head or support is considered an inferior family. A woman supporting her family actually degrades the family.

At this point in history, white working-class men will fight for nothing except those values associated with the masculine ideology, the ideology of the ruling class—family, home, property, country. This force, the organized or organizable working class, has been important in other social revolutions. However, because of the caste system which reigns here, the American "democracy" of white males, and the power of the nation in the world, white male workers are not now a revolutionary group in America. Among the most oppressed part of the white working-class males—Irish, Italian, Portuguese, French Canadian, Polish immigrants—the patriarchal Catholic church buttresses the masculine ideology with its emphasis on family. Even among lower-caste groups, Puerto Ricans and Mexican-Americans, the church reinforces masculine domination.

However, the women who "belong" to these men are going to revolt along with the women who belong to middle-class men, and women on welfare. Black women will probably continue to fight alongside men in the black liberation movement, with a reversal of the trend toward taking second place to the black man in order for him to gain his "proper" masculine status according to the prevailing masculine ideology. When the white male working class is confronted with the revolt of women against the family, their oppression as workers may become much clearer to them.

V

Feminism is opposed to the masculine ideology. I do not suggest that all women are feminists, though many are; certainly some men are oppressed by the masculine ideology, and some women embrace it in its most vicious forms. However, most women have been programmed for a role, maternity, which develops a certain consciousness of care for others, self-reliance, flexibility, noncompetitiveness, cooperation, and materialism. In addition, we have inherited and continue to suffer an oppression which forces us to use our wits to survive, to know our enemy. So we have developed the consciousness of the oppressed, not the oppressor, even though some women have the right to oppress others, and all have the right to oppress children. If these positive maternal traits, conditioned into women, are desirable traits, they are desirable for everyone, not just women. By destroying the present society, and building a society on feminist principles, men will be forced to live in the human community on terms very different from the present. For that to happen, feminism must be asserted as the basis of revolutionary social change. Women and other oppressed people must lead and structure the revolution and the new society to assure the dominance of feminist principles.[3] Our present female liberation movement is preparing us for that task, as is the black liberation movement preparing black people for their revolutionary leadership role.

The female liberation movement is developing in the context of international social revolution, but it is also heir to a 120-year struggle for women's rights. The nineteenth-century feminist movement as well as its child, the women's suffrage movement, were more modest in their demands. They fought from a base of no rights, no power at all. In the first movement, women began fighting for the right of females to speak publicly for abolitionism. The cause of female rights and the end of slavery were inexorably linked. The early feminists did not see the family as a decadent institution. They wanted to find a way to force

[3] *Feminism:* the theory of the political economic and social equality of the sexes (*Webster's Seventh New Collegiate Dictionary*).

men to share responsibility in supporting their families, and they saw alcohol as an enemy of family solidarity.

With the end of slavery, only black males received citizenship. Black women joined white women in being denied enfranchisement. Women, then, began the long struggle for suffrage. They felt they could make the large-scale changes in society which they saw as necessary through their influence in politics. They most certainly questioned the very foundations of civilization, but their strategy and tactics for gaining the desired upheaval of masculine society revolved around electoral politics. They believed they lived in a democratic society. In the process of their struggle, they opened the door for our present female liberation movement. They won not only the right to vote, but many other legal rights as well, including the custodial rights to their children. More than that, women began to fight their oppression and lift up their heads. They began to emerge from privacy and to know they did indeed have rights for which they must fight. They gained confidence in the struggle, and asserted a new independence, which we all inherited.

We also inherited an understanding of the weakness of single-issue tactics, and of "organizing" women around issues, rather than exposing a complete analysis of female oppression. Thanks to gains made by our feminist predecessors, though, we have the confidence to assert feminism as a positive force, rather than asking for equality in the man's world. We can think of men changing, and demand that they do so. We can consider leading a social revolution, not just benefiting from the benevolence and change of heart of those in power or of a single man. We can assert the necessity of industrializing all housework, of extending public education of children to birth, and of demanding the development of maternal skills and consciousness in men.

We are developing necessary skills—self-defense and physical strength, the ability to work collectively and politically, rather than privately and personally, and the ability to teach our ideas to many other women in such a way that they then can become teachers as well. From these new relations and skills will be built the values of the new society. Right now they are our tools of struggle. Though we may work in isolated and difficult situations, we can know our larger strategy and goals, and know that we are a part of a world-wide struggle for human liberation in just societies.

Sex equality:

the beginnings of ideology

ALICE S. ROSSI

The New Feminist movement has often been likened to the black civil rights effort. "Women know from personal experience what it is like to be 'put down' by men, and can therefore understand what it is to be 'put down' as a black by whites," says Dr. Rossi. However, there are obvious differences between the two drives against discrimination. Women are restricted because they are married to men, and their conditioning is such that a drive for sexual equality might create intolerable resistance and tension in the relationship.

Freudian theory has been a major contributor to status differentiation between the sexes, though Freud's ideas on the sexual development of the female are refuted by recent studies.

Dr. Rossi offers three potential models for dealing with the goals of sexual equality. The one most likely to work, she believes, would call for changes in traditional value systems of both men and women.

Alice S. Rossi is associate professor of sociology at Goucher College. She has held research appointments at Cornell, Harvard, Johns Hopkins, and the University of Chicago.

It should not prejudice my voice that I'm not born a man
If I say something advantageous to the present situation.
For I'm taxed too, and as a toll provide men for the nation
    While, miserable graybeards, you,
    It is true
Contribute nothing of any importance whatever to our
    needs;
    But the treasure raised against the Medes,
You've squandered, and do nothing in return, save that
    you make
Our lives and persons hazardous by some imbecile mistake.
What can you answer? Now be careful, don't arouse my
    spite,
Or with my slipper I'll take you napping
    faces slapping
    Left and right.
                              Aristophanes, *Lysistrata*, 413 B.C.

It is 2400 years since Lysistrata organized a sex strike among
Athenian women in a play that masked a serious antiwar opposition beneath a thin veneer of bawdy hilarity. The play is unique
in drama as a theme of women power and sex solidarity, and
takes on a fresh relevance when read in this tumultuous era.
Women in our day are active as students, as blacks, as workers,
as war protesters, but far less often as women qua women pressing for equality with men, or actively engaging in a dialogue
of what such equality should mean. Until the last few years,
women power has meant only womanpower, a "resource to be
tapped," as the manpower specialists put it.

It has been a century since John Stuart Mill published his
classic essay on "The Subjection of Women" in England, and
the Seneca Falls Conference in New York State gave public
recognition to the presence of women critical of the political
and economic restrictions that barred their participation in the
major institutions of American society. Thus, the time is propi-
tious in which to examine what we mean by a goal of equality
between the sexes, rather than to persist in the American pen-

chant for tinkering with short-run "improvements in the status of women."

The major objective of this article is to examine three possible goals of equality between the sexes, while a secondary objective is to pinpoint the ways in which inequality on sex grounds differs from racial, ethnic, or religious inequality.

MEANING OF INEQUALITY

A group may be said to suffer from inequality if its members are restricted in access to legitimate valued positions or rewards in a society for which their ascribed status is not a relevant consideration. In our day, this is perhaps least ambiguous where the status of citizens is concerned: we do not consider race, sex, religion, or national background relevant criteria for the right to vote or to run for public office. Here we are dealing with a particular *form* of inequality—codified law—and a particular *type* of inequality—civil and political rights of an individual as a citizen. There are several other forms of inequality in addition to legal statute: corporate or organizational policies and regulations, and most importantly, those covert social pressures which restrict the aspirations or depress the motivation of individuals on the ascribed grounds of their membership in certain categories. Thus, a teacher who scoffs at a black boy or white girl who aspires to become an engineer, or a society which uniformly applies pressure on girls to avoid occupational choices in medicine and law are examples of covert pressures which bolster racial and sexual inequality. *Forms* of inequality therefore range from explicit legal statute to informal social pressure.

Type of inequality adds a second dimension: the area of life in which the inequality is evidenced. There are inequalities in the *public* sector, as citizens, employees, consumers, or students; and there are inequalities in the *private* sector as family, organization, or club members. Throughout American history, the gains made for greater racial and sexual equality have been based on constitutional protection of individual rights in the public area of inequality, as citizens, students, and workers. But precisely because of constitutional protection of privacy of home, family, and person, it is more difficult to remove inequalities rooted in the private sphere of life. Attempts to compensate for emotional and nutritional deprivation of preschool, inner-city children are through three-hour Headstart exposure to verbal stimulation and nutritious food from caring adults. We have yet to devise a means to compensate for the influences of parents who depress a daughter's aspiration to become a physician, while urging a son to aspire beyond his capacity or preference. In both instances, the tactics used tend to be compensatory devices in the public sphere (counseling and teaching in the schools, for example) to make up for or undo the effects of inequalities that persist in the family.

There is, thus, a continuum of increasing difficulty in effecting social and political change along both dimensions of inequality: by *form*, from legal statute to corporate regulation to covert and deeply imbedded social mores; by *type*, from citizenship to schooling and employment, to the private sector of family. Hence, the easiest target in removing inequality involves legal statute change or judicial interpretation of rights in the public sector, and the most difficult area involves changes in the covert social mores in family and social life. It is far easier to change laws which presently penalize women as workers, students, or citizens than it will be to effect social changes in family life and higher education which depress the aspirations and motivations of women.

An example of this last point can be seen in higher education. Few graduate schools discriminate against women applicants, but there are widespread subtle pressures once women are registered as students in graduate departments—from both faculty and male peers. In one graduate department of sociology, women represent a full third of the students, and, hence, the faculty cannot be charged with discriminatory practices toward the admission of women students. On the other hand, it was not uncommon in that department to hear faculty members characterize a woman graduate student who showed strong commitment and independence as an "unfeminine bitch," and others who were quiet and unassertive as "lacking ambition"—women who will "never amount to much." Since it is difficult to be simultaneously independent and ambitious, but conventionally feminine and dependent, it would appear that the informal rules prevent many women from winning the game, although they are accepted as players.

Discrimination against women in hiring or promotion may be barred by statute and corporate policy, but this does not magically stimulate any great movement of women up the occupational status ladder. Progress on the legal front must be accompanied by compensatory tactics to free girls and women from the covert depression of their motivations and aspirations through ridicule and double-bind pressures to be contradictory things.

UNIQUE CHARACTERISTICS OF SEX INEQUALITY

Many women find an easy empathy with the plight of the poor, the black, and minority religious groups—not from any innate feminine intuition, but simply because a subordinate group is sensitive to both unintended and intentional debasement or discrimination where another subordinate group is concerned. Women know from personal experience what it is like to be "put down" by men, and can therefore understand what it is to be "put down" as a black by whites. But there are also fundamental differences between sex as a category of social inequality and the categories of race, religion, or ethnicity. I shall discuss three of the most important differences.

Category size and residence
In the case of race, religion, and ethnicity, we are literally dealing with minority groups in the American population, whether Mexican, Indian, Jewish, Catholic, or black. This is not the case for sex, since women are actually a numerical majority in the population.

While the potential is present for numerical strength to press for the removal of inequalities, this is counterbalanced by other ways in which women are prevented from effectively utilizing their numerical strength. The Irish, the Italians, and the Jews in an earlier period, and blacks in more recent history, have been able to exert political pressure for representation and legislative change because residential concentration gave them voter strength in large urban centers. By contrast, women are for the most part *evenly distributed throughout the population.* Women can exert political pressure in segmental roles as consumers, workers, New Yorkers, or the aged; but not as a cohesive political group based on sex solidarity. It is inconceivable that a political organization of blacks would avoid the "race" issue, yet the League of Women Voters does precisely this when it takes pride in avoiding "women's" issues.

Early sex-role socialization

Age and sex are the earliest social categories an individual learns. The differentiation between mother and father, or parent and child, is learned at a tender, formative stage of life, and consequently, we carry into adulthood a set of age and sex role expectations that are extremely resistant to change. Not only do girls learn to accept authority from the older generation and from men, but they learn this lesson in intense, intimate relationships. By the time they reach adulthood, women are well socialized to seek and to find gratification in an intimate dependence on men, and in responsible authority over children. They may be dominant and affirmative mothers with their own children, or as teachers in classrooms, but pliant and submissive as wives.

Sex role expectations tend to remain a stubborn part of our impulse lives. This is often not visible among young men and women until they become parents. Many young people are egalitarian peers in school, courtship, and early marriage. With the birth of a child, deeper layers of their personalities come into play. Since there is little or no formal education for parenthood in our society, only a thin veneer of Spock-reading hides the acting out of old parental models that have been observed and internalized in childhood, triggering a regression to traditional sex roles that gradually spreads from the parental role to the marriage and self-definition of both sexes.

As a result of early sex-role socialization, there is bound to be a lag between political and economic emancipation of women and the inner adjustment to equality of both men and women. Even in radical political movements, women have often had to caucus and fight for their acceptance as equal peers to men. Without such efforts on their own behalf, women are as likely to be "girl-Friday" assistants in a radical movement espousing class and racial equality as they are in a business corporation, a labor union, or a conservative political party.

Pressures against sex solidarity

Racial, ethnic, and religious conflict can reach an acute stage of political strife in the movement for equality, without affecting the solidarity of the families of blacks, whites, Jews, or gentiles. Such strife may, in fact, increase the solidarity of these family units. A "we versus them" dichotomy does not cut into family units in the case of race, religion, or ethnicity as it does in the case of sex. Since women typically live in greater intimacy with men than they do with other women, there is potential conflict within family units when women press hard for sex equality. Their demands are on predominantly male legislators and employers in the public domain—husbands and fathers in the private sector. A married black woman can affiliate with an activist civil rights group with no implicit threat to her marriage. For a married woman to affiliate with an activist women's rights group might very well trigger tension in her marriage. While there is probably no limit to the proportion of blacks who might actively fight racial discrimination, a large proportion of married women have not combated sex discrimination. Many of them fear conflict with men, or benefit in terms of a comfortable high status in exchange for economic dependence upon their husbands. There are many more women in the middle class who benefit from sex inequality than there are blacks in the middle class who benefit from racial inequality.

The size of a women's rights movement has, therefore, been responsive to the proportion of "unattached" women in a population. An excess of females over males, a late age at marriage, postponement of childbearing, a high divorce rate, a low remarriage rate, and greater longevity for women, all increase the

number of unattached women in a society, and therefore increase the potential for sex-equality activism. The hard core of
activists in past suffrage and feminist movements were women
without marital and family ties: exwives, nonwives, or childless
wives, whose need to support themselves triggered their concern for equal rights to vote, to work, and to advance in their
work. The lull in the women's rights movement in the 1950's
was related to the fact that this same decade saw the lowest age
at marriage and the highest proportion of the population married in all of our history.

Since 1960, the age at marriage has moved up; the birth rate is
down to what it was in the late 1930's; the divorce rate is up
among couples married a long time, and more married women
are in the labor force than ever before. These are all relevant
contributors to the renascence of women's rights activism in the
mid-1960's. The presence of older and married women in
women's rights organizations (like the National Organization
for Women) is also responsible for a broadening of the range of
issues that concern women activists—from the civil, political,
and economic concerns they share with feminists of an earlier
day, to a host of changes affecting family roles: repeal of abortion laws, revision of divorce laws, community provision of
child-care facilities, equal treatment under Social Security in old
age, and a debunking of the clinging-vine or tempting-Eve
image of married women that pervades the American mass
media.

The point remains, however, that movement toward sex
equality is restricted by the fact that our most intimate human
relation is the heterosexual one of marriage. This places a major
brake on the development of sex solidarity among women, a
brake that is not present in other social inequalities, since marriage tends to be endogamous with respect to class, race, and religion.

MODELS OF EQUALITY

Courses in social stratification, minority groups, prejudice, and
discrimination have been traditional fare in sociological cur-

riculum for a long time. Many sociologists studied immigrants and their children and puzzled about the eventual shape of a society that underwent so massive an injection of diverse cultures. From these writings, we can extract three potential models that will be useful in sketching the alternate goals not only for the relations between ethnic groups, but for those of race and sex as well.

Three such models may be briefly defined, and then each in turn explored in somewhat greater detail:

Pluralist model
This model anticipates a society in which marked racial, religious, and ethnic differences are retained and valued for their diversity, yielding a heterogeneous society in which it is hoped cultural strength is increased by the diverse strands making up the whole society.

Assimilation model
This model anticipates a society in which the minority groups are gradually absorbed into the mainstream by losing their distinguishing characteristics and acquiring the language, occupational skills, and life style of the majority of the host culture.

Hybrid model
This model anticipates a society in which there is change in both the ascendant group and the minority groups—a "melting-pot" hybrid requiring changes not only in blacks and Jews and women, but white male Protestants as well.

PLURALIST MODEL OF EQUALITY

It is dubious whether any society has ever been truly pluralist in the sense that all groups which comprise it are on an equal footing of status, power, or rewards. Pluralism often disguises a social system in which one group dominates—the upper classes (white Anglo-Saxon Protestants)—and minority ethnic, religious, or racial groups are confined to the lower classes. The upper classes may ceremonially invoke the country's cultural heterogeneity, and delight in ethnic food, art, and music, but exclude the ethnic members themselves from their professions, country clubs, and neighborhoods. Bagels and lox for breakfast, soul food for lunch, and lasagna for dinner; but no Jews, blacks, or Italians on the professional and neighborhood turf! Pluralism has been a congenial model for the race segregationist as well, rationalizing the confinement of blacks to unskilled labor, segregated schools, and neighborhoods.

In the case of sex, the pluralist model posits the necessity of traditional sex role differentiation between the sexes on the grounds of fundamental physiological and hence social differences between the sexes. This is the perspective subscribed to by most behavioral scientists, clinical psychologists, and psychoanalysts, despite the fact that the women they have studied and analyzed are the products of a society that systematically *produces* such sex differences through childrearing and schooling practices. There is no way of allocating observed sex differences to innate physiology or to socio-cultural conditioning.

Freudian theory has contributed to the assumption of innate sex differences on which recent scholars in psychology and sociology have built their case for the necessity of social role and status differentiation between the sexes. Freud codified the belief that men get more pleasure than women from sex in his theory of the sexual development of the female: the transition from an early stage in which girls experience the clitoris as the leading erogenous zone of their bodies to a mature stage in which vaginal orgasm provides the woman with her major sexual pleasure. Women who did not make this transition were then viewed as sexually "anaesthetic" and "psychosexually immature." Psychological theory often seems sterner and more resistant to change than the people to which it is applied. It is incredible that the Freudian theory of female sexuality was retained for decades despite thousands of hours of intimate therapeutic data from women, only recently showing signs of weakening under the impact of research conducted by Masters and Johnson and reported in their *Human Sexual Response*, that there is no anatomical difference between clitoral and vaginal orgasm.

Implicit in both psychological theory of sex differences and the Freudian, vaginal-orgasm theory was a basic assumption that women should be exclusively dependent on men for their sexual pleasure, hiding from view the realization that masturbation may be different from, but not necessarily less gratifying sexually than, sexual intercourse. Much the same function has been served by the strong pressures to disassociate sex from maternity. Physicians have long known that nursing is associated with uterine contractions and have noted that male babies often have erections while nursing, but no one has suggested that the starry-eyed contentment of a nursing mother is a blend of genital as well as maternal pleasure. The cultural insistence upon separating sex from maternity, as the insistence that vaginal orgasm is the only "normal satisfaction" of a mature woman, serves the function of preventing women from seeing that they can find pleasure and fulfillment from themselves, other women, and their children and do not have to depend exclusively upon men for such gratification.

Coupled with this is the further assumption, peculiar to American society, that childrearing is the exclusive responsibility of the parents themselves, and not a community responsibility to assure every child a healthy physical and social development (as it is, for example, in East European countries, Israel, and Sweden). This belief keeps women tied closely to the home for the most vigorous years of their adulthood. The "new" look to a woman's life span, now institutionalized by over 100 centers for continuing education for women in the United States, does nothing to alter this basic assumption, but merely adapts to our lengthened life span. Women are urged to withdraw from outside obligations during the childbearing and rearing years and to return for further training and participation in the labor force when children reach an appropriate mature age. The consequences of such late return to active work away from the home are lower incomes, work at levels below the ability of the women, and withdrawal for the very years all studies show to be the peaks of creativity in work, their twenties and thirties.

Why does American society persist in maintaining erroneous

myths concerning female sexuality, contrary to research evidence, as it does in urging women to believe their children's development requires their daily attendance upon them, again contrary to research evidence? I believe the answer lies in the economic demand that men work at persistent levels of high efficiency and creativity. To free men to do this requires a social arrangement in which the family system serves as the shock-absorbing handmaiden of the occupational system. The stimulation of women's desires for an affluent style of life and a bountiful maternity—to be eager and persistent consumers of goods and producers of babies—serves the function of adding continual pressure on men to be high earners. The combination of pronatalist values and aspirations for a high standard of living has the effect of both releasing and requiring men to give heavy psychic and time investment to their jobs, and requiring women to devote their primary efforts and commitments to homemaking. As a result, the broad sweep of many an American woman's life span is caught by the transitions from Bill's daughter to John's wife to Johnny's mother and Billy's grandmother.

Behind the veneer of modern emancipation is a woman isolated in an apartment or suburban home, exclusively responsible for the care of young children, dependent on her husband for income, misled to believe that sex gratification is only possible via a vaginal orgasm simultaneous with male ejaculation, and urged to buy more and more clothes and household possessions, which she then takes more time but little pleasure in maintaining. Complementing the life of the woman in the pluralist model of sex roles, the American male is prodded to seek success and achievement in a competitive job world at the emotional cost of limited time or psychic energy for his marriage or his children, tempted by the same consumption-stimulating media and promises of easy credit, expected to uproot his family if a move is "good for his career," and ridiculed if he seeks to participate more extensively in home and child care as "unmanly."

The odds are heavily stacked against the pluralist model of society as a goal in terms of which racial, ethnic, or sex equality can be achieved.

ASSIMILATION MODEL OF EQUALITY

This model anticipates that with time, the minority groups will be gradually absorbed into the mainstream of society by losing their distinguishing characteristics, acquiring the language, educational attainment, and occupational skills of the majority host culture. Concern for inequality along ethnic or racial lines is concentrated on the political, educational, and economic institutions of society. Little sociological interest or political concern is shown once men in the minority group are distributed throughout the occupational system in roughly the same proportion as mainstream males.

Feminist ideology is but one variant of the assimilation model, calling upon women to seek their place with men in the political and occupational world in sufficient numbers to eventually show a 50–50 distribution by sex in the prestigious occupations and political organizations of the society. The federal government has served as a pacesetter for the economy in urging the appointment and promotion of competent women to the highest civil service posts and encouraging private employers to follow the federal example by facilitating the movement of women into executive posts.

The feminist-assimilation model has an implicit fallacy, however. No amount of entreaty will yield an equitable distribution of women and men in the top strata of business and professional occupations, for the simple reason that the life men have led in these strata has been possible only because their own wives were leading traditional lives as homemakers, doing double parent and household duty, and carrying the major burden of civic responsibilities. If it were not for their wives in the background, successful men in American society would have to be single or childless. This is why so many professional women complain privately that what they most need in life is a "wife"!

The assimilation model also makes an assumption that the institutional structure of American society developed over decades by predominantly white Protestant males, constitutes the best of all possible worlds. Whether the call is to blacks or to women to join white men in the mainstream of American society, both racial integration and a feminist ideology accept the structure of American society as it now exists. The assimilation model rejects the psychological theses of innate racial or sex differences implicit in most versions of the pluralist model, but it accepts the social institutions formed by the ascendant group. This is precisely the assumption numerous blacks, women, and members of the younger generation have recently been questioning and rejecting.

HYBRID MODEL OF EQUALITY

The hybrid model of equality rejects both traditional psychological assumptions and the institutional structure we have inherited. It anticipates a society in which the lives of men and of whites will be different, not only women and blacks. In fact, it might be that this hybrid model would involve greater change in the role of men than of women, because institutional changes it would require involve a restructuring to bring the world of jobs and politics closer to the fulfillment of individual human needs for both creativity and fellowship. From this point of view, the values many young men and women subscribe to today are congenial to the hybrid model of equality: the desire for a more meaningful sense of community and a greater depth to personal relations across class, sex, and racial lines; a stress on human fellowship and individual scope for creativity rather than merely rationality and efficiency in our bureaucracies; heightened interest in the humanities and the social sciences from an articulated value base; and a social responsibility commitment to medicine and law rather than a thirst for status and high income. These are all demands for social change by the younger generation in our time that are closer to the values and interests women have held than they are to the values and interests of men. They represent an ardent "no" to the image of society projected by the new crop of male technitronic futurists—a machine- and consumption-oriented society that rewards technological prowess in a "plasticWasp9–5america."

"Because women have tended to play the passive, adaptive role in the past, they have not been prominent as social and political critics of American institutions. In fact, the traditional roles of women confined them to the most conservative institutions of the society: the family, the public schools, and the church. Women deviant enough to seek greater equality with men in professional, business, and academic life have tended to share the values of their masculine colleagues, while professional women who did not share these values have been quiet, either because they distrusted their own critical bent as a vestige of unwanted "womanliness," or because they feared exclusion from the masculine turf they have precariously established themselves on.

But there is a new groundswell in American society, which is a hopeful sign of a movement toward the hybrid model briefly sketched here. One finds it in women's liberation groups across the country, particularly on the university campus. I would predict, for example, that these young women, unlike their professional older sisters, will not bemoan the fact that academic women have been less "productive" than men, but will be critical of the criteria used to assess academic productivity. Up to now these criteria have been such things as "number of publications," "number of professional organization memberships," and "number of offices held in professional organizations." The new breed of women will ask, as many young students are now demanding, that the quality of teaching, the degree of colleagueship with students, the extent of service to both an academic institution and its surrounding community, become part of the criteria on which the productivity of an academic man or woman is evaluated. No one has conducted research on academic productivity with this enlarged net of criteria, and it is a moot point whether men would show greater productivity than women if such criteria were applied. Though it will be a difficult road, with all the money and prestige pulling in the opposite direction, this thrust on the part of the young, together with like-minded older humanist scholars and critics, creative artists, and natural and behavioral scientists, has the potential of developing oases of health and sanity in many educational, welfare, and cultural institutions of American society.

CONCLUSION

A *pluralist* model of social equality is implicitly a conservative goal, a descriptive model that accepts what exists at a given point in time as desirable and good. The *assimilation* model is implicitly a liberal goal, a Horatio Alger model that accepts the present structure of society as stable and desirable, and urges minority groups to accept the values and goals of the dominant group within that system as their own. The *hybrid* model is a radical goal which rejects the present structure of society and seeks instead a new breed of men and women and a new vision of the future. Applied to the role of women, these models may be illustrated in a summary fashion as follows: the pluralist model says the woman's nurturance finds its best expression in maternity; the assimilation model says women must be motivated to seek professional careers in medicine similar to those pursued now by men; the hybrid model says, rather, that the structure of medicine can be changed so that more women will be attracted to medical careers, and male physicians will be able to live more balanced, less difficult and status-dominated lives.

An analysis of sex equality goals may start with the reality of contemporary life, but soon requires an imaginative leap to a new conception of what a future good society should be. With the hybrid model of equality one envisages a future in which family, community, and play are valued on a par with politics and work for both sexes, for all the races, and for all social classes and nations which comprise the human family. We are on the brink not of the "end" of ideology, but its "beginning."

*Problems
and Goals
of the
New Feminism*

Women as a minority group

ELIZABETH DUNCAN KOONTZ

Women still comprise a minority in total employment figures. In the past, they have been considered a labor pool to be hired when the need is great, to be fired when the economy slows down. Post-Vietnam War adjustments, with thousands of men added to the labor force, a reduction of the military economy, and entrance into the labor market of workers born in the baby-boom years in the fifties, will have an impact on the position of women in the employment world. Many feminists feel it is imperative to consolidate their rights now.

In 1968, over 29 million women were working, about 40 per cent of the labor force. Their median pay in 1968, according to the Bureau of Labor Statistics in the Department of Commerce, was 58.2 per cent of men's: $4,457. In that year only 13.8 per cent of women were earning $7,000 or more, as compared with 58.6 per cent for males.

Some women urgently need part-time work, either for money or to keep up with their professions in childrearing years, but few employers are willing to make this adjustment. Those who have are reported to be usually pleased with the results: they may well benefit from the best efforts of two skilled people working at their peak for a few hours each day.

High-school or college counselors will have to help break the stereotype of the working woman's vocation if she is to venture into some of the better paying fields usually labeled "Help Wanted: Male," such as repairing household appliances, or in professions such as medicine and law. Mrs. Koontz in her article points out that a number of myths must be overcome before equality of opportunity on jobs will be possible for women.

Elizabeth Duncan Koontz is director of the Women's Bureau in the Department of Labor, and the first black woman to be appointed to this position. In 1968, she was elected president of the National Education Association, after a career as teacher in the public schools. She is also the United States Delegate to the United Nations Commission on the Status of Women.

The title "Women as a Minority Group" immediately raises the question, "Are women a minority group?" Many people think not.

Numerically, women are not in the minority; they comprise 51 per cent of the population.

As potential voters they outnumber men. In 1968, there were 62,071,000 women of voting age in the population as against 54,464,000 men. And, had women voted as a bloc in that year, they could have controlled the election, since those who voted outnumbered men by 2,938,000.

They also make up 51 per cent of individual shareholders owning stocks. However, this figure loses some of its significance when you consider that these holdings are usually managed by men. Consider also the volume of holdings of mutual funds, corporations, husband and wife joint accounts, and other owners of stock. Women account for only 18 per cent of the total ownership of stock.

The fact of the matter is that while women are not, in the overall picture, a minority group, they do constitute a minority in some facets of our society—in the work force, in labor unions, in the professions, and in public office.

And, of course, they are in many instances treated like a minority group. For example, women are not always equal with men before the law. In seven of the eight community property states in 1969 community property was generally under the control of the husband; in five states a married woman's freedom to venture into separate business is limited; and in nearly all states a wife does not have the same rights as her husband to establish a separate domicile.

The very fact that there is a debate as to whether or not women are equal under the Constitution implies minority status. One school of thought has held that women are guaranteed equality under the law in the Fifth and Fourteenth Amendments. The Supreme Court has thus far not dealt with any cases which raise this point.

Many feel that in order to adequately protect women we must have an Equal Rights Amendment to the Constitution. This proposed amendment states: "Equality of rights under the law shall not be denied or abridged by the United States or by any State on account of sex." As of March 11, 1970, it had been sponsored by 225 members of the House and 75 Senators, but for years has been held up in the Judiciary Committees of the House and Senate.

Education is another area in which women encounter discrimination. Not only are they discouraged from considering careers in fields generally considered "men's work," they are actually denied equal access to education. A few cases make the headlines, but I suspect those are only the top of the iceberg and the great bulk of injustice lies below the surface.

In one case a thirteen-year-old Brooklyn girl had to threaten court action to get into all-male Stuyvesant High School where she could get the kind of scientific education to fulfill the promise of a brilliant record.

The further such a brilliant girl goes up the academic ladder, the more difficult it may become for her. An example may illustrate what I mean. Not long ago I read that one department of a large midwest university had awarded fellowships over the years at a rate of 513 for men, 121 for women. It was the department of sociology, a field usually thought to be as open to women as to men.

Graduate schools, too, tend to give preference to male applicants. According to the United States Office of Education, women do well on entrance examinations in law and medicine, but their admission into those graduate schools is held down. Indeed, the percentage of women graduates in some fields is so constant over the years—7 per cent for women physicians, for example—that one suspects the existence of a quota system.

And once a woman has been through graduate school, how does she fare if she seeks a teaching career? A couple of examples suggest the answer. In that sociology department I mentioned, there have been exactly four tenured women since 1892. An unspoken doctrine of "No women need apply here" seems to prevail.

In another university it takes an average of three years for a male Ph.D. to move from assistant to associate professor. It takes a woman Ph.D. an average of nine years to achieve that rank.

Outside the women's colleges, how many women attain the rank of full professor? Such a woman is an exception, and it is a good guess that her road was harder, her qualifications superior to those of her male colleagues. Outside the women's colleges, how many women have become presidents, vice presidents, or deans, except deans of women? And we are not talking of a field like nuclear physics where one might expect men to dominate, but education, where women have traditionally played a strong role.

Is it any wonder, then, that the number of women in some professions is small, especially small when compared with some other industrialized nations today? Compared to our seven per cent for women physicians, the British have sixteen per cent and the Soviet Union 75 per cent. Only three per cent of our lawyers are women. In Germany nearly a third of the lawyers are women; in Denmark nearly half. Both France and Sweden have more women dentists and pharmacists than the United States. Women make up only nine per cent of our scientists, nine per cent of our professors, one per cent of our engineers.

Women one meets abroad and foreign women who visit this country usually ask the same question sooner or later: "In a country where women have so much freedom and where their voluntary organizations are so influential, why are there so few women in the Congress and in top government jobs?" Both India and Israel have women heads of government. Denmark has a woman on its highest court. How long will it be before a woman sits on the bench of our Supreme Court? When will we again have a woman cabinet member?

One obvious answer, of course, might be that the prospects are improving. The decade of the sixties has brought real changes in the prospects for women—changes in Federal Government hiring policy, as well as great advances in legislation. It helps us gain perspective if we recall that until 1962 it was the policy of Federal agencies to allow a hiring officer to specify a particular sex for a job if he chose to, regardless of the duties and without advancing any reasons.

Contrast that with government policy now: hire on the basis of merit alone, without regard to race, color, religion, national origin—or sex. The change has created a much more hospitable atmosphere for women, especially professional women. Between 1963 and 1968 the proportion of women among persons hired by the Federal Government from professional registers has doubled.

The change was set in motion in December 1961, when President Kennedy established the Commission on the Status of Women. One of his intentions was to make the Federal career service free of discrimination based on sex. The recommendations of the Commission laid the groundwork for legislation that followed, legislation rooted in the principle of equality. Because it was enforced, it altered the character of Federal hiring and will have, I believe, an even greater effect on the nation at large.

The first Federal legislative attack was on wage differentials based on sex. The Equal Pay Act of 1963 established in law the principle that men and women have a right to equal pay for equal work. " 'A fair day's work for a fair day's wages'; it is as just a demand as governed men ever made of governing. It is the everlasting right of man," said Thomas Carlyle in 1843. It took 120 years more to see that it was the everlasting right of women, too.

Enactment of Title VII of the Civil Rights Act of 1964 advanced still further the principle that men and women workers should be treated as equals, for it prohibited discrimination on the basis of sex in all phases of employment. Guidelines laid down for the interpretation of this law have established, for example, that a job cannot be limited to members of only one sex unless sex is a bona fide occupational qualification for that job; that help-wanted ads classified on the basis of sex, such as columns headed "Male" or "Female," constitute discrimination based on sex; that employers can no longer maintain separate lists for men and women for the purpose of deciding lines of progression for promotion or seniority; and that employers cannot discriminate in such areas as retirement and insurance plans.

The Equal Employment Opportunity Commission has issued a new guideline which provides that state labor laws applying to women, such as those regulating hours of work and weightlifting, may not be used by an employer as a defense to a charge of sex discrimination in failing to hire women. This has the effect of a ruling that Title VII supersedes a state's so-called protective labor laws.

The principle of equal opportunity was reinforced in 1967 when President Johnson amended Executive Order 11246 to outlaw discrimination on the basis of sex in Federal employment, in employment by Federal contractors and subcontractors, and in employment under federally assisted construction contracts. This order is a real boon to women workers in the private sector, since an employer who refuses to comply can lose existing contracts and be denied future contracts.

President Nixon has strengthened the position of women in Federal employment by issuing Executive Order 11478 in which he directs Federal agencies, under the leadership and guidance of the Civil Service Commission, to follow an affirmative program of equal employment opportunity which includes, of course, elimination of discrimination on the basis of sex. His order supersedes those sections of the amended Executive Order 11246 relating to Federal Government employment.

But it is not the legislative accomplishments alone that have changed the outlook on employment for women. What may have equal effect in the long run are the standards the government itself has adopted; for it is becoming a showcase of model employment practices.

I have been pointing to hopeful signs that all is getting better;

and it is. But no one believes that all is well. We know, for example, that discrimination against women still manifests itself in two major ways—the kind of salaries they receive, and the kind of work they do. What women won in the Equal Pay Act of 1963 was the right; we have yet to win the reality. There are still many ways around the law and still many situations in which it does not apply. It is not always easy to prove that jobs are virtually equal, and many intangibles are involved the higher up the scale one goes. As a result there are often great differences between what a man is paid to do a job and what a woman is paid to do the same job.

However, I would like to point out that the Department of Labor has had considerable success in enforcing the law. As of May 20, 1970, it had found $17,514,811 due in back wages to 51,160 persons in cases where the law had been violated. A big problem is that many violations are not reported. This is a responsibility that women themselves must assume, but many would rather settle for a lower wage than risk the displeasure of their employer by filing a complaint.

A common rationalization for permitting wage discrepancies to exist is the assertion that women do not need as much money as men do. This notion is patently ridiculous when one considers how many households, especially among the poor, are headed by women, and how many families would be living in poverty if it were not for the extra paycheck the working wife brings home.

While the salary gap affects the lower-income woman's pocketbook, women all along the line feel it. It injures the morale of the woman with a Ph.D. in chemistry who finds she earns less than a man with an undergraduate degree. Women near the top are constantly bumping their heads against an unseen ceiling. We know it's there even though some women break through it, and we suspect that the motto engraved on it is: "So far you may go and no farther." Its existence is confirmed in the statistics: less than three per cent of the fully employed working women have passed the $10,000 salary limit. Exactly 2.9 per cent are in that wage bracket. The proportion of men in that bracket is twenty-eight per cent.

When it comes to the jobs women do, we feel discrimination is practiced here, too; sometimes obvious, sometimes subtle. We know that women are crowded disproportionately into the menial, low-paying jobs. A majority become service workers, clerks, salesgirls, factory workers, perhaps secretaries. There is nothing wrong with these jobs. But there *is* something wrong in having so little choice. There are many other jobs that women could do, and do very well. They would be well-suited, for example, as upholsterers, optical mechanics, tool-and-die makers, or as repairmen for small electrical appliances, watches, office machines, computers, radios, and television sets. This is just a fraction of the occupations that should be open to young women and for which we should make the necessary training available. The horizons for young women today are needlessly narrow; and we have not done nearly enough to broaden them.

The same story of limited horizons applies to women in professional or technical fields. We educate a great many women; then we simply do not give them jobs in which they can use their real abilities. One statistic that has always distressed me is: of employed women in 1968 who had completed five or more years of college, 7 per cent had taken jobs as unskilled or semi-skilled workers. That represents an astonishing waste of the real abilities of highly educated women.

People call attention to the fact that women have penetrated almost every occupational field, and this, of course, is true. But the fact disguises the reality. For the educated woman, as for the uneducated, certain fields are considered women's work; other fields are considered unsuitable. Of the entire women's work force, only 14 per cent of the workers could be classified as professional or technical, and of these, almost two thirds are either teachers or nurses and other health workers. The question is not whether it is possible for a woman to enter almost any field she chooses; obviously it is possible. But she must have a lot more drive to succeed. She must at a comparatively early age have encouragement, self-confidence, and commitment to a goal to go her own way against the full weight of society's opinion and expectations. That is asking much more of a young woman than we ask of a young man. Not many of us can do it at any age.

In the final analysis, the most difficult barriers facing women are the invisible ones. All but unreachable by legislation, these are the barriers that will be lowered only when we have educated the human heart. For the real enemy lies within. It expresses itself in all those unadmitted prejudices, unthinking assumptions, and outworn myths which, often so subtly, oppose the full development of a woman as an individual. The grandmother of all these myths is: "A woman's place is in the home." But there are many, many more. To sample a few common myths:

> A woman must choose between home and a job; she cannot do both well.
> When a woman works, the chances are increased that her children will become neurotic or troubled.
> Women are overly emotional; they couldn't be cool under pressure.
> Women have a great deal of intuition but men have the logical, analytical minds.
> Women are practical and down-to-earth, but only a man can think abstractly, take the larger, long-range view.
> Women just don't have what it takes.

These are the kinds of prejudices women absorb from the world around them from the time they are little girls. From them a girl learns what is expected of her: that she may do things, but not too well; that she may aspire, but not too high. These are some of the myths which condition a woman to put limitations upon her own expectations, to narrow her vision of the world and what she might do in it. The really pernicious aspect of these myths is not that men believe them, but that women do. If *you* do, then ask yourself: "How can we really change the thinking of the world unless we change our own thinking first?" Perhaps the freedom we seek must begin in our own hearts.

Finally, let us be clear in our own minds about what we really want. Is it equal pay, equal job opportunities, equal rights? Or are these just victories along the way to some larger goal? I believe there is a larger goal that we pursue. I believe that what women must have is freedom—the freedom to choose different life styles, the freedom to fulfill the best that is in them. A philosopher once said: "The great law of culture is: Let each become all that he was created capable of being." I do not think we ask for more than that. I am convinced we cannot settle for less.

The liberation of black women

PAULI MURRAY

Should black women subordinate their fight against sex discrimination to the Black Revolution? Are black women gaining or losing ground in the drive toward human rights?

Pauli Murray makes cogent responses to these questions in her wide-ranging article on The Liberation of Black Women, *and dispenses with some of the stereotypes that plague the black woman in quest of equality of opportunity.*

The author writes from many years as an activist in efforts for human rights in both race and sex. In 1940, she was jailed for refusing to move to a segregated seat on an interstate bus, and as a law student in Washington in the forties she led sit-ins in Washington, D.C., restaurants which led to a Supreme Court decision in 1953 banning discrimination in public accommodations in Washington. In 1944, she challenged the sex bar against admission of women to Harvard Law School.

Pauli Murray is an attorney with a doctorate from Yale Law School. She has practiced privately, has taught constitutional law in Ghana, and is professor of American Studies at Brandeis University. She has also served as consultant to the United States Equal Employment Opportunity Commission. She joined with Betty Friedan and others in the founding of the National Organization for Women in 1966.

Black women, historically, have been doubly victimized by the twin immoralities of Jim Crow and Jane Crow. Jane Crow refers to the entire range of assumptions, attitudes, stereotypes, customs, and arrangements which have robbed women of a positive self-concept and prevented them from participating fully in society as equals with men. Traditionally, racism and sexism in the United States have shared some common origins, displayed similar manifestations, reinforced one another, and are so deeply intertwined in the country's institutions that the successful outcome of the struggle against racism will depend in large part upon the simultaneous elimination of all discrimination based upon sex. Black women, faced with these dual barriers, have often found that sex bias is more formidable than racial bias. If anyone should ask a Negro woman in America what has been her greatest achievement, her honest answer would be, "I survived!"

Negro women have endured their double burden with remarkable strength and fortitude. With dignity they have shared with black men a partnership as members of an embattled group excluded from the normal protections of the society and engaged in a struggle for survival during nearly four centuries of a barbarous slave trade, two centuries of chattel slavery, and a century or more of illusive citizenship. Throughout this struggle, into which has been poured most of the resources and much of the genius of successive generations of American Negroes, these women have often carried a disproportionate share of responsibility for the black family as they strove to keep its integrity intact against a host of indignities to which it has been subjected. Black women have not only stood shoulder to shoulder with black men in every phase of the struggle, but they have often continued to stand firmly when their men were destroyed by it. Few Blacks are unfamiliar with that heroic, if formidable, figure exhorting her children and grandchildren to overcome every obstacle and humiliation and to "Be somebody!"

In the battle for survival, Negro women developed a tradition of independence and self-reliance, characteristics which according to the late Dr. É. Franklin Frazier, Negro sociologist, have "provided generally a pattern of equalitarian relationship between men and women in America." The historical factors which have fostered the black women's feeling of independence have been the economic necessity to earn a living to help support their families—if indeed they were not the sole breadwinners—and the need for the black community to draw heavily upon the resources of all of its members in order to survive.

Yet these survival values have often been distorted, and the qualities of strength and independence observable in many Negro women have been stereotyped as "female dominance" attributed to the "matriarchal" character of the Negro family developed during slavery and its aftermath. The popular conception is that because society has emasculated the black male, he has been unable to assume his economic role as head of the household and the black woman's earning power has placed her in a dominant position. The black militant's cry for the retrieval of black manhood suggests an acceptance of this stereotype, an association of masculinity with male dominance and a tendency to treat the values of self-reliance and independence as purely masculine traits. Thus, while Blacks generally have recognized the fusion of white supremacy and male dominance (note the popular expressions "The Man" and "Mr. Charlie"), male spokesmen for Negro rights have sometimes pandered to sexism in their fight against racism. When nationally known civil rights leader James Farmer ran for Congress against Mrs. Shirley Chisholm in 1968, his campaign literature stressed the need for a "strong male image" and a "man's voice" in Washington.

If idealized values of masculinity and femininity are used as criteria, it would be hard to say whether the experience of slavery subjected the black male to any greater loss of his manhood than the black female of her womanhood. The chasm between the slave woman and her white counterpart (whose own enslavement was masked by her position as a symbol of high virtue and an object of chivalry) was as impassable as the gulf between the male slave and his arrogant white master. If black males suffered from real and psychological castration, black females bore the burden of real or psychological rape. Both situations involved the negation of the individual's personal integrity and attacked the foundations of one's sense of personal worth.

The history of slavery suggests that black men and women shared a rough equality of hardship and degradation. While the black woman's position as sex object and breeder may have given her temporarily greater leverage in dealing with her white master than the black male enjoyed, in the long run it denied her a positive image of herself. On the other hand, the very nature of slavery foreclosed certain conditions experienced by white women. The black woman had few expectations of economic dependence upon the male or of derivative status through marriage. She emerged from slavery without the illusions of a specially protected position as a woman or the possibilities of a parasitic existence as a woman. As Dr. Frazier observed, "Neither economic necessity nor tradition has instilled in her the spirit of subordination to masculine authority. Emancipation only tended to confirm in many cases the spirit of self-sufficiency which slavery had taught."

Throughout the history of Black America, its women have been in the forefront of the struggle for human rights. A century ago Harriet Tubman and Sojourner Truth were titans of the Abolitionist movement. In the 1890's Ida B. Wells-Barnett carried on a one-woman crusade against lynching. Mary McLeod Bethune and Mary Church Terrell symbolize the stalwart woman leaders of the first half of the twentieth century. At the age of ninety, Mrs. Terrell successfully challenged segregation in public places in the nation's capital through a Supreme Court decision in 1953.

In contemporary times we have Rosa Parks setting off the mass struggle for civil rights in the South by refusing to move to the back of the bus in Montgomery in 1955; Daisy Bates guiding the Little Rock Nine through a series of school desegregation crises in 1957-59; Gloria Richardson facing down the National Guard in Cambridge, Maryland, in the early sixties; or Coretta Scott King picking up the fallen standard of her slain husband to continue the fight. Not only these and many other women whose names are well known have given this great human effort its peculiar vitality, but also women in many communities whose names will never be known have revealed the courage and strength of the black woman in America. They are the mothers who stood in schoolyards of the South with their children, many times alone. One cannot help asking: "Would the black struggle have come this far without the indomitable determination of its women?"

Now that some attention is finally being given to the place of the Negro in American history, how much do we hear of the role of the Negro woman? Of the many books published on the Negro experience and the Black Revolution in recent times, to date not one has concerned itself with the struggles of black women and their contributions to history. Of approximately 800 full-length articles published in the *Journal of Negro History* since its inception in 1916, only six have dealt directly with the Negro woman. Only two have considered Negro women as a group: Carter G. Woodson's "The Negro Washerwoman: A Vanishing Figure" (14 *JNH*, 1930) and Jessie W. Pankhurst's "The Role of the Black Mammy in the Plantation Household" (28 *JNH*, 1938).

This historical neglect continues into the present. A significant feature of the civil rights revolution of the 1950's and 1960's was its inclusiveness born of the broad participation of men, women, and children without regard to age and sex. As indicated, school children often led by their mothers in the 1950's won world-wide acclaim for their courage in desegregating the schools. A black child can have no finer heritage to give a sense of "somebodiness" than the knowledge of having personally been part of the great sweep of history. (An older generation, for example, takes pride in the use of the term "Negro," having been part of a seventy-five-year effort to dignify the term by capitalizing it. Now some black militants with a woeful lack of historical perspective have allied themselves symbolically with white racists by downgrading the term to lower case again.) Yet, despite the crucial role which Negro women have played in the struggle, in the great mass of magazine and newspaper print expended on the racial crisis, the aspirations of the black community have been articulated almost exclusively by black males. There has been very little public discussion of the problems, objectives, or concerns of black women.

Reading through much of the current literature on the Black Revolution, one is left with the impression that for all the rhetoric about self-determination, the main thrust of black militancy is a bid of black males to share power with white males in a continuing patriarchal society in which both black and white females are relegated to a secondary status. For example, *Ebony* magazine published a special issue on the Negro woman in 1966. Some of the articles attempted to delineate the contributions of Negro women as heroines in the civil rights battle in Dixie, in the building of the New South, in the arts and professions, and as intellectuals. The editors, however, felt it necessary to include a full-page editorial to counter the possible effect of the articles by women contributors. After paying tribute to the Negro woman's contributions in the past, the editorial reminded *Ebony*'s readers that "the past is behind us," that "the immediate goal of the Negro woman today should be the establishment of a strong family unit in which the father is the dominant person," and that the Negro woman would do well to follow the example of the Jewish mother "who pushed her husband to success, educated her male children first and engineered good marriages for her daughters." The editors also declared that the career woman "should be willing to postpone her aspirations until her children, too, are old enough to be on their own," and, as if the point had not been made clear enough, suggested that if "the woman should, by any chance, make more money than her husband, the marriage could be in real trouble."

While not as blatantly Victorian as *Ebony*, other writers on black militancy have shown only slightly less myopia. In *Black Power and Urban Crisis*, Dr. Nathan Wright, Chairman of the 1967 National Black Power Conference, made only three brief references to women: "the employment of female skills," "the beauty of black women," and housewives. His constant reference to Black Power was in terms of black males and black manhood. He appeared to be wholly unaware of the parallel struggles of women and youth for inclusion in decision-making, for when he dealt with the reallocation of power, he noted that "the churches and housewives of America" are the most readily influential groups which can aid in this process.

In *Black Rage*, psychiatrists Greer and Cobbs devote a chapter to achieving womanhood. While they sympathetically describe the traumatic experience of self-depreciation which a black woman undergoes in a society in which the dominant standard of beauty is "the blond, blue-eyed, white-skinned girl with regular features," and make a telling point about the burden of the stereotype that Negro women are available to white men, they do not get beyond a framework in which the Negro woman is seen as a sex object. Emphasizing her concern with "feminine narcissism" and the need to be "lovable" and "attractive," they conclude: "Under the sign of discouragement and rejection which governs so much of her physical operation, she is inclined to organize her personal ambitions in terms of her achievements serving to compensate for other losses and hurts." Nowhere do the authors suggest that Negro women, like women generally, might be motivated to achieve as *persons*. Implied throughout the discussion is the sexuality of Negro females.

The ultimate expression of this bias is the statement attributed to a black militant male leader: "The position of the black woman should be prone." Thus, there appears to be a distinctly conservative and backward-looking view in much of what black males write today about black women, and many black women have been led to believe that the restoration of the black male to his lost manhood must take precedence over the claims of black women to equalitarian status. Consequently, there has been a tendency to acquiesce without vigorous protest to policies which emphasize the "underemployment" of the black male in relation to the black female and which encourage the upgrading and education of black male youth while all but ignoring the educational and training needs of black female youth, although the highest rates of unemployment today are among black female teenagers. A parallel tendency to concentrate on career and training opportunities primarily for black males is evident in government and industry.

As this article goes to press, further confirmation of a patriarchal view on the part of organizations dominated by black males is found in the BLACK DECLARATION OF INDEPENDENCE published as a full-page advertisement in *The New York Times* on July 3, 1970. Signed by members of the National Committee of Black Churchmen and presuming to speak "By Order and on Behalf of Black People," this document ignores both the personhood and the contributions of black women to the cause of human rights. The drafters show a shocking insensitivity to the revitalized women's rights/women's liberation movement which is beginning to capture the front pages of national newspapers and the mass media. It evidences a parochialism which has hardly moved beyond the eighteenth century in its thinking about women. Not only does it paraphrase the 1776 Declaration about the equality of "all Men" with a noticeable lack of imagination, but it also declares itself "in the Name of our good People and our own Black Heroes." Then follows a list of black males prominent in the historic struggle for liberation. The names of Harriet Tubman, Sojourner Truth, Mary McLeod Bethune, or Daisy Bates, or any other black women are conspicuous by their absence. If black male leaders of the Christian faith—who concededly have suffered much through denigration of their personhood and who are committed to the equality of all in the eyes of God—are callous to the indivisibility of human rights, who is to remember?

In the larger society, of course, black and white women share the common burden of discrimination based upon sex. The parallels between racism and sexism have been distinctive features of American society, and the movements to eliminate these two evils have often been allied and sometimes had interchangeable leadership. The beginnings of a women's rights movement in this country is linked with the Abolitionist movement. In 1840, William Lloyd Garrison and Charles Remond, the latter a Negro, refused to be seated as delegates to the World Anti-Slavery Convention in London when they learned that women members of the American delegation had been excluded because of their sex and could sit only in the balcony and observe the proceedings. The seed of the Seneca Falls Convention of 1848, which marked the formal beginning of the women's rights struggle in the United States, was planted at that London conference. Frederick Douglass attended the Seneca Falls Convention and rigorously supported Elizabeth Cady Stanton's daring resolution on woman's suffrage. Except for a temporary defection during the controversy over adding "sex" to the fifteenth Amendment, Douglass remained a staunch advocate of women's rights until his death in 1895. Sojourner Truth and other black women were also active in the movement for women's rights, as indicated earlier.

Despite the common interests of black and white women, however, the dichotomy of a racially segregated society which has become increasingly polarized has prevented them from cementing a natural alliance. Communication and cooperation have been hesitant, limited, and formal. In the past Negro women have tended to identify discrimination against them as primarily racial and have accorded high priority to the struggle for Negro rights. They have had little time or energy for consideration of women's rights. And, until recent years, their egalitarian position in the struggle seemed to justify such preoccupation.

As the drive for black empowerment continues, however, black women are becoming increasingly aware of a new development which creates for them a dilemma of competing identities and priorities. On the one hand, as Dr. Jeanne Noble has observed, "establishing 'black manhood' became a prime goal of black revolution," and black women began to realize "that black men wanted to determine the policy and progress of black people without female participation in decision-making and leadership positions." On the other hand, a rising movement for women's liberation is challenging the concept of male dominance which the Black Revolution appears to have embraced. Confronted with the multiple barriers of poverty, race, and sex, the quandary of black women is how best to distribute their energies among these issues and what strategies to pursue which will minimize conflicting interests and objectives.

Cognizant of the similarities between paternalism and racial arrogance, black women are nevertheless handicapped by the continuing stereotype of the black "matriarchy" and the demand that black women now step back and push black men into positions of leadership. They are made to feel disloyal to racial interests if they insist upon women's rights. Moreover, to the extent that racial polarization often accompanies the thrust for Black Power, black women find it increasingly difficult to make common cause with white women. These developments raise several questions. Are black women gaining or losing in the drive toward human rights? As the movement for women's liberation becomes increasingly a force to be reckoned with, are black women to take a backward step and sacrifice their egalitarian tradition? What are the alternatives to matriarchal dominance on the one hand or male supremacy on the other?

Much has been written in the past about the matriarchal character of Negro family life, the relatively favored position of Negro women, and the tensions and difficulties growing out of the assumptions that they are better educated and more able to obtain employment than Negro males. These assumptions require closer examination. It is true that according to reports of the Bureau of the Census, in March 1968 an estimated 278,000 nonwhite women had completed four or more years of college —86,000 more than male college graduates in the nonwhite population (Negro women constitute 93 per cent of all nonwhite women), and that in March 1966 the median years of school completed by Negro females (10.1) was slightly higher than that for Negro males (9.4). It should be borne in mind that this is not unique to the black community. In the white population as well, females exceed males in median years of school completed (12.2 to 12.0) and do not begin to lag behind males until the college years. The significant fact is that the percentage of both sexes in the Negro population eighteen years of age and over in 1966 who had completed four years of college was roughly equivalent (males: 2.2 per cent; females: 2.3 per cent). When graduate training is taken into account, the proportion of Negro males with five or more years of college training (3.3 per cent) moved ahead of the Negro females (3.2 per cent). Moreover, 1966 figures show that a larger proportion of Negro males (63 per cent) than Negro females (57 per cent) was enrolled in school and that this superiority continued into college enrollments (males: 5 per cent; females 4 per cent). These 1966 figures reflect a concerted effort to broaden educational opportunities for Negro males manifested in recruitment policies and scholarship programs made available primarily to Negro male students. Though later statistics are not now available, this trend appears to have accelerated each year.

The assumption that Negro women have more education than Negro men also overlooks the possibility that the greater number of college-trained Negro women may correspond to the larger number of Negro women in the population. Of enormous importance to a consideration of Negro family life and the relation between the sexes is the startling fact of the excess of females over males. The Bureau of the Census estimated that in July 1968 there were 688,000 more Negro females than Negro males. Although census officials attribute this disparity to errors in counting a "floating" Negro male population, this excess has appeared in steadily increasing numbers in every census since 1860, but has received little analysis beyond periodic comment. Over the past century the reported ratio of black males to black females has decreased. In 1966, there were less than 94 black males to every 100 females.

The numerical imbalance between the sexes in the black population is more dramatic than in any other group in the United States. Within the white population the excess of women shows up in the middle or later years. In the black population, however, the sex imbalance is present in every age group over fourteen and is greatest during the age when most marriages occur. In the twenty-five to forty-four age group, the percentage of males within the black population drops to 86.9 as compared to 96.9 for white males.

It is now generally known that females tend to be constitutionally stronger than males, that male babies are more fragile than female babies, that boys are harder to rear than girls, that the male death rate is slightly higher and life expectancy for males is shorter than that of females. Add to these general factors the special hardships to which the Negro minority is exposed—poverty, crowded living conditions, poor health, marginal jobs, and minimum protection against hazards of accident and illness—and it becomes apparent that there is much in the American environment that is particularly hostile to the survival of the black male. But even if we discount these factors and accept the theory that the sex ratio is the result of errors in census counting, it is difficult to avoid the conclusion that a large number of black males have so few stable ties that they are not included as functioning units of the society. In either case formidable pressures are created for black women.

The explosive social implications of an excess of more than half a million black girls and women over fourteen years of age are obvious in a society in which the mass media intensify notions of glamour and expectations of romantic love and marriage, while at the same time there are many barriers against interracial marriages. When such marriages do take place they are more likely to involve black males and white females, which tends to aggravate the issue. (No value judgment about interracial marriages is implied here. I am merely trying to describe a social dilemma.) The problem of an excess female population is a familiar one in countries which have experienced heavy male casualties during wars, but an excess female ethnic minority as an enclave within a larger population raises important social issues. To what extent are the tensions and conflicts traditionally associated with the matriarchal framework of Negro family life in reality due to this imbalance and the pressures it generates? Does this excess explain the active competition between Negro professional men and women seeking employment in markets which have limited or excluded Negroes? And does this competition intensify the stereotype of the matriarchal society and female dominance? What relationship is there between the high rate of illegitimacy among black women and the population figures we have described?

These figures suggest that the Negro woman's fate in the United States, while inextricably bound with that of the Negro male in one sense, transcends the issue of Negro rights. Equal opportunity for her must mean equal opportunity to compete for jobs and to find a mate in the total society. For as long as she is confined to an area in which she must compete fiercely for a mate, she will remain the object of sexual exploitation and the victim of all the social evils which such exploitation involves.

When we compare the position of the black woman to that of the white woman, we find that she remains single more often, bears more children, is in the labor market longer and in greater proportion, has less education, earns less, is widowed earlier, and carries a relatively heavier economic responsibility as family head than her white counterpart.

In 1966, black women represented one of every seven women workers, although Negroes generally constitute only 11 per cent of the total population in the United States. Of the 3,105,000 black women eighteen years of age and over who were in the labor force, however, nearly half (48.2 per cent) were either single, widowed, divorced, separated from their husbands, or their husbands were absent for other reasons, as compared with 31.8 per cent of white women in similar circumstances. Moreover, six of every ten black women were in household employment or other service jobs. Conversely, while 58.8 per cent of all women workers held white collar positions, only 23.2 per cent of black women held such jobs.

As working wives, black women contribute a higher proportion to family income than do white women. Among nonwhite wives in 1965, 58 per cent contributed 20 per cent or more of the total family income, 43 per cent contributed 30 per cent or more and 27 per cent contributed 40 per cent or more. The comparable percentages for white wives were 56 per cent, 40 per cent, and 24 per cent respectively.

Black working mothers are more heavily represented in the labor force than white mothers. In March 1966, nonwhite working mothers with children under eighteen years of age represented 48 per cent of all nonwhite mothers with children this age as compared with 35 per cent of white working mothers. Nonwhite working mothers also represented four of every ten of all nonwhite mothers of children under six years of age. Of the 12,300,000 children under fourteen years of age in February 1965 whose mothers worked, only 2 per cent were provided group care in day-care centers. Adequate child care is an urgent need for working mothers generally, but it has particular significance for the high proportion of black working mothers of young children.

Black women also carry heavy responsibilities as family heads. In 1966, one-fourth of all black families were headed by a woman as compared with less than one-tenth of all white families. The economic disabilities of women generally are aggravated in the case of black women. Moreover, while all families headed by women are more vulnerable to poverty than husband-wife families, the black woman family head is doubly victimized. For example, the median wage or salary income of all women workers who were employed full time the year round in 1967 was only 58 per cent of that of all male workers, and the median earnings of white females was less than that of black males. The median wage of nonwhite women workers, however, was $3,268, or only 71 per cent of the median income of white women workers. In 1965, one-third of all families headed by women lived in poverty, but 62 per cent of the 1,132,000 nonwhite families with a female head were poor.

A significant factor in the low economic and social status of black women is their concentration at the bottom rung of the employment ladder. More than one-third of all nonwhite working women are employed as private household workers. The median wages of women private household workers who were employed full time the year round in 1968 was only $1,701. Furthermore, these workers are not covered by the Federal minimum wage and hours law and are generally excluded from state wage and hours laws, unemployment compensation, and workmen's compensation.

The black woman is triply handicapped. She is heavily represented in nonunion employment and thus has few of the benefits to be derived from labor organization or social legislation. She is further victimized by discrimination because of race and sex. Although she has made great strides in recent decades in closing the educational gap, she still suffers from inadequate education and training. In 1966, only 71.1 per cent of all Negro women had completed eight grades of elementary school compared to 88 per cent of all white women. Only one-third (33.2 per cent) of all Negro women had completed high school as compared with more than one-half of all white women (56.3). More than twice as many white women, proportionally, have completed college (7.2 per cent) as black women (3.2 per cent).

The notion of the favored economic position of the black female in relation to the black male is a myth. The 1966, median earnings of full-time year-round nonwhite female workers was only 65 per cent of that of nonwhite males. The unemployment rate for adult nonwhite women (6.6) was higher than for their male counterparts (4.9). Among nonwhite teenagers, the unemployment rate for girls was 31.1 as compared with 21.2 for boys.

In the face of their multiple disadvantages, it seems clear that black women can neither postpone nor subordinate the fight against sex discrimination to the Black Revolution. Many of them must expect to be self-supporting and perhaps to support others for a considerable period or for life. In these circumstances, while efforts to raise educational and employment levels for black males will ease some of the economic and social burdens now carried by many black women, for a large and apparently growing minority these burdens will continue. As a matter of sheer survival black women have no alternative but to insist upon equal opportunities without regard to sex in training, education, and employment. Given their heavy family responsibilities, the outlook for their children will be bleak indeed unless they are encouraged in every way to develop their potential skills and earning power.

Because black women have an equal stake in women's liberation and black liberation, they are key figures at the juncture of these two movements. White women feminists are their natural allies in both causes. Their own liberation is linked with the issues which are stirring women today: adequate income maintenance and the elimination of poverty, repeal or reform of abortion laws, a national system of child-care centers, extension of labor standards to workers now excluded, cash maternity benefits as part of a system of social insurance, and the removal of all sex barriers to educational and employment opportunities at all levels. Black women have a special stake in the revolt against the treatment of women primarily as sex objects, for their own history has left them with the scars of the most brutal and degrading aspects of sexual exploitation.

The middle-class Negro woman is strategically placed by virtue of her tradition of independence and her long experience in civil rights and can play a creative role in strengthening the alliance between the Black Revolution and Women's Liberation. Her advantages of training and her values make it possible for her to communicate with her white counterparts, interpret the deepest feelings within the black community, and cooperate with white women on the basis of mutual concerns as women. The possibility of productive interchange between black and white women is greatly facilitated by the absence of power relationships which separate black and white males as antagonists. By asserting a leadership role in the growing feminist movement, the black woman can help to keep it allied to the objectives of black liberation while simultaneously advancing the interests of all women.

The lesson of history that all human rights are indivisible and that the failure to adhere to this principle jeopardizes the rights of all is particularly applicable here. A built-in hazard of an aggressive ethnocentric movement which disregards the interests of other disadvantaged groups is that it will become parochial and ultimately self-defeating in the face of hostile reactions, dwindling allies, and mounting frustrations. As Dr. Caroline F. Ware has pointed out, perhaps the most essential instrument for combating the divisive effects of a black-only movement is the voice of black women insisting upon the unity of civil rights of women and Negroes as well as other minorities and excluded groups. Only a broad movement for human rights can prevent the Black Revolution from becoming isolated and can insure its ultimate success.

Beyond all the present conflict lies the important task of reconciliation of the races in America on the basis of genuine equality and human dignity. A powerful force in bringing about this result can be generated through the process of black and white women working together to achieve their common humanity.

Women and legislation

MARTHA GRIFFITHS

Why is it that in the Congress of the United States there is only one woman in the Senate and ten women in the House from a total of 435 congressional districts? This is a challenge to which New Feminists must respond, if they intend to end the legal inequities which still exist under Federal law.

The growing ferment among women should have political repercussions that bring more women to policy-making positions not only on the national level, but in their state and local governments. But if women want to move out of the clerical pigeonholes to which they have mainly been assigned in government for a hundred years, they must become wiser in the ways of political organization.

Representative Griffiths believes that discriminatory laws and practices reflect the bias of men whose images of women confine her to the role of mother, wife, or widow.

In Title VII of the Civil Rights Act of 1964 we have an example of the special insights of a Congresswoman *in championing women's rights. Sex discrimination in employment is forbidden in this legislation because of the successful drive waged by Representative Griffiths.*

Among facts made clear in this personal account of her experiences as a lawmaker is the unfairness of present Social Security laws to the low-income husband and wife who both work. Though together they may have contributed more than a man

103

*who has made optimum payments, on retirement they may be
receiving lower benefits than the high-income man and his wife
who was never employed.*

*Representative Griffiths points out a number of areas in laws
where discrimination against women adversely affects the welfare of the whole family.*

*Martha Griffiths has represented Michigan's Seventeenth Con-
gressional District in the United States House of Representatives
since 1954. She has initiated or supported much legislation for
women's rights. She has worked as an attorney, and has served
as judge of Recorder's Court, City of Detroit.*

When I was elected as United States representative from Michigan's Seventeenth District, it never occurred to me that as a
woman I had any special insights to offer. I thought that all a
man or a woman legislator needed was a love of justice and an
urge to see that all laws were written to that end.

My political life began in 1948, when I was elected to the
Michigan legislature on my second try. From that day on, my
life has been devoted to either framing laws or, during my period as a recorder's court judge, to interpreting and enforcing
laws. As the years have passed, I have increasingly recognized
that every politician comes to his job with a unique view, created not alone by intelligence, but by the many things which
have made up his life—his environment, family, friends, experiences, beliefs, and finally, his prejudices.

I have always been a staunch supporter of the right of any
woman to hold any job for which her intelligence, training, and
experience prepared her, but women have not yet succeeded in
becoming direct participants in the world of government policy
making. I have attended countless meetings in which women
have laid wistful plans for putting women in these positions;
most of them have failed. Policy, even that affecting very directly the lives of millions of women, is made mostly by men. In
a man's view of the world, he earns the money; it is his duty to
love and honor his mother, to support his wife and children, and

to provide for his widow and orphans. In this rather simple view of today's world, a woman is a mother, a wife, or a widow. Laws made and interpreted in this country almost exclusively by men for 180 years have locked these views into the statutory and case law of the country. Thus, no woman litigant has ever stood before the United States Supreme Court and successfully argued that she is entitled to the "equal protection of the laws" clause of the Fourteenth Amendment.

While a Constitution largely written in the time of sailing ships and horse-drawn carriages has been quite adequate to cover the problems of automobiles, submarines, jet take-offs, and trips to the moon, it took a Constitutional amendment to allow women, who were also citizens, to vote, although the Constitution clearly states ". . . nor shall any State deprive any person of life, liberty, or property, without due process of law; nor deny to any person within its jurisdiction, the equal protection of the laws."

As late as twenty-two years ago, in *Goesaert vs. Cleary*, the majority of the Supreme Court denied the "equal protection" clause to women who wanted to be bartenders in the state of Michigan. They were not permitted to hold this better paying job. The Court adhered to the dream. They were not seeing women as workers. In the case of *Hoyt vs. Florida*, decided in 1961, the court protected the State of Florida in giving women an absolute exemption from jury service unless they volunteered for such service. They protected the dream—the childbearing duty of women to the exclusion of all other duties of women as citizens and the rights of all other persons, including women as defendants.

Check any set of statutory law, whether Federal or state, any ordinance of any city, town, or township, and you will find in almost every case special laws or ordinances enacted to distinguish between men and women in their rights and duties. These laws discriminate against women as workers. They are enacted and upheld as if women were not workers but the mothers, wives, or widows of the men who enacted them and toward whom those men had a special responsibility.

THE SOCIAL SECURITY LAW

Look at the Social Security law. A woman as a worker pays into the trust fund exactly the same percentage of her wages on the Social Security that a man pays. Once a man has established his right to Social Security, he can leave covered employment, work another fifty years elsewhere, and upon retirement draw Social Security, as could his dependents—his wife, his young children, and his aging parents. Before I became a member of the Ways and Means Committee of the Congress, the children or husband of a woman one and one-half years out of the work force, could draw nothing on her Social Security in the event of her death. In 1967, I offered an amendment, accepted by the committee and by Congress, which permits a woman worker's children to draw at her death, whether she was in the labor force at death or not. Actually, I wanted the surviving husband to be able to draw also, but the men, faithful to their training that a man should be the provider, refused to go along with this. Since very few working men earn less than their wives, and have their own larger Social Security benefits, this amendment would have covered generally aged men who never worked under Social Security and who are now in need; but the Social Security law remains faithful to the dream—only those husbands whose wives supplied more than half the family's total income, with both under Social Security, can draw on a wife's Social Security. However, Barbara Hutton or Doris Duke, like any other wife, would be able to draw Social Security on their last husband's earnings record without any problem.

The working wife pays into Social Security on exactly the same basis as her working husband. When she arrives at the age to draw the benefit she must choose whether to draw a benefit as a working woman or as a wife. If both husband and wife have worked at fairly low incomes, which is very frequently the case, you will find that while they have paid as much or more in Social Security taxes than the man who was the sole family earner and paid at the top base, they will draw less than the amount going to that man and his non-earning wife. It is estimated that it would cost 2 ½ billion dollars annually to correct this inequity, which shows the extent to which the working wife has endowed Social Security. As a worker, she has the responsibilities of any worker, but the Social Security law treats her as a wife, widow, mother, or daughter because this conforms to the needs of the men who made the law. It is only within the last few years that men workers have complained to me that their working wives are being unfairly treated.

WOMEN WORKERS

Some years ago, while explaining various laws to a woman reporter from a large midwestern daily, I pointed out that under the government health insurance policy that had been recently enacted, it cost me $2.80 more per month to cover myself and my husband than it cost any of my male colleagues to cover himself, his wife, and two small children. She replied that both she and her husband worked for the same newspaper to support their five children. If she had been the sole support of the children, it would have cost her $18.00 a month for the health policy, but that for her husband, the policy was a fringe benefit for which he paid nothing. In addition, his salary was substantially larger than hers.

In what I hope was the "last hurrah" for women losing their jobs first, a union in Detroit, during a 1950 recession, met and solemnly voted to require that all women employees be laid off so that the men could work. Fortunately, the management had sense enough to reject this proposal. The union had not bothered to inquire: (1) how many women workers were the sole support either of themselves, or of themselves and a family; (2) how many men workers employed in the plant had wives working elsewhere.

When I commented on this case at one time to the head of the National Labor Relations Board in Detroit, he said, "Well, I think it is wrong to permit a woman with top seniority to remain on a job and lay off a man supporting a wife and five kids when all the woman is doing with her money is buying good clothes, Cadillacs, and going to Florida."

I responded, "As far as I'm concerned, you could lay her off, but if you looked at the third and fourth people in line, and found that the third is a bachelor or a man whose wife is working elsewhere, and the fourth is a woman who is the sole support of five children, you should lay off the man and let the woman continue working."

When Willard Wirtz was Secretary of Labor, he appeared before the Ways and Means Committee and referred to "secondary workers." Questioning developed that "secondary workers" were wives and children. Obviously "secondary workers" have "secondary rights." Since most women are working for money to supply the necessities of life or to assist in educating their children, it would certainly be more realistic to define a primary worker as one whose salary paid the grocery bill and bought the children's books and clothes and a "secondary" worker as one whose salary paid for the outboard motor, the fishing tackle, the liquor, etc. Of course, the truth is that no one, certainly not the Secretary of Labor, should define any worker as a "secondary" worker. As a rose is a rose is a rose, a worker is a worker is a worker, and should receive exactly the same consideration as any other worker, whether she earns all of the family income or merely supplements it. It is unconscionable to define in law or by common usage a woman worker, married or not, as a secondary worker.

THE LAW AND MOTHER'S WELFARE

The welfare laws as no other laws have embodied the dream of legislators that the man is provider and the woman homemaker and mother. As written, they have done more to break up the American family by driving the unemployed father from the home and rewarding the woman for rearing her children alone, than if they had been written for the express purpose of breaking up the family. When aid to dependent children first became the law in the thirties, it provided that a mother and children could secure benefits if there were no "able-bodied man in the house." If the man was unemployed and couldn't find employment, naturally he left the house to permit his wife and children to draw the benefits. Under this rule, approximately 5 per cent of America's children were reared without a man in the house.

While a survey in New York City in 1969 showed that at least 70 per cent of the mothers would prefer work to welfare, the spokesmen for the welfare mothers usually ask only that the welfare be increased. Such spokesmen have accepted the world of the legislators as their own. They agree mothers should stay at home and be supported. Many welfare mothers would be far better off if they demanded a decent education, training, and a job at a living wage. Welfare will never be sufficient to pay a living wage, although in the large industrial states if a welfare mother has many children, she can draw more money on welfare than the average woman can make working. Jobs do not pay on the basis of how many children you have, and it is deplorable that welfare actually seems to pay you to produce children—whether you love them or can take proper care of them.

The new Family Assistance Program, suggested by President Nixon, and about to become the law as this is written, is an attempt to keep the indigent family together. It guarantees to a mother, father, and one child, an income of $1300, but it guarantees that same amount to a mother and two children, or $1,000 to a mother with one child, but nothing to an indigent couple without children. I felt it would have been better to have given the mother and child $800 or $1100 if there were two children, and add the extra amount for a husband on welfare, but at least two of the members of the committee drafting the bill were reared by widowed mothers. You could watch them go back in memory and take care of that widowed mother and help that little boy they used to be. They wanted the larger amount given whether the father was present in the home or not. Of course, the world has changed now and we are dealing with increased illegitimacy among teenagers. The law we are proposing is supposed to help solve the problem, but we are giving the teenage girl $1,000 if she has a baby, and only $300 more if she marries the baby's unemployed father, the same amount we would give her if the baby had a twin. This is setting too little value on fathers.

The legislators take care of women and children but not men. They believe that men must work; they are adamant that men support women and children. It has escaped the attention of the men legislators, although I mention the matter frequently, that men are no longer the sole support of women and children. Twenty-nine million women are working. They are paying more than their share of the taxes that are supporting other women and children. But the taxes, as I have shown, do not apply in an equitable way to their own husbands or children. For all women it would be better, cheaper, and fairer if they were regarded as first-class citizens, if they were regarded fairly at the hiring gate and in promotions. Both men and women should look to see who is paying for the legislators' world of "every woman at home." Twenty-nine million women workers are paying into the general funds of the Treasury, into payroll funds such as Social Security, into pension systems, medical systems, and other such earmarked funds that are giving to women at home rights and benefits that are not available to the woman worker herself, and certainly not to her beneficiaries or dependents.

When the legislators were children, mama was at home with them or they wanted her there; so they pass welfare laws that say "a woman with a child under six may stay at home if she wishes." It is my contention that the mother is rarely permitted to make a choice. Society, through its social workers, makes it for her. They make no real effort to get her a job at a living wage; day-care for her child is not provided. She lives outside the economic world. The different reactions of New York and California to the Work Incentive Program (WIN) provides a good example that with encouragment many mothers prefer work to welfare. Both states were funded for WIN for 12,000 training slots each for fiscal 1969. As of the end of March 1970, New York had completed 300,000 assessments (welfare agency determination of suitability), one-half of the 600,000 recipients provided for participation in the WIN program nationwide. Of these 300,000 assessments, the New York welfare officials had found only 21,341 recipients appropriate for referral and only 5,350 were actually referred to the WIN manpower agency. On the manpower side of the program only 586 were actually in education and training under WIN, and 106 of these were in New York City. This constituted only one welfare recipient for every 500 adults on the rolls in the state and one for every 2,000 adults on the rolls in New York City.

In California, on the other hand, there have been only 130,000 assessments, but from these have come 52,258 nominees and 47,248 actual referrals to WIN. At the end of March, 10,341 recipients were in WIN education and training (including employment follow-up) which was about 4 recipients for every 100 adults on the AFDC rolls. California reported that 20,577 welfare mothers had volunteered for the program.

As another example of society's blindness, can there be any question that the school-age mother, without a husband, should be permitted to go to school? Yet many school boards refuse to permit this girl to go to school. Is it possible that anyone else placed upon her so heavy a burden at so youthful an age? In a recent case, *Clydie Marie Perry vs. Grenada Municipal Separate School District* (June 1969), a United States District Court in Mississippi ruled that the school board's policy of excluding unwed mothers from high school admission violated the equal protection clauses of the Fourteenth Amendment. The court held that unwed mothers could not be excluded from high schools of the district for the sole reason that they are unwed mothers. The court, while noting that lack of moral character is a reason for excluding a child from public education, went on to clarify, "the fact that a girl has one child out of wedlock does not forever brand her as a scarlet woman undeserving of any chance for rehabilitation or the opportunity for further education."

In the 1970 welfare bill, I attempted to add an amendment that would require the local school to allow an unwed mother to continue her education or deny funds from the Family Assistance Program of the Federal Government for her. Under these circumstances, if her own parents could not provide for her, the general welfare funds of the state would have to do so. The Ways and Means Committee members opposed this amendment.

In this case, I do not feel that the legislators necessarily feel so strongly that she should remain at home with the baby, as they feel she should not contaminate the school. Therefore, she becomes an outcast. The father of the child is spared a similar fate, and society may have to support the girl—and her offspring for many years.

In a New Haven study of one hundred unwed pregnant adolescent girls prior to the establishment of any special program for them, it was found that these girls had given birth to 349 babies in five years. Only five of the girls did not become pregnant again.

In a comprehensive program for pregnant school girls in New York City, only 11 out of 492 girls had a subsequent out-of-wedlock pregnancy after two years.

Prejudice in these cases is a very costly thing for the general taxpayer as well as for the girl involved.

LEGISLATION ON EMPLOYMENT

Since I have been in Congress, there have been two major bills enacted which have aided women in the work force. I refer first to the "Equal Pay for Equal Work Act" passed in 1963. This bill is at last beginning to be enforced. The Third Circuit United States Court of Appeals in a unanimous decision issued January 13, 1970, ordered more than $250,000 in back wages to be paid to women employees at the Wheaton Glass Company of Millville, New Jersey (*Shultz vs. Wheaton Glass Company*).

The second bill which promoted women's rights was the Equal Employment Opportunities Act, known as the Civil Rights Act of 1964. This bill was drafted by groups who laudably sought to give Negroes the same employment and promotion rights as whites. It also wiped out discrimination based on religion.

When I looked at the bill, I realized that the committee had never really considered the rights of Negro women, or if it had, it had simply believed that they would get approximately the rights of white women. I made up my mind that all women were going to take one giant step forward, so I prepared an amendment that added "sex" to the bill. Then I learned that a woman newspaper reporter had asked Howard Smith of Virginia to offer such an amendment and he had agreed. Judge Smith was the Chairman of the Rules Committee and the leader of the conservative bloc which was trying to kill the bill. I realized that Mr. Smith would get more than a hundred votes just because he offered the amendment as a way of fighting the bill. I needed, if everyone voted, 218 votes to win. Without saying anything to anyone, I decided to let him offer it, and use my best powers of persuasion to get the rest of the votes. Every amendment offered had been defeated, so the task was not exactly easy.

Several had spoken before me on the amendment, and the House, which was crowded with both members and spectators, was enjoying to the utmost this laughable amendment. I began, "I rise in support of the amendment primarily because I feel as a white woman, that when this bill has passed this House and the Senate and has been signed by the President, that white women will be last at the hiring gate." There was silence.

I asked the chairman if the bill protected black men and women at the hiring gate equally. He agreed that it did. Then I sawed the limb off behind him. I pointed out that there were no laws that had ever protected white women, and this one would not do so either, without the amendment. It is history now that the amendment prevailed.

When it had passed the House, there were dark mutterings that it would be removed in the Senate or in Conference; so I called Liz Carpenter at the White House and asked her to tell the President that if that amendment came out of that bill, I would send my speech door to door in every member's district who had voted against it, and in my opinion those who voted against it would never return to Congress. Whether she did or not, I don't know, but the amendment stayed; and it has been through this amendment that most of today's court cases have been tried.

It has been particularly pleasing to me that men who helped draft the Civil Rights Act, and who opposed the "sex" amendment, have since come to me and told me that the amendment had certainly strengthened the bill.

A constitutional amendment which would have a great impact now would be the proposed Equal Rights Amendment, which says that "Equality of rights under the law shall not be denied or abridged by the United States or any state on account of sex." By the time the attitudes of the legislators have changed sufficiently to pass it, it may be unnecessary, but it would be a great morale booster for women if it could be passed now.

My efforts on behalf of women will continue to be primarily to see that women are recognized in their roles as workers; secondarily, to show that even in their traditional roles their actual economic contribution in the role of housewife and mother should be recognized. In these aspects, I think public policy-makers have a part, but as to who washes the dishes at home or burps the baby—that, in my opinion, is a private decision.

The educational establishment:
wasted women

DORIS L. PULLEN

Unwritten quotas are exercised by college graduate school admission boards to restrict the number of women enrollees, especially in the schools of medicine and law.

Key administrative positions even in women's colleges are more often than not held by men.

The percentage of doctoral degrees held by women has diminished since 1920. After the doctoral degree is granted, a woman seeking an academic career will meet rampant discrimination. Often her application will not even be considered. The girl seeking a position with a law firm will have the same experience.

Yet most of the women seeking higher degrees are serious about a career, though they may have to settle for jobs requiring less education. In 1968, 86 per cent of women forty-five to fifty-four years of age with five or more years of college were employed.

Educational establishments must adjust to the need of women for continuing education. University-connected child-care centers will help women faculty members as well as the woman seeking further education.

This author believes that women's colleges should lead the way as models of educational opportunities for women based on the needs and life styles of this day.

Doris L. Pullen is a professional journalist and instructor in journalism at Northeastern University's Burlington Campus in Massachusetts. She formerly was a writer and researcher on Fortune Magazine.

More than 400,000 girls arrive at college each fall, thoroughly indoctrinated by their parents, peers, and high school counselors, through television, movies, and advertising, and from personal observation of the behavior of most people with whom they've had contact. Only the rare girl arrives at college without a bone-deep feeling that as a female she is limited—intellectually, socially, emotionally, or biologically.

Colleges do little or nothing to dissuade her. Women's colleges—dedicated to educating women—are more guilty than coeducational schools where concern is for all students.

Who cares how women are educated?

Even those who do care, don't agree.

Some say, "Educate her for her special needs." Others say, "Educate her in the same way as men." Some believe American higher education is still so much under the European influence of what was, in centuries past, considered proper for well-bred gentlemen, that what does occur in the guise of education is so wrong that sex differences in education are of no significance.

But in an era when so many scapegoats present themselves for finger-pointing, the new feminists concentrate on the one institution which, by its very justification for existence, invites concentration of blame.

It is the American college for women.

In the new feminists' definition, the college stands either alone (Chatham, Skidmore, Vassar) or as a "sister" to a "brother" college (Pembroke-Brown, Barnard-Columbia, Scripps-Claremont), called a coordinate. Founded and dedicated to educating American women, these colleges have separate faculties, trustees, administration.

Among them are the pioneer women's colleges of America where once women were taught by excellent faculties and given full opportunity to develop their intellectual capacities, ambitions, and talents. Instead of continuing to set the example of academic excellence and preparing women for the proliferating needs of a society requiring the best brains of both sexes, the pioneers are accused by the new feminists of joining the current fashionable collective attitude that women have special needs: some training for semi-skilled short-term careers, but primarily "education" for marriage, childrearing, and dilettante community service.

In a study of women's higher education in America, the New York Chapter of the National Organization of Women (NOW) admonishes women's colleges to "either shape up or ship out," a conclusion based on the colleges' quality ratings, stated purpose, faculty, curriculum, and nonacademic and social regulations. The study, published in mimeograph (1968), is titled *Token Learning*, and has a cover drawing of a half-eaten apple—symbolizing that Eve, who nibbled first at knowledge, has long been detained by circumstance from getting her full share. Its conclusion is mild, compared with evidence demonstrating the abdication of women's colleges from their responsibility:

In the 1967-68 Gourman Report ratings for academic excellence, the top five women's colleges (Barnard, Smith, Bryn Mawr, Wellesley, Mount Holyoke) are far below the top five men's colleges; in overall averages (men's, coeducational, women's), the lowest rates in the nation are the women's.

In published statements of purpose, men's colleges assume the purpose of education is to create leadership; women's, to create followers, specifically home and community servants.

The sex split in curriculum is tacit but firm. The highest status fields are masculine, the lowest feminine, and bright girls are shunted to the humanities which, according to the study, are for some "inscrutable reason" considered ladylike.

As academic prestige and status increase (but not necessarily academic excellence) so does the ratio of male teachers over female teachers.

The coordinate colleges fare as badly, or worse.

Twenty-four pages of the 57-page *Token Learning* document the differences between the "brother" and "sister" schools of the coordinate colleges. The representative sampling studied shows that these partially coeducational schools offer the woman student either an inferior education (where faculties are separate) or an inferior status (when given the best male education, she is subtly taught she can't expect male-level success after graduation).

THE FACULTY AND STAFF

Systematic sex-role conditioning in both the sister schools and in the women's colleges is at its most subtle and perhaps most effective in the teaching staff. Even where the ratio of men to women is not strongly in favor of men, full professors and department chairmen are almost always men. The college girl sees in class, every day, the fact that men hold the authority.

Of the Seven Sisters, the counterpart of the Ivy League, only Wellesley, Barnard, and Radcliffe still have women presidents, and as both Barnard and Radcliffe are merging more and more with their powerful Columbia and Harvard brothers, one wonders about the difference between the titles "president" and "dean of women."

The announcement that Harris L. Wofford, Jr., had been appointed to succeed Katherine E. McBride as president of Bryn Mawr in 1970 prompted *The New York Times* to comment on the declining opportunities for women in the top management of American higher education. At the time of the Wofford appointment, Vassar had replaced president Sarah Blanding with Alan Simpson from the University of Chicago. President Esther Raushenbush of Sarah Lawrence had been succeeded by Dr. Charles DeCarlo, and Mt. Holyoke's new president, David B. Truman, was continuing a male precedent. Education editor of the *Times* Fred M. Hechinger suggests five reasons why women are being crowded out. He indicates that trustees fear that the good faculty they hope to attract and hold might shy away from female chief executives; few capable women are available;

with the trend toward coeducation, a woman president seems too feminine; as girls grow rebellious, virile charming male presidents can better maintain order; women in positions of power flourish in liberal times and the nation is now moving toward a new conservatism.

Trustees are also reported as fearing old finishing-school images, perhaps in part because they join the national race for Federal and foundation research grants.[1] While many probably believe in all honesty that they seek only the best possible president, regardless of sex *et al.*, the fact remains clear—women in positions of authority, power, and prestige are harder and harder to find in American colleges and universities.

In women's colleges, the loss is doubly severe. Not only are good women academics lost, but every day throughout their college years girls see that they may as well limit their expectations because there is no room for them at the top, even in the segregated schools. In coeducation, a girl's future is sharply mirrored. Female scholars and female administrators are rarely above assistant in level, and in men's colleges, they are nearly invisible.

The dual loss to higher education in teaching and administration is long term—a generation of excellent women is turned away from the academic life—and the effect on the next generation is the discouraged attitude, "Why bother?" The evidence demonstrates that authority is male.

Statistical evidence reveals a shattering lack of progress for academic women in the twentieth century. The most frequently quoted case of backsliding is the proportion of doctorates earned by women. In 1900, women earned 6 per cent of all doctor's degrees. The peak was 15 per cent in 1920; by 1950 the

[1] Their success in winning Federal contracts, though, will force them to end discrimination against women. Executive Orders (Executive Order 11246 as amended by Executive Order 11375) specifically forbid government contractors to discriminate by sex. In February 1970, the Women's Equity Action League (WEAL) requested the Office of Federal Contract Compliance of the Department of Labor to begin immediate action and compliance review of universities and colleges that receive Federal contracts, citing discrimination in hiring and promoting women faculty at the University of Maryland and other universities.

percentage dropped to a low of 10, and, by what must have been grim determination rose to 13 per cent in 1968.

Among faculty and other professional staffs in American institutions of higher learning, women have been kept at about the same low and erratic percentile. In 1964, women held 22 per cent of the positions, a tiny gain over 1910, yet in 1920 they held 26 per cent; in 1930, 27 per cent; and reached a sensational high 28 per cent in 1940, two years before the war manpower shortage offered temporary higher status jobs to women everywhere.

Those who think that that's not bad (after all, with all the other things women must do, a quarter—give or take—seems a fair proportion), need to note quality differential. In *Academic Women*, Jessie Bernard states: "By and large, academic women tend to be associated with the low-status or low-prestige institutions." [2] About a quarter are in teachers and junior colleges; the few in universities must have doctorates, and even they are more likely to be found at the less highly ranked institutions.

At Harvard University, there are 12 faculty women on tenure out of a full-time faculty of 700. In the Graduate School of Education, there are also 12 women faculty members out of 185. But women students amount to 63 per cent of degree candidates.

Another segment of the vicious circle in which the academic woman turns is the reputation of the school at which she earns her doctorate. True for both men and women is the "halo effect" of the prestige university; while it may send out its graduates to lesser schools, it rarely hires its new faculty from them. Only the uniquely gifted can ever expect to gain prominence in academia without the top schools' union card. For a girl to gain admittance to a high prestige graduate school, she must demonstrate extraordinary excellence, persistence, guts, and gall. If she can do this with winsome feminine delicacy, her chances are better.

Say she is one who makes it. With her new Ph.D., where can she go? In its January 12, 1970, issue, *The Chronicle of Higher*

[2] Jessie Bernard, *Academic Women* (University Park, Pa., The Pennsylvania University Press, 1964).

Education reported that the academic marketplace was tighter than it had been in recent memory, that some 40 per cent of the 1969 Ph.D.'s in physics were still looking for jobs, that the chairmen of modern language departments of several major universities reported receiving more than six hundred applicants for five openings, that two thousand history teachers are job hunting, that one university planning to graduate seventy Ph.D.'s in English in June 1970 expects to hire only one new faculty member in September. No one really expects the lucky person will be a woman. John Rumbarger, assistant executive secretary of the American Historical Association, noted that in a tight market "women don't get hired."

The ratio of male to female faculty, therefore, may favor males even more in the 1970's as the baby-boom graduates compete for positions to teach the post-baby-boom undergraduates. The ratios calculated by the NOW study at the close of the 1960's show the extent of discrimination against women faculty in women's colleges, the one place where the female scholar might expect a fair chance. Sex composition of the faculty at Bennington was 62 males, 13 females; at Sarah Lawrence, 70 males, 42 females. Where ratios are more equal or favor women, the schools usually specialize in traditionally feminine subjects. Mills College of Education, for example, had 27 women and 18 men on its faculty. In the majority of colleges, regardless of subject specialization, men dominate the high academic offices; women are clustered at the lowest teaching levels. Of tenured faculty at Chatham College for Women, to cite one of the cases in the NOW study, 26 were male and only 5 female; the total faculty favored men two to one—52 men and 26 women.

The belief persists that male faculty enhance status and prestige, a belief tragically underscored by the girl student's precollege social conditioning and then by her classroom observations. Women faculty even help sustain the belief because so many of them will work for less money than men and dollars are used as the yardstick of value, status, and prestige.[3] Whether in the tighter market of the seventies this will lead to the hiring of

[3] In 1965-66, the median annual salary at colleges and universities was $9,275 for men and $7,732 for women.

more women because they are cheaper, or whether the more customary economic pattern will prevail (i.e., women squeezed out entirely), remains to be seen. The answer most likely lies in industrial and business demands for Ph.D.'s.

A better answer for the future leadership of the nation—its college-educated men and women—lies in breaking, for all time, the vicious self-perpetuating circle that has kept women second-class citizens. First, every possible faculty vacancy ought to be filled by a qualified woman. Academically competent women are forced out of college teaching by overt discrimination and by less obvious means, such as nepotism rules, lack of day-care facilities, and by the convenient belief that qualified women don't exist. They do exist. The most minor recruiting effort, accompanied by fair pay, personnel, and promotion policies, will bring them into the classroom to the enrichment of their colleagues and their students. As the status of women improves, life for men also improves.

WOMEN STUDIES

Men and women teachers can begin breaking the vicious circle now and improve the quality of life by deliberately including in economics, mathematics, languages, sciences, the arts, and other curricula the contributions made throughout civilization by both sexes. Faculty who stand before the next generation without antiquated sex-role prejudices and who are supported in their honesty by forward-looking department chairmen, trustees, and administrators will not perpetuate sex stereotypes. Their men and women students will comprehend sexuality and its part in the disciplines of classroom, occupation, environment—of life.

Undoubtedly hundreds of individual faculty members, perhaps some trustees, administrators, and an occasional unfettered department chairman, already are convinced, as individuals, that liberal education ought to include such comprehension of human sexuality. Academic professionals within their group structure, however, feel otherwise and blame, as do women, an impersonal and impervious "they," about which little if anything can be done.

The NOW study specifies what can be done, and by whom:

> It is the clear obligation of the women's colleges. . . .
> While a new insurgent women's movement must start
> at the student level in the coeducational college, it is
> very likely destined to start at the faculty and
> administrative level as well as in the woman's college.
> When such institutions for women grasp that they
> have a way out of their moribund condition, they may
> discover they have a mission which could put them in
> the forefront of the academic community in the matter
> of revising the entire sex-role and trait assignment
> patterns of our culture—a great change certain to occur
> in the coming years, bringing with it a far more civilized
> and humane attitude toward human personality and
> the individual's freedom to define and develop his or
> her identity.

In addition, it may be that a brandnew coeducational college
will elect to pioneer in facing the educational issue of how to
deal with sex-role differences, to permit all students academic
excellence in faculty and full opportunity to develop their intellectual capacities, ambitions, and talents. Hampshire College in
Amherst, Massachusetts, will open in September 1970 with the
rich academic resources of its sponsoring neighbors, Smith, Mt.
Holyoke, Amherst College, and the University of Massachusetts. Among its intensive preparations toward creating an environment for excellence was a comprehensive study of women's
education and a model coeducation plan.[4] The recommendations (based on extensive published documentation available to
any who care to so search) specify that: in hiring faculty
Hampshire should consider teachers' "motivations and ability
to deal with the issue of sexuality; the Dean of Faculty should
meet annually with the faculty to talk with them about their attention to these issues in their classes and their counseling; there

[4] "Special Approaches to Women's Education: A Model Coeducational
Plan," a report to Hampshire College, by Barbara Currier.

should be a Committee of Coeducation to support faculty responsibility in this area."

> Hampshire should set out to hire a significant number of women faculty. Women should form no less than one-third of Hampshire's total faculty. They should be brought in at all levels. At least one dean should always be a woman. Hampshire should hire women faculty who have a variety of life styles.

Life-style variety means married and unmarried, with young children, with older children, with husbands who are teachers, businessmen, researchers, or artists.

The issue of sexuality has been swept into convenient corners of coeducation, into carefully labeled sociology or psychology courses, into closed conferences between deans, and into near oblivion in most men's colleges. If the purpose of education is to help individuals lead free and full lives, sexuality is far too important a part of all life to be swept into corners, eliminated from all but selected curriculum, treated as a slightly embarrassing joke, or distorted into "women's special needs."

The new feminists can work and hope toward the ideal coeducation that meets the true purpose of education; more immediately they can and do take issue with the absurdities in the name of higher education that perpetuate the notion that sexuality is woman's burden—and man's extracurricular activity.

WHAT ARE THE GOALS?

How to teach her to accept most gracefully her "burden" is, too often, the purpose of women's colleges. None use such blatant phraseology, but beneath the carefully worded official statements of purpose can be heard the promise. Leadership is rarely mentioned; life enrichment and social usefulness is stressed. Sweet Briar "tries to maintain an educational program that will produce . . . human beings capable of intelligent free choice." Hollins wants to "create an environment which generates a love of learning . . . and the strength of character and spiritual values needed for a productive life in modern society." Wellesley still holds as its goal the founder's purpose of education for "great conflicts, for vast reforms in social life, for noblest usefulness."

Emphasis is more often on adjustment to what is, than in leadership for making life better.

Few are as direct as Sullins:

> within a few years after graduation, most Sullins girls establish their own homes and assume the role of wife, mother, homemaker and community citizen. To meet these responsibilities successfully today, students urgently need to develop positive and attractive personalities, social competence and assurance, sound cultural values, and a sense of personal and social responsibility.

A woman's education is rarely expected to meet Simmons' purpose to "enable her to find opportunities for intellectual growth and professional advancement within her chosen career, and to equip her to assume expanding responsibility and leadership in her field of endeavor." Simmons has, perhaps, had more experience than other institutions with adult women returning for counseling ten and twenty years after their education— women who have found that a sense of usefulness is not enough.

Until very recently, women's colleges have also taken *in loco parentis* responsibility for outside-of-classroom regulation of students' private lives. Rules concerning curfews, keys, conduct, and clothing have assumed that women undergraduates are irresponsible little girls.

In parietals, though, changes are occurring rapidly.

In the last three years, for example, Smith girls have won the freedom to have alcohol in their rooms anytime and men in their rooms from 10 A.M. until 11 P.M. on weekdays and until 1 A.M. on weekends. Parietals have been a lively subject, well covered by the press, and one specific area where women students have made progress in convincing administrators that they are not children. Liberalized parietals are being adopted by a growing number of women's colleges—to the horror of tongue-cluckers and many parents who visualize sex orgies up and down what were once cloistered halls.

Sexual freedom, however, is not the issue to the new feminists. Love has always laughed at locksmiths. The basic issue is adult status. The NOW study states: "There is an insidious paternalism built into the housing situation completely at variance with the intellectual freedom, self-determination and independence which higher education is expected to foster and without which it is only a pretense."

An insidious paternalism, though, still seems to be built into curriculum and "choice" of major field. No evidence can be found to support the idea that men and women differ in educability. Yet girls are usually encouraged to major in what are called feminine subjects, i.e., helping services, decorative arts, and the humanities. Boys are pushed into science and math, toward the professions of medicine, law, engineering. Are colleges following the artificial labeling of society which bestows status and prestige on the so-called masculine fields? Over and over the NOW study finds women's colleges weak in the areas labeled masculine, strong in the low-paid service occupations. Higher education fosters the attitude of society-at-large that men lead and women follow. American education has arrived at a peculiar point if it sees as its mission the perpetuation of society's inequities.

Alibis and rationalizations, often couched in fine academic jargon, are paraded forth as truth. And do they not indeed contain a degree of truth? For, as Naomi Weisstein put it in "Woman as Nigger" (*Psychology Today*, October 1969):

> In the light of the social expectations about women, it
> is not surprising the women end up where society
> expects them to; the surprise is that little girls don't
> get the message that they are supposed to be stupid
> until they get into high school . . . until social ex-
> pectations for men and women are equal . . . answers
> . . . simply reflect our prejudices.

It is also true that a girl between sixteen and twenty-five is at the peak of her reproductive life. Physiologically determined to perpetuate the human race, she is inclined during these years to underestimate her intellectual potential. At this vulnerable point in her life span, she is encouraged by colleges to train for a lifetime of servitude, regardless of her abilities. Society apparently rewards her limited choice, her acceptance of the myth she is inferior, only to bemoan later the tragic waste of womanpower as our greatest underutilized natural resource. Which "society" should education placate? The one which rewards with prescribed status the titles Mrs. and Mom, or the one which at a later date decides it needs its female citizens mentally and emotionally healthy, in full utilization of their capacities?

It takes no advanced study to know the answer. Higher education has no excuse for placating society as it is. Higher education should not be training followers; it is the training ground of leaders. Coeducation, ultimately the better way, can and must acquaint men and women with the sexuality of human growth and development, so prejudices reflected in false expectations will disappear.

A highly favored alibi or rationalization for educating women for their "special needs" is "woman's nature" which claims women prefer an ordinary husband to an extraordinary career; women fear loss of femininity, and both men and women equate success with masculinity; women are harder on women than men are; nothing in life is as satisfying to a woman as her family. Jessie Bernard, in *Academic Women*, is compassionate in her understanding and brilliant in her analysis of these and other strengths and weaknesses exhibited by women who are college teachers—the women who, the new feminists say, must stand as role models for undergraduate women. In his introduction to *Academic Women*, David Reisman is more blunt (albeit in a footnote):

> In fact, there is a fair amount of evidence, though not stressed in this book, that women are their own worst enemies. The evidence lies in the tacit league of

educated housewives accusing working mothers of neglecting their families, or the preference of women college students for men teachers,* or the dislike of women to be "bossed" by other women.

More recently (*Saturday Review*, September 11, 1969, "What Did the Nineteenth Amendment Amend?") Reisman pointed out a more subtle barrier:

> Women are not able even in a woman's college to create the solidarity that is at least adumbrated or hoped for among other disadvantaged groups such as blacks. This is understandable since women are tied as daughters, sisters, girlfriends or spouses to men, whether they like it or not; they cannot create an autonomous subculture of women.

Or as Caroline Bird said in *Born Female: The High Cost of Keeping Women Down:* "The minority status of women goes unnoticed because they are the only minority in history that lives with the master race."

The degree of truth in these facets of the conundrum called "woman's nature" is important for men and women to know. Blame for the perpetuation of the interwoven myths is ubiquitous and indefinite. Of course parents are guilty when they want their sons to be doctors and lawyers and their daughters to be nurses and secretaries; home is the first place where girls' aspirations are depressed, motivations squelched. Of course society is guilty as it blindly pays the "high cost of keeping women down." Of course women are their own worst enemies, not only in their lack of solidarity as a sex and their peculiar intolerance of each other, but within themselves. As Matina S. Horner is

---

* Frequently cited as evidence that women college students have more respect for men than women teachers is the "Joan/John" experiment done at Connecticut College for Women. Two groups of sophomores were given the identical learned article to evaluate. The group who were told the article was by John McKay thought the work was impressive; those who believed Joan McKay was the author judged the work poor.

finding (see "Fail: Bright Women," *Psychology Today*, November 1969), bright girls fear that success in competitive situations will lead to unpopularity, unmarriageability, and lonely lives.

When the new feminists say to the women's colleges of America, "Shape up or ship out," they are placing the responsibility for cutting through the mishmash of myths about women where something can be done: in women's education, its curriculum and counseling.

Intelligent counseling for long-term commitment and planning requires a great deal more than the usual interview or two with the college vocational bureau just before graduation. Intelligent career guidance will begin in freshman or sophomore year. It will help a girl to examine in detail the careers that interest her, as well as ones for which she shows aptitude, but which have not interested her simply because it has never occurred to her that they are possibilities. It will help her to comprehend the advantages and potential difficulties in career commitment instead of just getting a dull menial job before marriage and maybe picking it up again after her children go off to school.

Such intelligent career counseling is not likely to precede a demand for it. It may be that intelligent and concerned women faculty at women's colleges, in league with intellectually curious women undergraduates, will undertake *ad hoc* counseling and careers information exchange centers. The demand for accurate career information exists. A study of 10,000 Vassar alumnae has shown that most graduates of the mid-fifties, at the time of their graduation, wanted marriage with or without a career; ten years later most were insisting on a career, with or without marriage.

CONTINUING EDUCATION

If additional evidence of the need for counseling exists, girls and college administrators need only to look at what happened during the decade of the sixties to older women and their desire to continue their education.

In 1960, the University of Minnesota pioneered a program to make the resources of the university available to adult women. Now called the Minnesota Planning and Counseling Center for Women, it offers individual counseling and information for women at all levels of education. Not only does it refer women to educational opportunities throughout the area, the program also offers scholarship aid, day-care facilities, and job-placement services.

The basic idea spread rapidly. Before 1970, some 1,300 American colleges and universities were accepting adult women back into the classroom and several hundred initiated special programs for them.[5]

Some indication of enrollment in these special programs is in Office of Education statistics: between 1950 and 1966, school enrollment rose from 26,000 to 214,000 among women twenty-five to twenty-nine years of age and from 21,000 to 92,000 among women thirty to thirty-four years old. Figures aren't available for women over thirty-four, although many schools find, such as Northeastern did in its 1965 survey of students in its new Program for Adult Women, that the typical student is a thirty-six-year-old housewife with three children, a husband whose education went further than hers, a high school graduate with two years of additional education. She now wants her degree and direction for future employment—paid or volunteer—with meaning.

The enthusiasm with which programs for adult women are oversubscribed from coast to coast also demonstrates the inadequacies of the American system of higher education for women. Women with previous college courses often find universities unwilling to accept transfer credits. Residency requirements defeat her desire for a degree. Few colleges credit life experience, or offer courses at convenient times for women who are also homemakers. Day-care facilities for her young children are nonexistent or expensive and inconvenient. Even though she is allowed back into the classroom, it is up to her to fit her life to

---

[5] *Continuing Education Programs and Services for Women*, U.S. Dept. of Labor, Wage and Standards Administration, Pamphlet #10, revised Jan. 1968, lists most.

the rigidity of a college designed for resident young single people. Notable exceptions exist. Comprehensive programs are offered the mature woman student at Oakland University (Michigan), the University of Michigan, the University of Wisconsin, Washington University (Missouri), Simmons College (Boston) and others. Comprehensive child-care facilities are being planned at Radcliffe, Boston University, Brandeis, and a few other schools to serve women faculty, returning women students, and the community.

Residency requirements, though, remain an anachronism. Goddard College (Plainfield, Vermont) demonstrates it needn't so remain. Goddard conducts an adult degree program for men and women at least twenty-six years of age who have not graduated from college. Two-week resident seminars with lectures and discussions are alternated with 6-month periods of independent home study supervised through correspondence with faculty.

Another solution has been proposed that takes into account the high mobility of current society. The girl who drops out of college for marriage or a job (often to support her husband's education) may move several times during the years she could be continuing work toward her degree. In "A Modest Proposal for the Educating of Women" (*American Scholar*, Fall 1969), Elizabeth Cless, one of the creators of the Minnesota Plan, believes that the college that originally accepted the girl student indicated its confidence in her, and therefore must assume lifelong responsibility for her academic counseling, whenever and wherever she wishes. This would mean "an immediate joint attack by all responsible institutions . . . on the problems of admissions procedures, credit transfers, residence requirements, and informal accumulation of learning. It means a new approach to record keeping, perhaps a national credit bank under the auspices of the Federation of Accreditation Commissions."

Responsible institutions concerned with women's education don't argue with the proposal; so far, though, few have gone beyond an occasional private arrangement permitting the senior year to be taken elsewhere. They are moving faster toward co-education.

Coeducation, most educators believe, is better than separate education, but one strong argument in favor of colleges for women will remain valid for as long as society preconditions girls to defer to men. In coeducational classrooms, many girls are unwilling to participate in discussions; at a woman's college they can be helped to overcome their fear that they have no contribution of value.

The trend, however, toward coeducation is accelerating. Fall enrollments for 1969-70 listed full-time male students at many women's colleges: for example, 47 at Bennington, 93 at Bryn Mawr, 2 at Goucher, 8 at Mount Holyoke, 26 at Skidmore, 45 at Smith, 47 at Vassar. Men's colleges enrolling full-time women students included Amherst, 23; Bowdoin, 13; Colgate, 38; Trinity, 159; and Williams, 62.[6]

Numbers, however, prove nothing, and some of these minority coeds see themselves as sex-tokens. The Yale coeds who broke into an alumni luncheon to protest that Yale's new experiment is a myth, that women are crowded out, were later answered by President Kingman Brewster, Jr., that some of the complaints were true but "we must not, unless it is absolutely necessary, increase the number of women at Yale at the expense of the number of men."

It will be necessary in ending discrimination, though, to stop the numbers, or quota, game. Colleges and universities discriminate by having quotas for women in admissions to undergraduate and graduate programs, and in scholarships and financial assistance. It often costs parents more to educate daughters than sons at the same institution. Girls can be required to live on campus and pay full room and board fees; boys can rent a cheap room off campus and eat where they want. Also, a girl needs higher marks than a boy does to get into most coeducational colleges. For example, at Penn State University a boy's chance of being accepted was reported to be five times as good as a

[6] The 50th Annual Report of Statistics of Attendance in American Universities and Colleges, 1969-70, Garland G. Parker, *School and Society*, January 1970, published by the Society for the Advancement of Education, Inc.

girl's. In Virginia, according to a report cited at the debate in the United States House of Representatives on Title VII of the Civil Rights Act, 21,000 women were turned down for college entrance during a period when not one male applicant was rejected.

EDUCATION AND THE NEW FEMINIST

Higher education has failed women.

Many intellectually capable women in this country do not receive the education for which they are qualified. Among students capable of college level work, 65 per cent of the men enter college and 45 per cent graduate. Among women of comparable ability, only 50 per cent enter and 30 per cent graduate.

Even those women who do graduate have not utilized their abilities constructively, having settled for the easiest courses or the traditional women's majors, because they have been convinced that, as women, they are less capable and less important than men. Every successful woman verifies that for comparable positions and salary, a woman must be more capable, have more ability than a man, and simultaneously play up to stereotyped notions of femininity.

The first problem is getting bright girls to go to college; the second is in motivating them for academically appropriate reasons.

If women ask for and receive an expensive education (the cost is not only in money and parental sacrifice to meet the bills, but is in classroom space and faculty attention) women have an obligation to make a return to society on its investment. If, however, society wants this kind of woman also to have a family, society has to make it possible for her to keep professional proficiency in her field while she is bearing children. Instead, now she must take time out, and when she returns she is employed below her capacity. She both short-changes and is short-changed by society.

For a woman, a college degree means she is more likely to be employed, and the higher the degree, the higher the likelihood. In March 1968, the United States Department of Labor reported that 71 per cent of women who had completed five years or more of college were in the labor force, 54 per cent of women with four years of college were employed or looking for work, compared with 48 per cent of women high school graduates and only 24 per cent of women with eight or less years of schooling. As the educated woman grows older, her employment expectations are greater: in 1968, 86 per cent of women forty-five to fifty-four years of age with five or more years of college were employed.

These bare statistics alone should provide a girl with academically appropriate reasons to pursue studies that have lifelong meaning for her as an individual. Instead, the average college girl admits that her pursuit of the bachelor is more important to her than her bachelor's degree—at the age of twenty. Ask her what she expects to be at fifty, and she will shrug off the question as unimportant, that she will meanwhile be a cultured and enlightened mother and wife. Such enlightened homemakers are a nice by-product, but not the main aim of higher education, and it is little wonder that educators often despair of going beyond training women college students for short-term jobs and longer-term homemaking.

Education has failed women, and women have failed education. In *Developing Woman's Potential* (Iowa State University Press, 1968), Edwin C. Lewis says, "The failure of women to recognize an obligation, both to themselves and to society, to make productive use of their education and training has produced a cynical attitude on the part of men responsible for that training. Only the women themselves can demonstrate that their attitudes have changed and that they are willing to accept the responsibility implied in the education provided them."

Women have failed education. The "average" and the "typical" women have failed, but a revolution—a second wave—is under way.

As with all revolutions, the work is on the part of a tiny minority of the people affected. The new feminists who are demonstrating changed attitudes are expected to accept the responsibility implied in the best higher education. The women's colleges can do no less. Many were founded during the earlier feminist period. Once more they are called on to be pioneers in the new revolution of women.

Toward partnership in the church

MARY DALY

At a time when churches are so deeply involved in the problems of civil rights of minorities, it is curious that in general the religious establishment has seemed indifferent to the civil rights of women.

Women ministers in Protestant churches are a rarity and almost a curiosity. Directors of religious education and women executives within the church are deliberately underpaid in comparison to men with equal education and experience. Women are scarce in the higher echelons of denominational organization and as heads of local church boards. When a woman was recently elected to the presidency of the National Council of Churches, her accomplishment received wide notice.

The church's women's organization in many cases is still oriented to money raising and church housekeeping, but the New Feminism is having an impact there, also. Members of the Unitarian Universalist Women's Federation, for instance, have initiated efforts for abortion law repeal within several states. "Civil rights of women" is a UUWF program priority. In the National Council of Churches, Church Women United delegates joined other women at the 1969 General Assembly in a Women's Caucus that asked for liberation of women.

Dr. Daly writes from the point of view of a Roman Catholic when she asks that women be ordained as priests. She is also a modern feminist, and has been part of a NOW task force study-

136

ing the discrimination against women in all religions. Her call for recognition of ability rather than sex as qualification for church leadership applies to all denominations.

Mary Daly is an assistant professor of theology at Boston College. She is the author of The Church and the Second Sex *(1968) from which this excerpt is taken.*

> God created man in his image. In the image of God
> he created him. Male and female he created them.
>
> *Genesis* 1:27

> There is neither Jew nor Greek, there is neither
> slave nor free, there is neither male nor female; for
> you are all one in Christ Jesus.
>
> *Galatians* 3:28

Some believe that those concerned with the problem of eradicating sexual discrimination should concentrate their energies upon the secular milieu rather than upon the Church. It is said that if truly equal educational, professional, and political opportunities are attained for women in secular society, and if psychological and social pressures which hinder them from using these opportunities can be combated successfully, the Church will grudgingly but inevitably follow suit. There is something to be said for this approach, but it is incomplete. First of all, it is seen as incomplete by those who recognize value in the church itself and who therefore feel the urgency of the need for its reform. Furthermore, it is incomplete because it considers the Church simply as a superstructure without influence upon society. This view fails to take into account the great power which the Church has as pressure group and image maker. It would be as foolish to ignore its power at this point in history as it would be to ignore that of any great cultural institution. It is important to take into account the fact that, while it is true that ecclesiastical attitudes are conditioned by the secular milieu, it is also true that the Church has influence upon the whole environment.

Our problem now is to understand the basic nature of our task of exorcising, on the level of practical activity and within the context of evolving structures, the "demon" of sexual prejudice in the Church. We have already seen the need for exorcism on the level of theory, particularly through the expulsion of the demonic myth of the eternal feminine from theology. Now we must ask what will be the operative principle which will direct our efforts on the level of social action.

The answer to this question must be sought by first considering the nature of the disease which we are attempting to cure, for an adequate cure must be appropriate to the illness. The disease can be understood in terms of self-fulfilling prophecy, a process by which the dominant class projects its unwanted characteristics, its lower self, upon the members of the oppressed class, who in turn introject the despised qualities. Thus, the creation story speaks the truth in declaring that Eve came from Adam. Moreover, the workings of the process—the whole vicious circle of role psychology—are understood neither by the oppressor nor by his victim, both of whom are inclined to accept the myths, such as the myth of fixed natures, which serve as its justification.

If the resultant fixed roles were harmful only to the class of persons who have been made inferior (the slave, the Negro, the woman) there would be compelling enough reason to seek a cure. However, there is more to it than this. Thus the white supremacist is rent at the core of his being. Thus also the male, through the mutilation of woman, has been caught up in a process of self-destruction. In relation to woman as mother, wife, companion, he is doomed to frustration if he cannot find in the other an authentic, self-activating person—with precisely the qualities which are stunted by the imposition of the eternal feminine. Fated to partnership with "true woman," he may find this dissociated, narcissistic being less satisfactory than the companion of his dreams. What is more, the "eternal masculine" itself is alienating, crippling the personalities of men and restricting their experience of life at every level. The male in our society is not supposed to express much feeling, sensitivity, aesthetic appreciation, imagination, consideration for others, intuition. He is expected to affirm only part of his real self. Indeed, it may be that a good deal of the compulsive competitiveness of males is rooted in this half existence.

It is the nature of the disease, therefore, to inhibit the expansion of the individual's potential, through conditioned conformity to roles, and through a total identification of the individual with them. It contrasts starkly with free acceptance of roles by integrated personalities, for its effect is to hinder the integration of personality. The healing which we seek must not be understood as a return to a state of health presumed to have existed in the past. This would be nothing but an abortive quest for the state of dreaming innocence, for primitive unconsciousness, or for the paradise lost by the Fall. Rather, we must strive for that forward leap into the future of human history which is now demanded of us. Then perhaps it will be understood that our sickness was only the growing pains of a species on its way to maturity.

The nature of the effort demanded of us is revealed by the nature of our predicament, of our alienation. Disintegrated and dissociated by processes which may have been necessary for the development of civilization, we must seek integration by confronting each other in a way which is qualitatively different from that of the past. Men and women are in history, in time, existing only in dynamic relationship to each other. We have in the past been chained to the wheel of psychological processes whose nature was not understood, living out roles which seemingly were predestined, written in the heavens. There is evidence that a few privileged souls in every age transcended the blindness of the culture and achieved communication which was profound and genuinely personal, but the literature of all ages attests to the general failure. In our time, however, we appear to be at the threshold of liberation from this ancient servitude. The developing sciences, particularly psychology and anthropology, have given us insight at last into the mechanisms which had enslaved us. The advance of technology has provided us with a situation in which, for the first time in history, we have the required leisure, mobility, control of our environment to experiment on the basis of this insight.

Our efforts, then, must be toward a level of confrontation, dialogue, and cooperation between the sexes undreamed of in the past, when the struggle for biological survival of the species and numerical multiplication had to take precedence over any thought of qualitative development of relation between the sexes. The directing principle of our thoughts and plans concerning the future relations of men and women in the Church and society must be commitment to providing the possibility of ever more profound, complete, dynamic, and humanizing relationships, in which we may hope to transcend our alienation through understanding of each other and of ourselves.

A concerted effort should be made to work toward this eradicating of discrimination on all levels. On the parish and diocesan levels, wherever boards and councils of laymen are established, women should be represented, significantly and proportionately, not merely by a few token appointments. They should be found in positions of importance in the national Catholic organizations. In particular, efforts should be directed to seeking out and using the talents of gifted and highly trained women specialists in influential and decision-making roles within the Church. Relevant areas of specialization in which competent women are now to be found include advanced theological research and teaching, sociology, political science, psychology, educational administration, business administration, journalism, law, social work. Such specialists should be recruited for postconciliar commissions and other organizations which may be set up to continue the work begun by the Vatican Council.

In liturgical affairs, as participation of the laity becomes more active, equally active participation of both sexes must be insisted upon. If laymen serve as lectors and acolytes, if they preach and distribute Holy Communion, then women should do the same. Moreover, it is evident, if one faces the problem with consistency, courage, and sincerity, that the process of eradicating discrimination must not stop here. The question of women clergy must be faced.

THE QUESTION OF WOMEN PRIESTS

In the question of whether women may be ordained priests, the whole problem of the situation of women in the Church is reflected, symbolized, and crystallized. Indeed, it is evident to anyone who has repeatedly engaged in discussions of the subject that this can serve as a touchstone for attitudes concerning women and the man-woman relationship. Many who would see the appropriateness of some kind of active role for women in the Church recoil in horror when the priesthood is mentioned. Often, conversations which had been rational up to this point suddenly become wildly emotional and hidden prejudices blossom forth, dramatically revealing the insincerity of earlier admissions that women should be recognized as equal to men in the Church.

What is at stake is the character and quality of the man-woman relation in the Church of the future. There will be no genuine equality of men and women in the Church as long as qualified persons are excluded from any ministry by reason of their sex alone. Those who point to the rising position of the laity in the Church and then argue that women are attaining equality because of this are ignoring the fact that the situation of men and women is not the same here. Men have the option of becoming priests or remaining laymen. Women have no choice. As long as the Church maintains a significant distinction between hierarchy and laity, the exclusion of women from the hierarchy is a radical affirmation of their inferior position among the people of God. By this exclusion the Church is, in a very real and effective way, teaching that women are not fully human and conditioning people to accept this as an irremediable fact. It is saying that the sexual differentiation is—for one sex—a handicap so crippling that no personal qualities of intelligence, virtue, or leadership can overcome it.

That there is no valid theological objection to the ordination of women has become increasingly evident in recent years. Discussion by scholars in the various Protestant churches which have decided to ordain women has helped to manifest the absurdity of objections on theological grounds. Of particular interest is the dispute which occurred concerning the ordination of women in Sweden in the 1950's. Biblical scholar Krister Stendahl has pointed out that scholars on both sides of the dispute were in agreement concerning the historical meaning of the texts of St. Paul concerning women. The real problem and disagreement concerned application to modern times. Those who took the conservative position assumed that Paul's view could be taken as a generally valid Christian view, normative for all times. This is precisely the weakness of the conservative position. Professor Stendahl maintains that in all the texts where the New Testament speaks about the role of women in the Church, when a reason is given, it is always by reference to the subordinate position of women in creation. In fact, "the question of women's place in the cult and ministry and in the Christian home and in society is dealt with on the selfsame principle: the subordination in creation." [1] This implies that the question about the ordination of women cannot be separated from the total problem of the emancipation of women in our society. Thus, Professor Stendahl argues, it is almost impossible to assent to the political emancipation of women while arguing on biblical grounds against the ordination of women.

There is further reason to reject the position of those who accept the political emancipation of women but, on supposedly scriptural grounds, reject their ordination. The New Testament (Galatians 3:28) suggests that if there is to be a change in the man-woman relationship, it will be in Christ. It is a peculiar reversal of this to claim that emancipation is all right in "the world" but not in the Church. It would be more consistent, although quite mad, to crusade in the name of the Bible against all emancipation and try to regain the social situation of the first century. Professor Stendahl summarizes the case succinctly: "If emancipation is right, then there is no valid 'biblical' reason not to ordain women. Ordination cannot be treated as a 'special'

[1] Krister Stendahl, *The Bible and the Role of Women: A Case Study in Hermeneutics,* translated by Emilie T. Sander (Philadelphia: Fortress Press, Facet Books, Biblical Series 15, 1966), p. 39.

problem since there is no indication that the New Testament sees it as such." [2]

A frequent type of objection takes the form of an argument from fact. Some have based their opposition upon the fact that Jesus called only men to be his apostles. The weakness of this sort of reasoning is evident. It is impossible to move with logical certitude from this to the conclusion that only men should be priests —such a conclusion requires quite an unjustifiable leap. How do we know that this was the point of his choice? He also chose only Jews, which hardly can be interpreted to mean that only Jews can be priests. The objection fails to take into account the cultural climate of the time. It reflects a kind of Docetism, which refuses to recognize the implications of the full humanity of Jesus. That is, it simply does not take into account the fact that, being truly human, Jesus lived and thought within the cultural context of his age.

Similar to this objection is the argument based upon the fact that Jesus was male. It is argued that the priest represents Christ and therefore must be male. This type of fuzzy, symbol-oriented thinking leaves itself open to objections at both ends. It betrays a distorted understanding of the meaning of Christ, giving prior importance to his maleness, rather than to his humanity. Moreover, it is forced to be inconsistent in order to avoid the assertion that women cannot represent Christ at all—and few would want to go this far.

Some forward-looking Catholic writers (notably Monsignor J. D. Conway) have suggested that Pope John was opening just a crack the door to the priesthood for women, perhaps without realizing it, when he wrote in *Pacem in Terris*, "Human beings have the right to choose freely the state of life which they prefer, and therefore the right to establish a family, with equal rights and duties for man and woman, and also the right to follow a vocation to the priesthood or the religious life."

After quoting this passage, Monsignor Conway commented:

> Pope John might object to my taking his words
> literally but they deserve meditation. He noted with

[2] *Ibid.*, p. 41.

approval the fading of a stratified society, in which
some persons are put in an inferior condition, and
others assume superior position, "on account of
economic and social conditions, of sex, of assigned
rank." [3]

It is possible that Pope John's words have prophetic implications
which will be recognized only after the passage of time.

A procedure similar to that employed by Monsignor Conway
could be used in connection with a passage from Vatican II's
Pastoral Constitution on the Church in the Modern World:

With respect to the fundamental rights of the person,
every type of discrimination, whether social or cultural,
whether based on sex, race, color, social condition,
language, or religion, is to be overcome and eradicated
as contrary to God's intent. For in truth it must still be
regretted that fundamental personal rights are not yet
being universally honored. Such is the case of a woman
who is denied the right and freedom to choose a husband, to embrace a state of life, or to acquire an education or cultural benefits equal to those recognized for
men. [4]

It is clear that women cannot "embrace a state of life" on the
same terms as men, as long as they are excluded from the hierarchy.

The vast theological developments which have taken place in
recent years have implications for the specific question of
women's ordination which have not been lost upon progressive
theologians. Recognizing the weakness of theological objections, they have openly shifted the whole question to the arenas
of sociology and psychology. Thus, in 1966, Father Hans Küng
stated:

There are two factors to consider regarding the
ordination of women to the Sacred Ministry of the

[3] *NCR*, 16 November, 1966, p. 8.
[4] *Pastoral Constitution on the Church in the Modern World*, n. 29.

Church. The first is that there are no dogmatic or biblical reasons against it. The second is that there are psychological and sociological factors to be considered. The solution to the problem depends on the sociological conditions of the time and place. It is entirely a matter of cultural circumstances.[5]

It can hardly be denied that cultural circumstances, as far as women are concerned, have changed enormously during this century. We live in an age in which women have gained access to nearly all the professions, including the Protestant ministry, and have demonstrated their competence in them, often to an unusual degree. There are few thinking people who would deny this, or who would deny that in the face of this social evolution the situation within the Church is anachronistic. However, there is by no means unanimity concerning the nature of the problem and its solution.

Among those who recognize that something is amiss and who do sincerely wish to see the female situation improved, a variety of attitudes exists. We shall consider two extremely opposed approaches, both of which betray inadequate understanding of the dimensions of the problem at hand. The first approach favors some modest reform of women's situation among the laity but looks upon the question of women priests as premature, peripheral, and unrelated to the more immediate problems of women and of the Church. It ignores the fact that exclusion of women from the clergy not only reflects but also serves to perpetuate a certain restrictive style of man-woman relationship. The second attitude supposes that the ordination of women will be a panacea for the ills of the Church in general and women in particular. It naively ignores the complexity of the problems which are the concern of sexual anthropology. We shall examine each of these approaches in turn.

Despite the evidence of social evolution, there are many—including many women—who feel that people are not ready for

[5] Hans Küng, quoted in *Progress Report to the House of Bishops* (Episcopalian), from The Committee to Study the Proper Place of Women in the Church's Ministry (an unpublished report), October 1966, p. 111.

so radical a change as the introduction of women priests. They choose to keep a prudent silence on this issue, or at least leave the matter in abeyance. They wish to avoid what they consider to be extremism and to work realistically for small changes. Briefly, they think that the question of women's ordination has surfaced prematurely. Although this position may appear to reflect a sense of "balance" and good judgment, it has inherent difficulties.

First of all, the question simply cannot be ignored as premature, since many Protestant churches now ordain women. Thus it inevitably enters into the ecumenical frame of reference. This is not to say that the "argument from ecumenism"—i.e. what one church does, another must do—is valid. It does mean that the question has been raised and must be faced.

Second, the argument that it is "too soon" to consider seriously women's ordination puts an exaggerated emphasis upon the factor of psychological resistance to social change. There is always some resistance to any social change. This will be the case no matter how delayed the reform movement may be in coming. Indeed, if there were no unwillingness to change, there would be no discriminatory situation. In fact, it is to a large extent true that prejudice is overcome only by the fact of change itself. A prejudice against women university professors, for example, is not overcome by refusal to hire them. Rather, it is defeated by demonstration, that is, by the presence and influence of excellent women professors.

Nevertheless the factor of psychological resistance should not unrealistically be ignored. If in a given time and place the opposition to change is overwhelming, and if it is reinforced by other cultural institutions, then delay or gradualism will be necessary. Today, however, it is clear that in the United States and a great part of Europe, the basic conflict is not between cultural circumstances and the admission of women to the ranks of the clergy. On the contrary, there is a basic incongruity between present social conditions and the absolute exclusion of women from the official ministry of the Church. Indeed, at this point in history the Church is in the somewhat comical position of applauding women's legal, professional, and political emancipation in secular society while keeping them in the basement of its own edifice.

Much of the insistence that the discussion of women's ordination is premature is rooted in the belief that it is a peripheral and unimportant issue, having little relevance for the immediate problems of men and women. Thus, many will dismiss this topic as unimportant but will favor raising the status of women among the laity. This reveals a notion of the man-woman relation which is narrow and short-sighted. Such persons are willing to accept discrimination on the basis of sex up to—or rather down to—a point, and fail to affirm that this is wrong in principle and justifiable only when circumstances make it impossible to avoid. This position is weak and inconsistent. It would be more consistent to hold that whatever deficiency or mysterious difference makes women universally unfit for membership in the hierarchy would also disqualify them from equality with men among the laity. If sexual discrimination is desirable or at least justifiable where the hierarchy is in question, there is no compelling reason for not perpetuating it where the functions of the laity are in question.

When this principle of consistency is understood, it throws some light upon the unfortunate fact that in post-Vatican II years, rather than gaining ground at an equal pace with laymen, women have been kept in an inferior status. This has become so painfully obvious that in 1967 the executive director of the National Council of Catholic Women in the United States—traditionally a very cautious organization—publicly issued a strong protest. Her comments had been prepared for discussion by the National Council of Catholic Bishops, which was held in Chicago in April of that year. Significantly, the topic was never discussed, but the report was issued to newsmen who were covering the bishops' meeting. In it the NCCW director stated that women now seem destined to become third-class Christians, despite the emphasis upon the laity as the "people of God," which was voiced at Vatican II. She said:

> As the participation of laymen in liturgical and
> ecclesiastical affairs continues to increase, it becomes

painfully obvious that women are being left behind
in a class by themselves. The position of the Catholic
woman in the spiritual worshipping community is
exactly the same as it was before the Council.

The statement further bemoaned the fact that women still
have no active role in the liturgy, that they are very much in
the minority on parish boards and councils, that they are not in
positions of importance in national Catholic organizations. Finally, it declared that the present situation is "an unhealthy climate" for the Catholic woman, who "waits for her talents and
abilities . . . and, indeed, her personhood, to be recognized and
acknowledged by the Church." [6]

The difficulty is that the Catholic woman will wait in vain for
such acknowledgment, unless organizations such as the NCCW
come to see and publicly affirm the full implications of the personhood which they want to be recognized by the Church. Because Catholic women and their organizations have been too
timid in affirming their worth and their rights, because they
have asked for too little, they have in fact failed to make progress. Until they have the clear-sightedness and courage to reject
discrimination totally, it is to be expected that women will be
the losers on all levels. The perverse consistency in the present
trend toward third-class citizenship in the Church can be challenged only by those who think and act with consistency.

Just as it is short-sighted to dismiss the question of women in
the hierarchy as premature and irrelevant, so also it is a mistake
to think of their acceptance as a panacea. There are lessons to
be learned in this matter from the experience of Protestant
churches which have ordained women. From the testimony of
these women ministers it is clear that being ordained does not
guarantee the removal of all discriminatory practices. In fact,
they do suffer from such practices in a variety of ways. This experience indicates that the problems involved in relations
between the sexes in the Church, as in any society, are profound
and complex. There is no instant cure for them. Progress on any

[6] Quoted in *The Catholic Transcript*, Hartford, Conn., April 21, 1967
(Religious News Service).

level toward recognition and development of the full potential
of women should be the occasion of rejoicing but not of unrealistic optimism. In the long run, particular advances will not be
very effective unless they are accompanied and supported by
developments in many parts of the social organism.

When studying the problem of women's situation vis-à-vis the
Church, it is essential to realize that the solution is inseparably
bound up with the whole issue of evolving structures. It would
be rash to pretend that one can predict with certainty what
form the Church community of the future will take. However,
there is a serious danger of short-sightedness, of being fixated
upon presently existing forms which are already fading into the
past or which are doomed eventually to disappear. A consciousness of social evolution counteracts the temptation to simplistic
activism, to the search for panaceas for a problem which is all-
pervasive and extremely complex. This is not to say that an
awareness of evolution should spawn a sort of quietism which
chooses to "wait and see" what will happen. On the contrary, it
is essential to see that man is the being who shares in the shaping
of his own destiny. Thus it is necessary to work within the existing situation, to rectify injustice within existing structures
insofar as this is possible, and at the same time to anticipate and direct toward future developments.

It is most important, then, to go beyond thinking in terms of
the institutional Church as it has existed until the present time.
We are living in a time of social upheaval. Indeed, it appears that
we are entering upon a new stage in human evolution, and it
may be that many social structures which are still with us and
many accepted patterns of behavior are really dead remnants of
an earlier stage. Characteristic of our age is the breakdown of
class distinctions which have persisted for thousands of years—
indeed, since the human race moved from its infancy, the state
of primitive society, into its adolescence. These class distinctions
have been expressed in hierarchical patterns of society. Master
and slave, feudal lord and serf, husband and wife—all lived out
their existence in fixed roles, more or less modified according to
circumstances and individual disposition. The fundamental dialectic was between oppressor and oppressed. This hierarchical

vision of the world was reflected in the structures of the Church and justified by her theology. Today these structures remain, but modern man is experiencing them more and more as suffocating anachronisms.

At the same time, modern man experiences an anxiety about the disappearance of these structures. There is an awareness, in some cases explicit, in others half-buried in the unconscious, that we stand at a turn in the road and that there is no going back. This is the reason for the strange power of the women priests issue to arouse violent and irrational responses. In fact, the very expression "women priests" juxtaposes in the most striking way two symbols which in a former age, the age from which we are emerging, had been understood as occupying opposed positions in the hierarchical scheme of things. The very suggestion that the same individual could be the bearer of these two images is a declaration that an age has ended and another has begun.

It is quite possible, many would say inevitable, that the distinction between hierarchy and laity as we now know it will disappear. Since our age is characterized by the emergence of oppressed minorities, it is unlikely that the Church can hold out against this rising tide. The existence of a separate and superior priestly caste, of a hierarchy, appears to modern man as a quaint leftover from an earlier stage of human development. Modern theologians, recognizing this, stress the point that the clergy exist in order to serve the faithful, not in order to accumulate power, honors, and prestige. A prominent theologian has pointed out that whereas for several centuries the Catholic idea of the priest was almost exclusively that of an "offerer of sacrifice," doctrinal development has moved away from this. Vatican II's Constitution on the Church reflects growth from a cultic notion of the priest to a ministerial one.[7]

This is an important transition. The priest, formerly detached, a "sacred person," an object of veneration and almost superstitious awe, is beginning to be seen as a presence in the midst of the world rather than an overseer, as brother rather than as father. Thus there is a shift toward democratization. The priest now

[7] Gregory Baum, in *The Ecumenist*, November-December, 1965, p. 6.

sees himself and is seen in terms of mission to the world, which requires dialogue and cooperation with his fellow men. Since dialogue and cooperation are two-way processes, the priest's temptations to accept false prestige and to appraise himself unrealistically will be greatly diminished.

The emphasis upon service and cooperation has the effect of putting sharply into focus the problem which is nagging many priests, who discover that they are, in fact, in a less advantageous situation for serving the Christian community than many professionally competent laymen. Indeed, a large percentage of the clergy, in this age of specialization, are in the uncomfortable situation of being nonprofessional dabblers competing with experts in a variety of fields. Their work touches many areas requiring special competence: theology, teaching, preaching, social service, counseling psychology, business administration, recreational leadership. Any of these areas of work can be handled by qualified members of the laity, men and women, and any of them can be handled better by lay specialists than by clerical nonspecialists. It is not surprising, then, that some are beginning to look upon clerical caste as we now know it as irrelevant and doomed to extinction, and to envision the Church of the future as a community based upon charismatic ministries, and transformed into a higher and more adequately human social order.

It is essential that those who are concerned with relations between the sexes in the Church give serious attention to this modern development in the direction of democratization and specialization. When the emphasis is shifted away from symbolic roles which are identified with fixed states of life and toward functional roles freely assumed on the basis of personal qualifications and skills, away from caste systems and toward specialization based on ability, there will be hope for realization of that higher level of dialogue and cooperation between men and women which we seek.

Emerging

Life Styles

of the

New Feminism

The status of women in Sweden

REPORT TO THE UNITED NATIONS, 1968

The excerpts here given of the 1968 report to the United Nations on the Status of Women in Sweden offer much encouragement to the New Feminist movement everywhere.

Sweden is engaged in a campaign for total emancipation of women, a fact probably not unconnected with the low birth rate in the country. However, the developments in Sweden involve, according to this report, the emancipation of men as well. Men are assuming a greater share of responsibility for the upbringing of children and the care of the home, and in return are not relied upon as the sole breadwinners for the family, forever chained to particular jobs.

Women are expected to receive parity not only in the matter of rights, but also to assume duties formerly held by men in trade union and political work. They are urged to work for election to positions of trust in the community and the nation.

A modern family policy is emerging, which includes a basic child allowance, expansion of child-care centers, free maternity care, a maternity-benefit payment, a special treatment allowance to families with handicapped children, free school meals, municipal domestic help for emergencies, subsidized holiday camps for children, and the like.

The total report is well worth the study of men and women to whom some of the demands of the New Feminists seem bizarre and radical.

The Government of Sweden has noted with satisfaction resolution No. 1133 (XLI) of the Economic and Social Council concerning a long-term program within the framework of the United Nations aimed at raising the status of women and the suggestions put forward by the Secretary-General in conjunction with this resolution. In a world where human rights in various areas of society are still largely limited with respect to women either by law or in practice, the Swedish Government feels that any effort likely to promote greater equality between men and women should be accorded high priority. Continued and intensified efforts on the part of the UNO to make member countries conscious of the need for active measures to achieve better utilization of the talent and labor potential represented by women are an important phase of the work of realizing human rights. A long-term program adopted by the UNO and containing both a definition of policy and proposals to concrete measures in this respect would undoubtedly represent a major contribution to the emancipation of women all over the world.

Before proceeding to a more detailed account of the activity which has taken place and is taking place in Sweden with a view to achieving greater equality between the sexes, the Government wishes to give its general views on what it considers to be important aspects of the *aim* of such an international program.

The measures to raise the status of women recommended in resolution No. 1133 as well as in certain of the suggestions included in the Secretary-General's "Annex II" are felt to be relatively isolated from the general policy in various fields aimed at economic and social progress for the population as a whole. However, experience from both Sweden and other industrial countries suggests that the question of women's rights must be viewed as a function of the whole complex of roles and the division of labor imposed on both women and men by upbringing, tradition, and practice (and to a lesser extent by legislation). A decisive and ultimately durable improvement in the status of women cannot be attained by special measures aimed at women alone; it is equally necessary to abolish the conditions which tend to assign certain privileges, obligations, or rights to men. No decisive change in the distribution of functions and status as between the sexes can be achieved if the duties of the male in society are assumed *a priori* to be unaltered. The aim of reform work in this area must be to change the traditional division of labor which tends to deprive women of the possibility of exercising their legal rights on equal terms. The division of functions as between the sexes must be changed in such a way that both the man and the woman in a family are afforded the same practical opportunities of participating in both active parenthood and gainful employment. If women are to attain a position in society outside the home which corresponds to their proportional membership of the citizen body, it follows that men must assume a greater share of responsibility for the upbringing of children and the care of the home. A policy which attempts to give women an equal place with men in economic life while at the same time confirming woman's traditional responsibility for the care of home and children has no prospect of fulfilling the first of these aims. This aim can be realized only if the man is also educated and encouraged to take an active part in parenthood and is given the same rights and duties as the woman in his parental capacity. This will probably imply that the demands for performance at work on the man's part must be reduced: a continued shortening of working hours will therefore be of great importance. In this context it would be advisable to study how reductions in working hours could best be distributed over the working week with a view to making it easier for husbands to do their share of work in the home.

In this connection the Swedish Government would refer to the Memorandum of October 23, 1963, delivered to the Secretary-General in connection with General Assembly Resolution No. 1777 (XVII) concerning UN aid to improve the status of women in the developing countries. With reference to the proposal to draft a long-term program for women in these countries, the following comment, among others, was made:

> The aim of such a program must be to establish a situation where community efforts are directed as a matter of course toward all citizens within the respective countries, without any discrimination as to

race, religion, or sex. This implies that women must be integrated completely into the work of developing the community. . . . It is therefore necessary to emphasize that, in the long run, specific "programs for women" and specific "efforts for women" should be abolished —as obviously the whole community shares the benefits.

The same principle applies, in the opinion of the Swedish Government, now that the question has been raised of a long-term program within the United Nations framework covering all its member states. The aim of a *long-term* "program for women" must be that every individual, irrespective of sex, shall have the same *practical* opportunities, not only for education and employment, but also in principle the same responsibility for his or her own maintenance as well as a shared responsibility for the upbringing of children and the upkeep of the home. Eventually to achieve complete equality in these rights and obligations, a radical change in deep-rooted traditions and attitudes must be brought about among both women and men, and active steps must be taken by the community to encourage a change in the roles played by both. The view that women ought to be economically supported by marriage must be effectively refuted—also in the legislative field—as this view is a direct obstacle to the economic independence of women and their ability to compete on equal terms in the labor market. Similarly, the husband's traditional obligation to support his wife must be modified to constitute a responsibility, shared with her, for the support of the children. This concern for the children should also be manifested in a greater degree of participation in the supervision and care of the children on the husband's part.

The Government is well aware that this view appears revolutionary and unrealistic in the eyes of the representatives of many other countries. A growing opinion in Sweden has however rallied to its support. In Sweden, as in the other Scandinavian countries, a lively debate has been going on for the past six or seven years in mass media, in organizations, and in public bodies concerning the tasks of men and women in society and the home. This debate has brought forth a new approach which involves a departure from the traditional habit of regarding these problems as "women's questions."

The debate has received great support from scientific research concerning the roles of the sexes; the research has been conducted mainly by sociologists, although economists are now also beginning to make a contribution. The analyses hitherto available show that no rapid advancement of women in employment and the professions, politics, trade union activity, etc. is possible as long as men fail to assume that share of the work of the home which falls to them as husbands and fathers. The expression "male emancipation" has therefore been coined in Sweden to denote the right of a husband to remain at home while the children are small where it is found more appropriate for the mother to devote herself to gainful employment. The demand for male "emancipation" in family life is also supported by the results of recent psychological research, which have proved that the identification of growing boys may become uncertain in a one-sided, mother-dominated home environment.[1] This lack of certainty in identification (of what is "manly" behavior) may lead to overcompensation expressed in exaggerated aggressiveness and may be one explanation of the higher crime rate of boys as compared to girls. In recent years demands have been made for a change in legislation whereby the father, like the mother (when she interrupts her career) would be entitled to a certain leave of absence with pay while the children are small. The need for male staff in child-care institutions, day nurseries, nursery schools, and the lower schools has been emphasized in many quarters.

In the discussion of woman's role which has been going on in Sweden, it has been particularly pointed out that the mothers— or fathers—of small children ought to be afforded a free and open choice between working inside or outside the home. This emphasis on the married woman's right to continue in gainful employment during the years when the family has small chil-

[1] Per Olav Tiller, "Parental role division and the child's personality development," see *The Changing Roles of Men and Women*, ed. by Edmund Dahlström (London: Gerald Duckworth and Co. Ltd., 1967), pp. 79-104.

dren has done a great deal to break down the negative attitude to mothers going out to work which was formerly common. It is another matter that society has not as yet been able to provide the facilities, e.g. for looking after children, that would be needed to guarantee full freedom of choice to all parents of small children. According to a survey made in 1967, there were over 200,000 mothers with children below the age of ten who would like to go out to work if they could arrange to have their children looked after.

The great majority of married women in Sweden, however, do not have young children. The period of active motherhood now occupies only a comparatively small portion of a woman's adult life owing to the tendency to marry younger, have fewer children than in former times, and concentrate the bearing of children to an early age. A married woman can therefore devote the greater part of her adult life to gainful work. It is important in the discussion of gainful employment for married women to distinguish, on the one hand, between women with children at an age when they demand supervision and, on the other, women who no longer have children who require their mothers' presence in the home (the latter group forms the great majority in Sweden). It can therefore hardly be argued that married women without young children should be regarded differently in any essential way to unmarried women as far as the labor market is concerned; on the contrary, the professional ambitions of women must be encouraged. The old idea that women bear the main responsibility for work in the home must be countered, as gainful work by married women is otherwise liable to be regarded as a mere supplement to housework.

It is further clear that the possibility of remaining at home which is open to many married women, even though their children no longer require their presence, cannot by any means always be taken as a manifestation of true freedom of choice. A woman's decision to remain at home often means in reality that she has limited the choices open to her on the labor market if she should wish to go out to work later. It may prove to be a great handicap if a woman is absent from the labor market for an extended period of time, for she finds, when she later wishes to return to work—or is compelled to do so for economic reasons—that she is at a considerable disadvantage as compared to someone who has been in continuous employment.

However, it would be unreasonable to presume that married women should devote themselves to gainful employment to the same extent as men and at the same time do all the work of the home. Surveys in both western and eastern Europe show that working married women today have less leisure time than any other group in society. Nor can one expect that women who devote themselves to permanent gainful employment will have access to the same opportunities for promotion as men under the present system of sex roles, as the individual employer considers the risk of women's leaving his service on marriage too high to justify the investment of training and promoting them. The character of matrimony as an institution for the support of women according to the occidental tradition has thus come to be an indirect obstacle to her emancipation in modern industrial society.

Swedish opinion, therefore, has made a great point of stressing the economic independence of every individual both inside and outside marriage. Instead of a one-sided emphasis on the function of motherhood, the importance of greater contact between father and children has been stressed. At the same time, the care and upbringing of children have come to be increasingly regarded as essential services to the community, which in principle ought to be paid for in cash in the same way as services to an employer. It has been felt that the social security of the parent who stays at home to look after the children should be equivalent to that of the one who goes out to work. This view is also reflected in the directives issued to the Committee currently reviewing our family policy.

The new view set forth here represents a sharp break with older tradition. Young married couples with children have been among the keenest supporters of the new equality. Incidentally, it is interesting to note that men have taken an active part in the debate on future sex roles. This new opinion, which is represented in practically all organizations, will undoubtedly exert a strong influence on future reform policies in Sweden.

Through a comprehensive social insurance system, the State in Sweden has assumed the main responsibility for the individual in case of sickness, disability, and unemployment. Thus women are no longer so economically dependent on their husbands for their personal security.

It is however most important that social welfare legislation should be applied to the married woman as an individual and not indirectly via her husband. Studies now in progress in Sweden are aimed at putting men and women on an equal footing with regard to social security insurance.

Notwithstanding its basic attitude—that community measures and reforms must be clearly directed toward all citizens irrespective of sex—the Swedish Government fully appreciates the additional necessity of special action on behalf of women in the present situation and, in many countries, during a lengthy period of transition. Special efforts on the part of the community to strengthen the position of women will be necessary until the gap between men and women as regards the practical exercise of human rights has narrowed appreciably. The need for special action to stimulate female emancipation is certainly present in other countries besides those which have traditionally assigned a subordinate role to women. Steps must also be taken to ensure that women can *maintain* the strong or economically independent position which they have traditionally held in certain countries now embarking upon industrial development. It is most important that the UNO and its various special bodies should be conscious of the risk that women may be forced into greater economic dependence upon their men folk when their country abandons a barter economy in favor of an industrial monetary economy. This happened in Sweden and a number of other European countries at the end of the nineteenth century and the beginning of the twentieth. It is so much more difficult to put right the defects afterward.

Special efforts are clearly also called for to overcome prejudices against certain groups of women, e.g. unmarried mothers. This group undoubtedly has to face a difficult situation in many countries owing to prejudices against women who become mothers without benefit of matrimony. Experience from Sweden indicates that such prejudices can be broken down, partly through a series of measures on society's part to improve the economic and social status of unmarried mothers.

The special reforms affecting women must however be so designed as to encourage the *full integration of women into all the facets of society*. It is essential to keep this aim clearly in mind, as the risk otherwise arises that special action on behalf of women may serve to entrench a traditional division of labor which *in the long view* will hinder the achievement of practical equality between the sexes. A further complication attendant upon a division of various types of community effort according to sex is that it is all too easy to give the impression that public reform policy is mainly directed toward satisfying the needs of the male population, while questions affecting women must be resolved by special arrangements or supplementary regulations. At the same time as special provisions are made for giving women equality of opportunity with men, it is necessary to induce women to move into areas traditionally regarded as male preserves.

It is also important to the realization of the program to stress that the object of the action taken is to achieve parity not only in the matter of rights, but also of the duties of women. Women, just as much as men, have an obligation to take an active part in, for example, trade union and political work and to share the economic responsibility for the support of children. They should not be able to acquire social status and privileges automatically by virtue of their husbands' contributions to public life. On the contrary, women must be made aware of their personal responsibility as citizens. They must be encouraged to exercise the franchise and the opportunity of being elected to positions of trust in political life. Women should further be conscious of their obligation to give some return on the capital which society has invested in their education and training, as society has a right to expect this capital to pay dividends. This aspect is becoming all the more important now that education is rapidly becoming more widespread among young people and courses of training are becoming longer and longer.

The grounds for initiating a long-term program for women

should preferably also be given a broader content than the simple objective of creating equality in respect of rights and obligations. The economic profit and the more rapid economic progress that both the community as a whole and the individual business stand to gain through greater equality between the sexes must be emphasized. It should further be stressed that increased *efficiency* and more rapid economic progress are dependent on the abandonment of scales of evaluation based on physical characteristics such as sex and race instead of individual aptitude and ability. A Swedish economist and labor market researcher has calculated that the Swedish national income could be increased by some 25 per cent if the unused labor potential of women were to be fully utilized and by some 50 per cent if sex discrimination and other barriers were to be totally abolished. According to a calculation made in France, the standard of living of that country would rise by 35 per cent if women were professionally active to the same extent as men. Experience from Sweden shows, moreover, that many private employers are little inclined to show interest in the recruitment of female labor for what are traditionally regarded as "male" jobs simply in response to appeals for "fair play between the sexes." One must in the first instance be able to show proof of the economic gains a company can effect by increasing its recruitment of women. A number of Swedish industrial firms took a greater interest in part-time employment of women after it had been demonstrated that the average productivity of two women employed part time to fill one full-time vacancy was higher than that achieved by one male worker employed full time. In an area where there is a shortage of labor, it is possible to arouse interest in the employment of women if one can show that the company gains in productivity by broadening its field of recruitment to include women also. Unfortunately, however, the female skill that could be turned to profit is still an unknown quantity in many occupations where it has never been given a chance to prove itself.

Provided that the special program for women is so formulated that it directly encourages the full integration of women into the work of the community outside the home, a program designed to improve the status of women over the period 1968-1978 will be of great value. In view of what was said earlier about the need to modify the traditional division of roles between the sexes, it would, however, be advantageous if a long-term program adopted by the UNO were to be formulated as a program of equality between women and men. There can be no doubt that even the title of such a program would be significant, and it would be valuable if the designation of the program were such as to avoid giving the impression of being concerned with questions relating to women that could be dealt with and solved by women. It may be mentioned that the term "woman question" as applied to these problems is now being largely abandoned in Sweden in favor of the sociological term "sex-role question."

With reference to the international conventions listed in "Annex II Suggestions, etc." to the Secretary-General's note, Sweden subscribed to all of these. Swedish law contains no formal obstacles to the exercise of civil, social, or economic rights by women. Of some significance, however, are the limitations placed upon the entry of women into certain special spheres of activity with a particularly great aura of "male prestige" which tend to preserve the philosophy of segregation. In Sweden nowadays this applies only to the profession of arms; formerly it also applied to holy orders. The ultimate reason why women have been unable to achieve a status in society equal to that of men is to be sought in the traditional division of functions whereby women are by upbringing, habit, and tradition assigned the prime responsibility for the care of home and children. It is this so-called primary female role which deprives women of equality in vocational training and employment and of equal representation in political and trade organizations.

To promote greater equality, one must always determine which political instruments will directly or indirectly encourage a more equal division of labor between the sexes, for every act on the part of the community affects the status of men and women—in a favorable or unfavorable direction. The question of the roles of the sexes must therefore be regarded as one of the chief problems in the continual work of reforming educational, employment, social, family, and taxation policies.

As explained in the following, studies are now in progress in a number of fields which will make a direct contribution to greater equality. These studies are not being conducted by any special organization for women, but by commissions charged with the task of making a general review of legislation within their respective fields.

Point A (*General*) in the Secretary-General's Annex II raises the question of the "establishment of machinery to assist in the development of measures and techniques for the advancement of women, including national planning." Examples of such machinery quoted in the Annex include special sections within a department, a central unit of government, a national commission on the status of women, a joint committee, or a group of liaison officers. The Swedish Government on its part, however, would question the appropriateness of setting up a special body for women's questions in the present situation, since so many of these questions have been integrated into the general policy of reform. Had such a body been established in Sweden four years ago, it would presumably have been charged with the task of resolving important questions relating to policies of employment, social welfare, taxation, family matters, and education, which are now being dealt with by the committees working on the general reform of large areas of these policies. The problem of women's wages, which is an important component of the low-wage problem as a whole, is thus being dealt with by the Government commission set up to study the matter of low incomes. If these questions insofar as they affect women had been divorced from their context and handed over to a commission on women, there would have been a risk that the proposals might have been delayed owing to the many and widely varied aspects with which such a commission would have had to deal.

The fact that Sweden for its part feels best able to solve the problems of women's status in this "integrated" manner does not of course prevent the UNO from issuing a general recommendation to member states to set up a body of the type envisaged.

Such a body may prove necessary to point out deficiencies and problems in this area and thus provide a stimulus to further reform in various special bodies, a work that might not otherwise have been undertaken.

FAMILY POLICY

Out of Sweden's 7,843,000 inhabitants on January 1, 1967, 1,752,000 (or about 22 per cent) were children under sixteen years of age. Sweden is probably one of the few countries in the world with such a low proportion of children. In 1966, the birth rate (i.e. the number of live births per 1,000 of the mean population) was 15.8.

According to the 1960 census, half the families in Sweden with children under sixteen living at home had only one child. Only 16 per cent of families with children had three or more children. However, the children included in this last group amounted to a third of all the children in the country. This means that 7 per cent of the population between the ages of eighteen and sixty-six were responsible for rearing a third of the next generation. Families with children are naturally taken to include families with only one parent, and these amounted to a tenth of the total.

Sweden has for a long time provided extensive protection for the safeguarding of the right of children to good care and upbringing. Each of the 900 municipalities in the country has a child welfare committee charged with the task of working for improved child and youth welfare.

(a) *Important points of modern family policy*

A *basic child allowance* of 900 kronor per annum is paid to every child under sixteen resident in Sweden, regardless of the parents' incomes. The allowance is intended to provide for the maintenance and upbringing of the child. Another objective is to reduce the difference in the standards of living of families with and without young children. The allowance is paid quarterly to the mother or to whomever has custody of the child instead of the mother. An *extended allowance* is paid to pupils over sixteen years of age attending comprehensive schools or similar institutions.

Kindergartens, where children can be taken care of during the daytime while their parents are at work are at present undergoing considerable expansion.

Great importance has been attached to measures designed to safeguard the health of mother and child in connection with pregnancy and childbirth. All expectant mothers and mothers with newborn children are entitled to *free examination* and advice at *maternity and pediatric clinics* providing regular services; pregnancy can be established here and treatment given for illnesses caused by pregnancy or childbirth. These clinics also provide instruction in child care and birth control. Prophylactic medicines such as vitamin preparations and certain other medications are supplied free of charge.

The actual *confinement* is also *free of charge* at maternity hospitals as is the care given by midwives. Most deliveries nowadays take place in maternity hospitals or the maternity wards of general hospitals. When confinement takes place at home and the help of a doctor is required, three-quarters of the expenditure incurred by the parents in connection with treatment by a doctor are refunded. The cost of traveling to the nearest hospital in connection with confinement is refunded in full.

During pregnancy and for 270 days after childbirth, the mother can receive dental treatment on very favorable terms, up to three-quarters of the cost of such treatment being refunded. Every mother receives a special *maternity benefit* or 1,080 kronor when her child is born (even if it is stillborn). If she gives birth to twins, the sum is increased by 540 kronor for every additional child. Three hundred kronor of this benefit can be drawn prior to confinement.

In addition to the maternity benefit an employed mother receives supplementary sickness benefit if immediately before childbirth she has been insured for sickness benefit at her place of work for at last 270 days in succession. This supplementary sickness benefit is graduated according to income (though the income must exceed a certain minimum) and is payable for a maximum of 180 days.

In order to facilitate the formation of families, the State also grants *homemaking loans* for the purchase of furniture and other items for the home. Loans of this kind are granted, subject to a means test, to newly married couples and couples wishing to get married, and are also available to unmarried mothers or fathers with children under sixteen.

Special *family housing allowances* are also available, subject to a means test, to families with two or more children. The Swedish Riksdag has recently approved a Government proposal providing for an increase in the amount paid in allowances of this kind.

A *special treatment allowance* of 3,420 kronor is paid to people with handicapped children at home in need of special care and attention.

(b) *Principles of family policy*

The number of families in which both spouses are gainfully employed is continually increasing. The employment incidence of young married women without children is almost as high as that of the men. Also, an increasing number of mothers are going out to work. Thus Sweden is approaching a situation in which it is normal for a family to have two members earning incomes.

The increasing part played by married women in the labor market has resulted in entirely new demands being made on family policy. This policy must be adopted to the changed roles of the sexes and be designed in such a way as to promote equality on the labor market and in the division of labor at home. This means that increased prominence will be given to care of the children and the cost thereof.

Families with small children generally solve the problem of taking care of them by one of the following methods:

1. The father or mother stops going out to work and stays at home with the children full time for a number of years.
2. The parents engage somebody to supervise the children in the home during the day or else make use of a kindergarten.
3. Both parents try to obtain part-time employment and cooperate in taking care of the children. However, this alternative

is not generally feasible owing to the prejudices still surrounding the role of the father in taking care of the children.
In all these cases the care of the children costs money: in cases
No. 1 and 3 by reason of reduced income and in case No. 2
through direct costs of supervision reducing retained income.
As it becomes more common for women to acquire vocational
training, they will wish to an increasing extent to go on working outside the home. Consequently, it is to be expected that the
demand for services from families in which both parents go out
to work will increase considerably. The other category of families with small children will, as previously, prefer one of the
parents to refrain from earning money so as to be able to devote
a shorter or longer time to looking after the children. Nevertheless, it will be considered unjust for a family to have to reduce
its living standards to any appreciable extent during these years
of increased need.

Society has therefore every reason to maintain the living
standards of families with children as far as its resources permit.
After all, the result of the care devoted to the children is to
bring up a new generation which eventually will guarantee the
incomes of the present working population when that population retires and begins to draw its pension.

Up to now, the Swedish Government has adhered to the principle of evening out living standards, as far as possible, between
the period when the family's needs are greatest and the period
when its maintenance burdens are most lenient. Failing this kind
of evening-out, living standards are bound to fall considerably
during the years when the children need care and attention.
There is call, therefore, for additional support over and above
the basic child allowance during the period when the children
are most in need of attention. The political program for women,
adopted in 1964, laid down the following three guiding principles for family policy:

Social insurance comparable to that available to the working
population should be provided for the spouse looking after the
children.
Payment should be made for such care.

The direct consumption costs incurred through the child should be provided for.

Since it is to be expected that women will continue to play a more active part than men in looking after the children for a long time ahead, a family policy based on these principles would be of considerable importance to them. Social insurance during the period when children require most attention would also encourage parents to resume working when the children are old enough to take care of themselves. In this way child care and outside employment combined would give parents the same old-age pension as persons with full-time employment are guaranteed through the general supplementary pensions scheme alone.

(c) *Reforms in Progress*

There has been a considerable amount of discussion in recent years concerning the future structure of family policy. Particular emphasis has been placed on the connection between family policy and equality of status between men and women. Today there seems in general to be a high degree of unanimity that the costs of child care should rank on the same level as outside employment. It has also been found appropriate for the parent, whether father or mother, who stays at home to look after the children, to be able to include this period to his or her credit in connection with the calculation of pension rights.

There has also been a great deal of unanimity concerning the need for society to increase the general economic support given to families with children. One expression of this demand has taken the form of the introduction of a special child-care allowance for families with small children. Attention has also been drawn to the need for a special supplementary payment for families with three or more children, in addition to the basic child allowance. As a rule, it is the mother who has to stay at home and look after the children; her absence from the labor market is considerably prolonged in families with several children, and with it the loss of her income from gainful employment.

A special drafting committee on family affairs was appointed by the Government in 1962, the main task of which was to investigate and analyze the various problems affecting social services to families with children and to submit proposals based on its findings. Since the committee submitted its report in 1964, the State has increased its grants to local authorities for the building of kindergartens. The committee's terms of reference also included a closer study of the question of a child-care allowance. The committee considered that extra support for families with small children over and above the basic child allowance was particularly called for while the children were in their infancy. Extra support of this kind should be given to all families with children in the age group it is decided to help, regardless of whether both parents are gainfully employed or not. The committee proposed that an investigation be made into the question of gradually extending a system of child-care allowances and the possibility of gearing such a system to social insurance through financing it with contributions.

The drafting committee also considered the question of special support for families with three or more children. The committee drew attention to the fact that the proportion of the costs incurred through the children and borne by the families becomes more and more noticeable as the number of children increases. It is unjust for children in large families to have to grow up in less favorable circumstances than other children. The drafting committee therefore found good cause for families with three or more children to receive a supplementary family allowance rising in proportion to the number of children in the family.

The memorandum of the drafting committee has since been submitted to a number of authorities and organizations, all of whom—insofar as they have expressed any opinion—have been in favor of the basic idea of increased support for large families.

In view of the favorable response encountered by these statements of principle concerning future family policy, the Government appointed a committee on family policy in 1965, and this committee is now engaged in investigating the question of economic support for families with children. One particular task of the committee is to test the effect of different types of support as well as their structure and demarcation. According to the committee's directives, family policy is to be differentiated so as to provide support when and where it is most needed.

As can be seen from the foregoing, housing policy has been regarded as an important part of family policy in Sweden. A law passed by the Riksdag in 1968 provides for a considerable increase in the *housing allowance* payable as of 1969 to families with children. This allowance has been reshaped in order to make it available to far more families than previously. The amount payable varies according to the number of children, the family income, and size of the house or flat. About 430,000 families with several children out of a total of approximately one million are expected to be eligible for allowances of this kind. It is important for families with several children to be guaranteed decent housing, not only from the point of view of the children, but also with a view to reducing the work to be done in the home by the parents.

SERVICE TO FAMILIES

Good *facilities for child supervision* are of direct significance to the promotion of equality between men and women in the labor market. A survey carried out in 1967 showed that there were more than 300,000 children under ten years of age in Sweden whose mothers went out to work for more than fifteen hours a week. The same survey revealed that there were more than 200,000 mothers with children under ten who would like to go out to work if they could arrange for the supervision of their 350,000 children. Thus there is a very great demand for supervision facilities for children of employed parents.

In Sweden there are two forms of State-subsidized institutions for the supervision of children, viz. *kindergartens* and *family day nurseries* (supervision in private homes). The main responsibilty for the extension of kindergartens rests with the 900 municipalities in the country, who receive subsidies from the State, mainly toward investment costs. Kindergartens are establishments where children of gainfully employed parents can be looked after all day or for half the day by qualified staff (nursery-school teachers and children's nurses). Places providing super-vision all day are called *whole-day* places. Some of these can also be used for the supervision of children under school age for three hours a day or for the looking after of school children out-side school hours (known as leisure-time homes). There are at present 24,000 places for the part-time or full-time supervision of children whose parents are gainfully employed. About 20,000 of these places are in kindergartens and the remainder in leisure-time homes. However, these places are quite insufficient to meet the demand, and there are still a number of urban areas without kindergartens. In order to increase the rate of expansion, State subsidies for the building of kindergartens were raised consid-erably as of July 1, 1966. During 1968, the Government is to put forward a bill for a further increase of State support by 40 per cent, which will make it possible to provide 10,000 new places during 1968 and 1969 respectively.

Over the past five years the number of places at training col-leges for nursery-school teachers has been doubled in order to increase the supply of personnel. The number of places now available is 1,110, and this will be increased to 1,560 in 1970. Efforts are also being made to recruit male trainees.

In addition to kindergartens, day supervision is also available in a number of private homes. Some of these places are made available by local authorities, who refund a certain amount of the cost to the daytime mother. A resolution has recently been passed by the 1968 Riksdag providing for a State subsidy starting in 1969 and amounting to 35 per cent of the costs in-curred by local authorities through payments for day supervi-sion in private homes, though in the case of the larger municipalities this is made subject to the condition that at least an equal number of places are available (whole-day) in kinder-gartens. This rule has been proposed in order not to discourage the local authorities from extending the institutional form of child supervision.

It can be added that the question of reliable child supervision during the parents' working hours has attracted the attention of both trade unions and employers. Out of their joint bodies, the

Women's Labor Market Committee has done a great deal to increase the interest of local authorities in expanding facilities.

Popular opinion used to regard kindergartens as a sort of poor relief for families where mothers were forced by economic necessity to go out to work. Today they are regarded as a service providing the most reliable supervision possible, under the direction of qualified staff, and teaching children the rudiments of social behavior before school age. The popularity of the kindergartens among young parents is shown by the fact that 200,000 mothers of small children desire this form of supervision for their children. Previously it was possible for better-situated families to solve the problem of child supervision by engaging maids. Today, however, there are only 20,000 home helps in Sweden as opposed to 205,000 in 1930.

Another facility is provided by *nursery schools,* where children can be left for three hours per day. These are less frequently used by parents who are gainfully employed, but they make the same contributions toward the social acclimatization of children as do kindergartens providing supervision all day. Nursery schools have a total of about 32,000 places and can thus take care of about 64,000 children.

The Swedish Government wishes in this connection to emphasize the significance of organized child supervision to the attainment of equality between the sexes. The Government considers the question of child supervision to be as important for fathers as for mothers. Responsibility for the supervision and care of their children rests with both parents in the same way as both of them are responsible for the children being provided for. However, the rapid expansion which the Government expects to result from the increased subsidies in practice make kindergartens of greatest consequence to mothers, since it will enable them to go out to work. The costs incurred by society in building and running these institutions can pay dividends in a number of ways. The social acclimatization of the children is stimulated, and their health is regularly checked through medical examinations. The mother is enabled to make use of her vocational qualifications or to acquire the qualifications she desires, and she retains her job longer. The rewards reaped by society take the form not only of increased taxation revenues through the income tax paid by the mother and through increased turnover in the consumer sector, but also of the filling of positions in the economy and social services, which might otherwise remain vacant through lack of personnel.

Another service available to all families with children of school age is that of *free school meals*, a service which has now been extended to certain other school forms even after the comprehensive school. This service probably has been and still is of the utmost importance to the parents' possibilities of going out to work. At the same time it has fulfilled a particularly important nutritive function since it was first introduced on a more general scale during the 1940's.

Free *health checkups* for children of school age by school doctors and nurses and free dental care for children are other important aspects of the development whereby the school has assumed a greater share of responsibility for children.

Yet another form of service to families with children is provided in the form of *municipal domestic help*. Domestic help employed by the local authorities are detailed to help families with children in the event of sudden crises, e.g. when a parent is taken ill and the children must be looked after and supervised by somebody else in the home. Similar problems arise when the mother must be away from her children for a short time because of childbirth.

Most of the larger municipalities also employ *children's nurses* to take care of sick children at home who cannot be admitted to kindergartens.

Organizations also contribute to services for families with children. The State gives grants to a number of organizations which provide *children's holiday camps* in the country so that children can get out into the sun and bathe and play during the summer. There are also *holiday homes*, i.e. private homes in rural districts which provide accommodation for children during the summer. The grants are paid to cover, among other things, the travel costs of the children. Children on holiday with their families can also travel more or less free of charge.

Service in housing areas has been the subject of lively discussions during the last few years. Demands have been voiced from many quarters for the creation of service facilities, e.g. in the form of service centers within convenient walking distance of housing areas. Part of the reason for the growing demand for collective service facilities in housing areas is, of course, to be found in the rising employment frequency of married women. But other population groups, too, such as pensioners and unmarried persons desire more such facilities. A service center may, for example, have a reception desk where cleaning, childminding, and messenger services can be booked. It should also include a post office, dispensing chemists' shops, a shop open in the evenings, a restaurant and café, as well as a kindergarten and leisure-time center for the children. Another alternative would be to build special service houses, i.e. large multidwelling houses with their own kindergarten, restaurant, cleaning staff, etc.

In 1967, the Government appointed a special service committee to investigate, among other things, the regulations applying to Government loans for the service facilities with which such houses need to be provided. Service blocks, centers, or houses are at present being built in the Stockholm and Gothenburg areas.

Editor's note: Other sections of the report are illuminating on developments on the status of women in Sweden. They deal with "Previous Measures for the Advancement of Women," "Review of Current Efforts to Promote Equality between the Sexes," and include a detailed account of reforms in education, family law, social insurance, taxation of families, and labor market policy. Tables giving statistics on the employment of women are also given. The complete report from which this excerpt was taken was published by the Swedish Institute in Stockholm, and was written by Maj-Britt Sandlund, Head of Section at the Halland County Administration.

The androgynous life

CAROLINE BIRD

*Life in the United States is changing, as salaries and career op-
portunities for women improve. While the progress toward a
more androgynous life style for couples is mainly an upper-
middle-class movement at present, it will doubtless spread. With
it, will come obligations as well as rights.*

*There will be changes in laws on divorce and alimony. Cus-
tody of children of divorce will more commonly go to the best
qualified parent, and not so generally to the mother.*

*Caroline Bird discusses the trends that indicate that women
will be living in ways that parallel rather than complement the
lives of their husbands—the decline in the birth rate, the availability of college education to women, the experience of working side by side with men in an increasing variety of jobs, and
the decline of "women only" or "men only" social facilities and
organizations. Women, too, she believes, are less prone to
"female" troubles in modern society, although more of them are
afflicted with ulcers, formerly considered a male occupational
disease.*

Caroline Bird is author of Born Female: The High Cost of
Keeping Women Down *(1968), in which this article appears.
She writes for many national periodicals and is at present at
work on a book on the effects of population growth. She has
been director of research for a New York public relations firm.*

178

People talked New Masculinism in 1968, but a growing number of young couples were living New Feminism.

People noticed, with distaste, that men seemed to be growing more feminine and women more masculine, and they feared for the moral fiber of the country. The fact of the matter was that trends in marriage, education, and employment conspired to make the lives of men and women similar, so that they found themselves reacting in ways associated with the opposite sex in spite of conscious efforts to be "masculine" or "feminine." Androgyny seemed to be one of the dismaying consequences of progress.

The most obvious reason was the contraceptive pill, which more than the other methods of birth control made it possible for women to be as uninhibited about sex as men. At first, this possibility was hailed as an unadulterated blessing. Sex would at last be really free from both fear and bother. Marriages would be happier.

In 1960, when the pill first became generally available, married couples offered themselves as subjects for experiments to test the theory, and the initial results confirmed the happy forecasts. In reporting the first long-term study of the impact of the pill on marriage, Dr. Frederick J. Ziegler of the Cleveland Clinic Foundation noted that after four years on the pill, wives in the study not only felt freer sexually, but actually wanted sexual intercourse more frequently than husbands. This seemed all to the good.

For generations, marriage counselors had been urging husbands to consider the lesser sexual appetite of their wives. In the 1950's, studies of marital adjustment reported that college-educated women thought that they should enjoy sex, but few of them reported that they really wanted it as much as their husbands. Psychiatrists, psychologists, and even endocrinologists had explanations. Psychiatrists found that sexual response required a modicum of self-confidence and self-esteem which many women lacked. Psychologists discovered that women who scored high on "masculinity" in written psychological tests achieved orgasm more frequently than women who scored high on "femininity." Endocrinologists reported that sexual response in both sexes depended on androgens, the male sex hormone, which women only secrete in small quantity. Women treated medically with synthetic testosterone, a male sex hormone, were sometimes troubled by unaccustomed sexual urges.

Then in the 1960's, the idea that sexiness was somehow masculine began to fade. Women were no longer penalized for seeking sexual satisfaction. On the contrary, they were being brought up to enjoy sex, and they did. In 1967, Robert T. Bell, a sociologist from Temple University, reported a study of 196 college-educated young wives which showed that a fourth wanted sex more frequently than their husbands, while only 6 per cent said their husbands wanted sex more frequently than they. "The results may be far more serious for the sexually inadequate or uninterested male than they were for the personally unfulfilled female of the past," he warned.

By late 1967, psychiatrists were genuinely worried about reports of this ironic switch from the patriarchal past. "Women aged forty to fifty now expect—in fact, it would be more precise to say they *demand*—sexual satisfaction," Dr. Ralph Greenson, professor of psychiatry at the University of California, complained. "It is not rare to find men who act in bed as though the sexual act is a dangerous obligation." Dr. Richard E. Farson, director of the Western Behavioral Sciences Institute, told a conference of leading women that educated career women enjoyed sexual relations more than women of lesser attainments or women of their kind in the past, but he did not seem to think they were happier for it. "Women really want to be dominated by men," he said. "The trouble with women is weak males."

This shift in sexual interest challenged the traditional foundation of marriage itself. How can a woman expect a man to support her in exchange for sex if she wants sex relations more ardently than he does? The answer is that an increasing proportion of college-educated, career-bound young wives simply don't think that they are trading sex for financial support. A surprising number don't even know they are entitled to support.

We discovered this curious blind spot by accident. We were trying to explain to a friend why some employers think it is right to pay men more than women. "It's because men have to support women," we reminded her. She looked so puzzled that we jokingly repeated the Old Masculinist answer to pleas for equal pay: "After all, *you* don't have to support your husband, but *he* has to support you."

"Does he?" she said with transparent innocence. And it turned out that she really did not know the laws of family support.

"You just ask your husband," we told her. "It's really so. He has to support you. By law."

For several weeks afterward we told the story to working wives as a believe-it-or-not anecdote. But many of them found nothing peculiar about her question. A surprising percentage just had never thought about marriage in terms of legal support.

"What about alimony?" we asked one newly married girl. "Why do divorced wives get alimony?"

"Do they still?" she asked, with enormous indifference. "I thought that had been abolished."

Her comment reflected the increasing opposition to alimony. The proverbial golddigger who takes a divorced husband for all he is worth is giving way to the woman who would rather support herself than accept money from a man she does not love. As one talented divorcee put it, "Who cares about money? You can make that." Young college-educated couples do not expect a wife to press her legal right to alimony unless there is some reason why she cannot support herself.

Family-support laws are being challenged in the courts. In 1966, Mary McLeod, president of the National Association of Women Lawyers, warned that wives and mothers had been required to pay alimony to divorced husbands if they were financially able to do so. Some local welfare laws make an employed wife responsible for the support of a husband who would otherwise become a public charge. And support works both ways, theoretically at least, in some European countries.

One of the young brides we queried thought the family-support laws we told her about were reciprocal in this country, too. "If my husband supports me," she reasoned with us, "don't I have to support him, too?"

For these young women, at least, the sex-for-support bargain is a thing of the past. They have not married for money. Their husbands have not married for sex. These young couples do not think they have a vocational relationship. They think of themselves, rather, as companions, carrying the androgynous pattern of school life into marriage, family, and work. They marry almost as early as the girls who expect to make marriage a career, and like them they get a job or go on studying. But they work or study for different reasons.

Instead of waiting on table to put a husband through medical school, these young, college-educated brides seek out jobs which pay in experience and opportunity rather than in cash. They work for token pay or no pay at all on small-town newspapers, in nonprofit organizations, in the Peace Corps or poverty programs. They make jobs for themselves in museums or in local government or community colleges. Like alert young men beginning careers, they are working for the work itself, for what it can teach them, or where it can lead.

Because her work is important, this kind of young woman often marries a man in her own field, often a fellow student or fellow worker. Graduate students marry each other. Law students marry law students. Medical students marry medical students. College faculty members marry each other. Research workers marry each other. Actors and actresses marry each other. In 1966, one of the engineers inspecting telephone installations in Orange County, California, was a woman married to another telephone company employee. These wives are not helpmeets of their husbands. If they happen to have the same employer, they are colleagues, even competitors.

The first home these couples live in is temporary, and they readily accept barracks-like public housing for its convenience, or even a furnished room for the duration of the course, the project, or their first, trial jobs. Housework is minimized and shared.

They often head for the big city where both can find work. One may go to school while the other earns, but the earner is not always the wife, and the arrangement is short-term.

If they are in the same profession, they are tempted to work together, like the famous French scientists Marie and Pierre Curie, who discovered radium, and the English social reformers,

Sidney and Beatrice Webb. Some contemporary couples have become famous, among them the theater team Lynne Fontanne and Alfred Lunt, Oregon Senators Richard L. and Maurine Neuberger, historians Will and Ariel Durant, Lila and DeWitt Wallace, founders of the *Reader's Digest,* and Robert and Helen Lynd, the sociologists who immortalized Muncie, Indiana, in *Middletown.* Thousands of less celebrated couples have demonstrated that two can combine marriage and a career more successfully than either might have done working alone. Many pediatricians are husband-and-wife teams who can spell each other on phone calls and office hours so that they both have time to spend with their own children. Anthropologists who marry each other make a handy team for field work which needs investigators of both sexes.

Usually, however, it is impractical for the couple to work together, and as both careers develop, it may be hard for them to stay in the same part of the country. But it can be done. In 1967, Bob and Barbara Williams were serving as Army nurses within enemy mortar range in Vietnam and living together in a hut made out of materials Bob had scrounged. They met and married while studying nursing at the Columbus State Hospital in Ohio. When Bob was drafted three months after their marriage, Barbara volunteered and joined him overseas a few months later. Both were First Lieutenant Army surgical nurses.

Sometimes it is the husband who moves. Men teachers have found jobs in Los Angeles or New York to be with actress wives. Henry Luce accompanied Clare Boothe Luce when she was Ambassador to Italy and spent most of her term with her, managing Time, Inc., from an office in Rome. In 1966, Ambassador-at-Large Ellsworth Bunker took up official residence with his bride, Carol Laise, the United States Ambassador to Nepal, Asia, because residence was a requirement of her job but not of his.

For the affluent, air travel can solve the geographical problem, at least temporarily. When Rosemary Park, president of Barnard College in New York, married Dr. Milton V. Anastos, Professor of Byzantine Greek at the University of California at Los Angeles, in 1966, she kept in touch with her new husband by cross-country jet until Barnard found a new president. Then she got a job near her husband's as vice-chancellor for educational planning and programs at UCLA. That same year, Senator Maurine Neuberger of Oregon was jetting between her constituency on the West Coast and her new husband's home in Massachusetts.

Two-career families may have children, but they do not build their whole lives around them. "It's simply not true that they are as involved with their families as women who want to stay at home," Alice Rossi of the Department of Social Relations at Johns Hopkins University reports after studying 15,000 women three years out of college who planned careers. She found that the career-committed women didn't want as many children, on the average, as the homemakers, and that they were far more willing to let others care for their children. One of Dr. Rossi's tests for career-commitment was a woman's willingness to postpone having a baby in order to stay in graduate school.

In two-career homes, the babies do not come all at once, at the beginning of the marriage, but in phase with the wife's work commitments. Teachers can plan to have their babies during vacations; Professor Ilse Lipschutz of Vassar has had four children without losing time from class. Almost every graduating class now has pregnant wives in the procession, and sometimes a husband and wife are graduated together while their small child looks on. In June 1967, for instance, Stephanie Beech and her husband Charles were graduated from Park College, in Parkville, Missouri, five months after their baby was born. Stephanie was able to make up the month of classes she missed and to do her part earning the money needed to keep them both in school. She and her husband shared her job on the early-morning shift at a cafeteria. He did it while she was in the hospital, and after the baby was born, they took turns, one doing the job, the other the baby's three o'clock feeding.

Many employers believe that pay isn't an inducement to a woman worker because "you can't compete with a baby." The fact is, of course, that you can. With money. The more money a woman makes, the more likely she is to come back to work after a baby. "You can afford to stay home with your baby," a woman executive once told her secretary. "At my salary, I can't." The better-paid a woman, the more apt she is to keep working.

Fathers in two-career homes are often closer to their children than men whose wives make a career out of motherhood. They share child care in various ways. A woman television director in New York who is married to an optometrist spends her days off with their two boys while he keeps his office open. On the days she has to work, he closes his office and takes care of the boys. In 1966 he took them over alone while she tested a job in California. In another family, the mother is a public relations executive and the father is a teacher. Like mothers who teach, he uses his shorter day and longer vacations to spend more time with the children. Husbands with flexible schedules cook, run errands, baby-sit, and shop for wives who have less control over their time. Two-career families either forgo the social life wives usually arrange or share the work of organizing it.

Two-career homes undoubtedly form the character of children in a different way than homes where mothers do most of the rearing alone. Mother-child relationships are cooler than the early Freudians advocated, and parents have more rights than they have recently enjoyed in America, particularly rights to privacy and a shared adult life. Dr. Rossi speculates that wives in two-career families are more interested in a relationship with their husband than the homemaking women, who tend to seek their major satisfaction from their children.

Sociologists report that they can't find any important difference between the children of mothers who work and the children of mothers who stay at home. In fact, in some cases they discovered that the children suffered in homes where the mothers wanted to work, but stayed at home out of a mistaken sense of duty. They also found that the children of working mothers were sometimes more self-reliant than children reared by full-time, child-centered mothers.

Two-career couples are New Feminists, but they are not militant. The women are more friendly to men than the pioneer career women, partly because they have undisputed control over the timing of their children and no longer need to fear the strength and spontaneity of their own sex drives. They are not missionary about their life style, and tend to minimize and even ignore their departure from the traditional pattern.

New Feminists' husbands tend to be academic or professional men who for one reason or another are out of the rat race of middle-class suburban life. Some are graduate students. Some are handicapped. Some are artists or scholars. And a good many are gentle and sometimes charming souls who aren't ambitious themselves, but wholeheartedly admire their energetic wives. Women married to these departures from the standard pattern are freed—and sometimes goaded—to pursue goals and make money of their own. Dr. Rossi found that the career-committed women she studied in 1964 did not see their husbands as driven, career-oriented men. "Many of the males in this room are businessmen who may make erroneous appeals to employed, college-educated women by assuming that the husbands of those women are like themselves," she warned a workshop on the "Homemaker Who Earns" organized for clients of the New York public relations firm Dudley-Anderson-Yutzy in January 1967. "Women who have married businessmen or professional men—doctors, lawyers, ministers—are far less apt to show a high degree of career commitment than women who are married to academic men, to men in any of the applied aspects of the humanities or the humanities themselves, the social sciences, or the people-caring professions."

How many women are leading this kind of life? The idea of self-determination is aristocratic. New Feminist women are so often frankly upperclass that they seem snobbish. Advertising, television, and popular magazines ignore them on the ground that there aren't enough of them to matter. But if you want to know what's going to happen in the future, you must pay them very serious attention indeed. Their life style will become more common when more women are given a chance to do what they want to do.

What do these girls want? It certainly seems as if they are reacting against the preoccupation with personal relationships that characterized the 1950's and choosing instead an almost Puritanical commitment to causes such as peace, the poor, science, art, or even scholarship. *Newsweek* reported that for women graduating from college in 1966, the "career drive exceeds the mating drive." This impression can be tested on the changing values of Vassar alumnae. Although Vassar was drawing students from a much broader base than formerly—in the 1960's, a majority of freshmen came from coeducational public high schools instead of private preparatory schools—the alumnae group has remained unusually homogeneous. In 1967, this remarkably stable population was the subject of a bigger and more intensive study than has ever been made of any group of American college women.

Vassar alumnae of all ages were asked to choose one of four patterns to describe their lives after college. Most chose the life style that could be labeled "Home with some outside interests," but the classes of 1954 to 1958 indicated a shift to "Home with whatever career could be fitted around it." The real surprise, though, was in the youngest alumnae. The classes of 1964 to 1966 voted for "Career with as little time out for family as possible," and there was even a notable rise in the number of girls who said they were pursuing a Career, period. Many of the younger graduates were just founding families, so their lives were likely to change. But these brides who described themselves as career-oriented seemed to be marrying, as their husbands did, for a meaningful private life rather than to enter the vocation of wife and mother, as their older sisters had done in the 1950's.

All the measurable data—vital statistics, education, and job patterns—indicate that women will increasingly find themselves living in ways that parallel rather than complement the lives of their husbands. Even fashions in clothing, homemaking, recreation, and social life are emphasizing the similarities between men and women and playing down the differences. The signs pointing to the future are clear if you examine the trends, one by one.

First, the *vital statistics* of birth, marriage, and death are changing to give women more years of life during which they are not bearing or rearing children. Birth control has upset patterns that demographers regarded as inevitable. Before birth control was standard practice, men waited to marry until they were well enough established to support wives and children. When they could afford to marry, they could and often did choose brides much younger than themselves. This age gap reinforced the patriarchal authority of husbands over wives and confirmed the impression that men were wiser, calmer, and less "emotional." But this is no longer true. Husbands and wives average closer to the same age, and to older people today's young couples sometimes look like Hansel and Gretel toddling hand in hand into the woods, both equally inexperienced.

In the mid-1960's, the birth rate began to drop sharply from its post-World War II high. Demographers at the United States Public Health Service and the Population Reference Bureau, a foundation devoted to warning against the danger of overpopulation, give two reasons: young wives may be planning smaller families than the young wives of the 1950's, or they may simply be postponing their babies.

In 1960, the foundation survey *Growth of American Families* reported that young wives then eighteen to twenty-four said they wanted only 3 children instead of the 3.4 average that wives twenty-five to twenty-nine years old said they wanted. It was no secret, at least to obstetricians, that the fertile wives of the 1950's were not as eager to have the third and fourth babies as they thought they ought to be.

By the middle of the 1960's, young couples were realizing that they had time for everything if they planned ahead. Young mothers spoke of spacing their children so that they would have more years in which to enjoy watching them grow. More mothers talked about having babies at times that fitted into specific plans they had for their own or their husbands' careers, instead of getting their babies "over with" as fast as possible.

Postponing babies gives young wives a chance to look around at a time of life when careers are being established. Even a year's breathing space is important. Most successful women did not bear children in their early twenties. The reason why is not as important as the fact.

In 1967, young women in the peak marrying ages were experiencing involuntary delays. Girls born in 1946, 1947, and 1948, the baby-boom years, outnumbered boys born during the war. Since girls usually marry men a few years older, this created a problem. According to Robert Parke, Jr., and Paul G. Glick of the United States Bureau of the Census, this "marriage squeeze" will be resolved in several ways: more boys will marry at younger ages; more girls will marry later, or not at all; or more of them will marry older divorced or widowed men. However it works out, these girls in their early twenties will be marrying later, and what they do with their waiting years can make a lot of difference in their lives.

Some of them, of course, have been swept into the booming job market. But some stayed at school. Fewer girls dropped out of college, and more went on to graduate school. "When a girl doesn't get married right away when she is graduated from college and she can't find a job that she thinks is worthy of her, she gets her father to send her here for a year," one dean of a graduate school said. He may, of course, be right about her motives. But there is always the chance that once she gets to graduate school, she will be hooked on her field of interest. Women students are not quite as impervious to education as some college professors pessimistically declare.

The second powerful influence that is working to make the lives of women more like those of men is *education*. As we have seen, we educate boys and girls together so that women are conditioned to work with men. Not unexpectedly, the more years a woman has spent in school, the more likely she is to get a job. Mary Keyserling startled the Dudley-Anderson-Yutzy workshop on women by asking the participants to guess what percentage of women over forty-five with five years of college held down paying jobs. Even the sophisticated market researchers in the audience could hardly believe that 84 per cent of these privileged women were out earning money. The percentage and the surprise it occasions are significant because women with postgraduate education will be much more common in future. As recently as 1956, for instance, less than 15 per cent of the senior class at Vassar College went directly to graduate school. In the mid-1960's, about a third were moving directly into a fifth year of college. The trend has not lasted long enough to raise the proportion of doctoral degrees awarded to women to the high prewar levels attained in the Depression, when many women went on to graduate school because they could neither marry nor earn, but the proportion as well as the number of higher degrees awarded to women is increasing.

Meanwhile, more women than ever before are staying in school through high school and beyond. In 1966, half of the white women in the United States over twenty-five years of age reported more than twelve years of school, almost a whole year more than in 1960. The trend must be interpreted with caution. College may not mean as much in the future, when "everybody" goes, as it has meant in the past; girls may be staying in school because their parents can afford to keep them there and college is now where all the boys are. But whatever her intent, a girl increases her chances of working as she increases her schooling. In 1966, Mary Keyserling put her slide-rule to work on the relationship and reported that schooling was a stronger pull to work in 1966 than in 1952 or 1962. Education pulls women into the job market not so much because it makes them dissatisfied with the home—although it may well—but because it increases their earning power.

The third factor making women's lives more like those of men is the *experience of employment* itself. Nine out of ten women will now earn at some time in their lives. Census reports predicting the number of women who would be working in 1968 have generally fallen short of the fact. Before World War II, economists assumed that wives worked only because they had to. In their experience, a wife who had to "go out" to work was either lowerclass or the victim of misfortune. They discerned what they rather snobbishly called a "respectability pattern," and they assumed that it operated quite simply and universally: the richer the country, the better the times, the higher a husband's income, the less likely it would be that a wife would work. In 1946, home economist Hazel Kyrk listed forces dissuading women from working: ". . . movement upward of men's real earnings, a longer period when children are in the home, higher standards of child care, and a standard of living that requires a large amount of home-centered time." Another analysis of the time gave "inadequacy of income of male members of the family" as the number-one reason why married women worked, and emphasized the "opportunity presented to employers to obtain cheaper labor."

This reasoning simply did not account for the rising tide of women workers during the affluent period that followed World War II. On the contrary, the women who flocked to work were not the unfortunate but the best-off.

The young women college graduates whom educators criticized for "throwing their educations away to raise families" surprised everybody. According to a study made by the Women's Bureau, 85 per cent of the class of 1957 married soon after leaving college. By 1964, seven years later, two-thirds of them had children. According to every rule and all the professional advice, these privileged mothers should have been out of the job market, yet more than a quarter of those with children under six were working. The mothers of preschool children who were most likely to work were not the poorest, but those with five or more years of college whose husbands could presumably support them.

Economists began to re-examine their old theories. As family incomes increased into the five figures, wives began to retire, as predicted, but nowhere near as fast as the "respectability pattern" suggested. In 1963, the Labor Department reported that the highest proportion of working wives was in families which enjoyed a total income of $12,000 to $15,000.

The figures accorded with everyday experience. Almost everyone knew some wife who was working in spite of the fact that her husband could keep her. Far from a shameful necessity, earnings have become a point of pride for wives of the frankly rich. Society pages herald their ventures into business and the professions.

In the 1960's, two economists, Professor Jacob Mincer, of Columbia University, and Dr. Glen G. Cain, of the University of Chicago, constructed mathematical equations to weigh the influence of such factors as the presence of children, husband's income, the education and earning power of the wife, and even the value of her home services on her decision to go out and get a job. Both reported that the most important influence in her decision was not her husband's income, as the old attitudes toward her role assume, but the amount of money she herself could earn.

This financial "pull of the job" is a sufficient reason for the educated young mothers to go out to work. It isn't necessary to assume, as some social critics have done, that they are "pushed" out of the home because they find it boring. As long as every additional year of schooling increases their earning potential, education will continue to motivate women into employment. And since workers with education are in such short supply that their wages are rising, it is not surprising that the percentage of educated women working outside their homes is rising.

Women themselves have known this, all along. When asked why they were working, wives always said "for money." In April 1964, 42 per cent of working wives told the Bureau of Labor Statistics they were working out of "financial necessity," and 17 per cent more said for "extra money," but they did not seem to be propelled by the stark necessities the Women's Bureau implies when its spokesmen insist that working women "have to" work. "Husband lost job" was one category, and it accounted for fewer than 7 per cent. Almost 20 per cent, on the other hand, said they were working for "personal satisfaction," and 10 per cent simply because they were "offered job."

Financial "necessities" vary dramatically with families. For some wives, the necessity is a boat, a second car, a vacation, camp for children. Many work to send a child to college. Many volunteer to breadwin for their men. One reason that the census forecasts erred was that they did not expect so many men to drop out of the labor force. When young men go to college instead of to work, employers are more receptive to women, many of whom are now working so that their husbands can continue their educations. And since 1955, the percentage of men who continue to work after they are 65 has declined 1 or 2 per cent a year as more men covered by pensions reach retirement age. Wives of men eligible for Social Security are often young enough to get jobs so that their husbands can afford to take early retirement. Most people are surprised to learn that in

10 per cent of all American families the husband does not work at all. He may be disabled, retired, or going to college. Without his earnings, the income of the family is often low, but the family may not be living in poverty. (The absence of the father is one of the salient features of the "culture of poverty," described by Michael Harrington as the way the poor live which dooms their children to poverty, too.)

All of these influences snowball. The temporary-help agencies know that a woman who has worked previously is more likely to work again in the future and to want a permanent rather than a temporary job when her children are grown. Every time opportunity widens for women, some women escape into employment never to return home. The Hudson Institute, a private social science research organization, figures that by the year 2000, a majority of women will work at every age between eighteen and sixty except during the heavy child-bearing and childrearing decade from twenty-five to thirty-four years of age.

The daughters of women who work are more likely to work themselves. Dr. Rossi thinks the daughters feel less guilty about working when their children are young because they do not think that their mothers hurt them by working. The snowball effect is, of course, an answer to Old Masculinists who insist, somewhat hopefully, that women "don't want to work." The proposition can only be tested when a woman is offered a well-paying job and turns it down in order to pursue a home role. It happens, of course, but not as often as claimed. And the fact that a woman is staying home at the moment does not mean that she is going to stay there indefinitely. Some surveys report that half of the full-time homemakers say they expect to get a job at some time in the future.

A fourth force that is making women's lives more parallel to men's is the growing *desegregation of work*. The sex labels remain, as we've pointed out, but a number of influences are whittling them down in certain areas. Most hopeful, perhaps, is the rise of *new* jobs that have not been sex-typed, and that have cropped up and had to be filled—with anyone qualified—during a period when employment is tight. Skill is more important than sex in computer programming, so girl mathematicians are being recruited to learn the work, even though men dominate the big jobs and the repair work in the field.

Meanwhile, the increasing use of machinery in offices is giving office jobs more status for males at a time when many young men need temporary or part-time work to stay in school, so the "girly" atmosphere of many offices is changing. At the same time, the mechanization of office work is reducing the number of supervisory jobs for which men have been preferred. When work that formerly required a roomful of girls under a straw boss is done by one highly skilled person operating a special machine, the sex of that person is of no consequence, and if the job is new, it is likely to be filled by the first qualified applicant of either sex.

The fastest-growing occupations are in services such as teaching and government work where women have always been more welcome than in business. Rapidly expanding research programs need talent too desperately to discriminate against women.

Even in business organizations, the new jobs added are likely to be "inside" jobs providing special services to salesmen or executives and so off the direct ladder to promotion. In spite of the word "public," public relations is really a staff service to managers; in 1967 about a third of those in this explosively growing field were women. Mechanization and the addition of new services created new jobs in telephone troubleshooting and internal research. In 1966, an official of the New York Telephone Company estimated that more than 10 per cent of its jobs paying $10,000 or more were held by women, double the percentage of women in this salary bracket generally.

The slowest-growing occupations, on the other hand, have been those generally reserved for men. The number of farmers is declining, fewer workers all the time are needed for factory production, and fewer jobs are developing that require physical strength or exposure to the weather. Engineering, for instance, is no longer primarily concerned with heavy construction in the field but is directed to design and research.

"There is nothing inherently feminine about mixing a given batch of materials, exposing it to a definite temperature for a definite time, and producing a cake," Dr. Rebecca Sparling, of General Dynamics, declared. "There is nothing inherently masculine in mixing a batch of materials, exposing it to a definite temperature for a given time, and producing *iron castings*. I have done both and find them satisfying occupations."

Opportunities for women in occupations once reserved for men were publicized by banks, governments, and companies that were having a hard time finding qualified employees. Newspapers cooperated by giving publicity to any "first" for a woman that her organization's public information officer could verify. In the summer of 1967, we clipped, at random, news of the "first" woman assistant vice president of the New York Federal Reserve Bank, "one of the first" woman court psychologists in New York State, the "first" woman pilot to be hired by a French Government airline, and the "only" woman to be elected to the board of governors of the American Oil Society. Publicity exaggerates the progress women are making, but it also weakens the psychological barrier against them.

The fifth trend toward androgyny is a general *desegregation of the sexes*. Stag sanctuaries are being challenged, most often by their own members. Luncheon clubs in most cities are quietly beginning to admit women or are making it easier for them to use their facilities. In 1967, the National Press Club invited women to its traditionally stag "Congressional Night" honoring members of Congress. Previously, even women members of Congress had been excluded. In February 1968 the United States Military Academy at West Point appointed its first woman faculty member.

Professional and special-purpose organizations formed by women when the barriers against them were high are rethinking their reasons for existing. Members of the National Association of Bank Women, Theta Sigma Phi, the women's journalistic fraternity, and American Women in Radio and Television began to wonder if they should not try to join the men's organizations. Many distinguished women simply did not bother with *Who's Who of American Women*. If they weren't well-known enough to be in *Who's Who in America*, they didn't want to be in a woman's *Who's Who*.

The Medical Women's Association addressed itself to public

issues on which it felt women doctors could make a special contribution, such as sex education and medical education for women. Women were, of course, admitted to the American Medical Association, which represents the profession as a whole, without question, but they were underrepresented in its House of Delegates and on its committees. In June 1967, the Episcopal Church Women of Iowa disbanded because they felt it would be "more efficient" to work with the men of the church. In September 1967, the National Secretaries Association, a formerly all-female organization, broke with "one of its basic precepts" and admitted C. J. "Bucky" Helmer, Jr., a man who had been trying to get in for years. When he was rejected in 1964, he had formed the Male Secretaries of America and built it up to 315 members.

Other customs which separate the sexes are also being challenged. The most dramatic example can be seen in the liberal wing of the Roman Catholic Church. Nuns are no longer invariably hidden away from the world, as traditional wives used to be. Some are doffing their habits. "I have come to believe that the notion of cloister—in physical enclosure or in social regulations or in dress—is not valid for some of us who must live our lives as dedicated women in the public forum," Sister Jacqueline Grennan told reporters when she left the Order of the Sisters of Loretto.

During the 1960's, the notion of cloister has been breaking down so fast on college campuses that graduates of the 1950's can hardly recognize their own alma maters today. Rules restricting the hours and activities of women in college dormitories are being relaxed and even abolished. Girls are rebelling against the whole idea of living under supervision, and on many campuses have taken apartments together "off campus," and, on some avant-garde campuses, even with men students. College authorities have tried to avoid the issue with parents or the press, but many have given up any attempt to regulate the private lives of their students. In 1967, Stanford University converted four dormitories into "demonstration houses" mixing men and women in the hope of reducing "distracting social pressures" and enhancing "more natural relationships between men and women."

As recently as thirty years ago, pretty girls were warned not to go to Radcliffe, the first woman's college to be affiliated with an Ivy League men's school, because no Harvard man would look at a girl who went to school just across the street. In order to preserve their chances, many girls entered Vassar or Wellesley instead. But relations between affiliated colleges such as Radcliffe and Harvard, Barnard and Columbia, Tulane and Sophie Newcomb have grown more intimate. In the 1960's, a Radcliffe girl was made editor of the Harvard *Crimson*, and a Barnard girl became editor of the Columbia *Daily Spectator*.

Admissions statistics for the Seven Sister colleges reflect the changes. Radcliffe is currently the most popular college, while women's colleges unaffiliated with men's colleges have been complaining that they are not getting the cream of the freshman crop. In 1966, Vassar and Yale announced a joint study to determine whether and how the two might affiliate. Yale students had long been for the merger, and although older Vassar alumnae feared that the presence of men might deprive women of opportunities for campus leadership or class discussion, Vassar undergraduates of 1967 saw no difficulties.

Although outsiders ribbed Vassar for its apparent eagerness to join Yale, it was Yale who first suggested the merger. Harvard's sociologist David Riesman, a staunch supporter of his Radcliffe students, warned that without girls Yale would lose the brightest young men (presumably to Harvard, which had Radcliffe) and might even attract "boys who are frightened by women and who prefer to see them only on weekends." Gone was any thought that the presence of women might lower standards.

In the end, Vassar turned down Yale's proposal. After a year of soul-searching, the Vassar trustees decided in November 1967 to stay in Poughkeepsie and explore the establishment of a coordinate men's college on Vassar-owned land that formerly had been operated as a college farm. In February 1968, Sarah Lawrence announced it was admitting men. Meanwhile, in May 1967, President Robert F. Goheen of Princeton announced that it was "inevitable that, at some point in the future, Princeton is going to move into the education of women. The only questions now are those of strategy, priority, and timing."

The whole trend is encouraged by the rising proportion of

college faculty that has been educated in coeducational colleges as well as by the number of students who come from coeducational high schools rather than sexually divided prep schools.

Segregated recreation is dying out along with segregated education. Most men no longer stop at bars to drink together after work; instead, they hurry home to help with the children, have a drink with their wives, or watch television. Poolrooms, once refuges for men, have had to try to attract family groups in order to stay in business. Girls are going on camping and biking trips with men friends, as they long have done in Europe.

The de-emphasis on sex is also altering supposedly immutable feminine biology. Now that her sex no longer determines a woman's social destiny, now that she chooses whether to conceive or even bear a child already conceived, she has fewer miscarriages, menstrual pains, and "female" troubles, real or imaginary, than when her status depended on her sexual relationship to a man. In their places, however, doctors are noticing a rise in the proportion of women afflicted with ulcers, asthma, respiratory diseases, and alcoholism—health problems formerly considered male.

Hormone therapy is expected to increase radically in the future. It is already being used to overcome some of the traditional handicaps of female physiology. Estrogen replacement can compensate for the irregular output of hormones which causes some menstrual and menopausal disturbances. Women athletes sometimes take male hormones to increase their strength.

These trends to the androgynous life—longer years for women without childbirth, more education for women, more work outside the home, less segregation of the sexes—are all part of a more general trend to individual choice. We are affluent enough and command sufficient technological knowledge to be able to live in many different ways. There will be more styles of life, and more people will be able to enjoy the style that fits them best. The choice is especially rich for women, if only because their old role is breaking down and no single new role is taking its place.

Program

for the

Future

Forecast for feminism

MARY LOU THOMPSON

The New Feminism, though widely publicized, still involves actively only a minute fraction of the female population of the United States. It differs from the black revolution in that it is much more fragmented even among its most intent participants; its scope of ideology is divisive; public opinion does not support it as yet; and it has no appeal for thousands of middle-class women apparently content with their present condition.

Yet I believe that the situation of women is certain to change, and with it will change styles of architecture, family life, patterns of marriage, and the consumer market. As they develop sophistication in techniques of political power, in cooperation with other reform groups women may bring about a number of changes in our economic and political system.

Take the matter of housing and the nuclear family, with each woman now in her own kitchen in her more or less elaborate big or little wooden box, often with her family totally cut off from the warmth, support, or acquired wisdom of an extended family. With space in urban and suburban areas critical in the future, family apartment house living will be more customary, and apartment houses of the future will probably be built with central dining rooms operated economically for family use. There will be central child-care centers under expert supervision and other services as mentioned in the *Status of Women in Sweden* report (page 155).

Young people are even now experimenting with the commune system of living, patterning their living somewhat on the Israeli kibbutzim. The Fort Hill section of Boston, in Roxbury, has a number of communes of both married and single young people, and children. Similar arrangements are being tried in New York, San Francisco, and other cities, as well as in rural communities in the United States and Canada. Whether these arrangements will be permanent cannot be predicted at present; earlier publicized efforts at communes in this country such as the Brook Farm experiment in Boston did not last.

The welfare of children will be more closely guarded by the state of the future, as families grow smaller and more women elect not to become mothers. Hopefully those so unfortunate as to be born to parents who reject them may have more opportunity to grow up as whole persons with proper care.

With population pressures creating a tendency toward smaller families, or no children, some women who normally would be emotionally suitable mothers may choose to forego that experience. Yet must they, and some men, also, be deprived of the happiness of contact with children? Dr. Roger Revelle, Director, Center for Population Studies, Harvard University, has said:

> Our typical Anglo-Saxon Protestant attitude is that children are a kind of property. They are "my children and belong to me." If we could think of children as belonging to a larger group, to the neighborhood or to the community, so that all of us could share, so that everyone could share in the joy of having children, it might be that there wouldn't be this proprietary need for families to have three or four or more children.[1]

The new feminist revolution may benefit the older woman as well. Certainly with women engaged in more remunerative and rewarding occupations, with more adequate retirement benefits, the life of the aging, impoverished widow or spinster should be

---

[1] Hearings before a Subcommittee of the Committee on Government Operations, House of Representatives, 91st Congress. September 15 and 16, 1969.

less miserable. Perhaps there will be more experimentation with new models for living in the older years. The extended family concept in apartment living should give the elderly person more opportunities for rewarding contacts with others, and health service centers in housing complexes will become more common.

Will the divorce rate continue to climb, as women become more independent? Probably so; but it has already escalated under our present system. Substantial numbers of prosperous executives find it easier to divorce a first wife for a younger, more glamorous, possibly more subservient woman than ever before in our history. What happens to the woman who is discarded, if she has no skills or resources, if she has depended for her status on the accomplishments of her husband and her children?

Possibly the world of the future will not be so determinedly organized into a culture of couples, a custom that is cruelly excluding to the mature unmarried, widowed, or divorced woman. One of the by-products of the feminist movement already familiar to members of women's organizations has been the discovery that women enjoy each other's company when they are not rivals for the attention of a man. They can work together for a common cause; they like and trust each other.

Of course, most women will continue to prefer a heterogeneous sexual relationship. Emancipated woman may make a better, less passive, sexual partner in marriage. Man is not the enemy, except to the more radical female liberationists one finds, and many of them manage somehow to accommodate to marriage. The more moderate National Organization for Women admits men to membership; a number participate in the business sessions of the annual conference. Some undoubtedly became involved along with their wives, and others view the women's movement as another struggle for civil rights which deserves their support.

The consumer market will change with the emancipation of women. For one thing, as more go to work, they will have less time for the compulsive shopping that brings so many to the department store. The consumerism of the abundant society is due for a revaluation anyway, with waste disposal of everything from wrappings to wornout automobiles a serious environmental problem in this throw-away generation. And it might just happen that more women will elect to wear their clothes until they are worn out, and thereby emancipate themselves from the fashion czars—almost all men.

Probably no happening of the liberation movement has produced more comment than the bra-burners who picketed the Miss America contest. In the rush to call it an act of the lunatic fringe of feminism, hardly anyone stopped to consider what these modern-day Carrie Nations were really saying. Were they not protesting the commercialization of the female sex symbol in which the uplift bra has, shall we say, figured so prominently?

The image of women is the subject of a number of task forces within the feminist movement, and advertisers are hearing increasingly from lady customers who object to being pictured either as female sex symbols or joyful washers of floors with a new magic cleaning fluid. Right now there may not be enough of them to worry executives in the advertising agencies, but they were probably equally indifferent when blacks first started being articulate about their image. Now blacks are a dignified part of the advertising scene, and they represent only 12 per cent of the population.

The pill has been widely heralded as the emancipator of women, but since hearings at the capitol raised questions on its long-term safety, feminists have taken a new look at the whole contraception question. Men will probably have to take more responsibility for birth control techniques, and there is talk of a male pill for temporary sterility. Vasectomy for the male is a minor operation as compared to sterilization for the female; when the small family of the future is complete it would seem to be a logical procedure.

Abortion will be available on the request of the woman, as an emergency method of birth control.

The whole volunteer scene may change as we approach a more androgynous life. Men as well as women will have time to assume more roles in volunteer work, and not so often as chairman of the committee or president of the organization. The growing complexity of social problems will require more professional skills, but unless the federal budget is freed of its burden for defense, these problems will also engage more volunteers who will take the time to develop expertise in worthwhile volunteer jobs. The number of young lawyers giving free time to concerns of the poor, of racial minorities, or to the environment is heartening, and we may expect to hear more from the female lawyers caught up in the new feminism.

It will not be so easy to involve highly qualified women in almost full-time volunteer responsibility as they move into the professions and the working world. Most certainly, unless there is more of a sharing of topflight volunteer offices with women, they will either retreat into women's organizations, as some of the best do at present, or they will just not be available for hewing the wood and drawing the water for the male officer of the organization.

One thing that characterizes the feminist revolt is the way it cuts across ethnic lines, as Pauli Murray has indicated in her article (page 87). Possibly women in their campaign for common goals will keep the lines of communication open toward an integrated society.

Will the woman in poverty benefit from the liberation of women? Thus far the revolution has been based mainly in the middle class, under the guidance of the experienced professional woman or the college-educated young woman. Some way must be found to include the economically deprived woman in the leadership of the feminist movement so that she can assume control over her own economic destiny. Whether her letters are addressed "Miss," "Mrs.," or "Ms." may seem inconsequential to the poor woman, but she does want public education facilities extended to include day-care centers, and she may join her more affluent "sister" in making this demand. Just as the plight of the mill girls working sometimes fourteen hours for pittance wages concerned earlier feminists, so this revolution must be extended to improve the lot of the nearly two million United States families in poverty headed by women.

Most clear-eyed young feminists are realistic enough to accept the fact that with any freedom attained, responsibility is inevitable, and some protections will be withdrawn. This has been pointed out in the excerpts from the *Status of Women in Sweden* (page 155) and in the article by Caroline Bird (page 179). If the Equal Rights for Women Amendment is finally passed by Congress and adopted by the states, it will void a number of highly discriminatory state laws on family property, employment, longer punishment for a woman than a man committing the same crime, and the like. At the same time protective legislation limiting hours women may work will be ended. In reality this legislation has often been used to limit a woman's advancement on the job. There will inevitably be changes in alimony laws, and some women will find themselves paying alimony to a dependent husband, instead of the other way round. As in Israel, women may be drafted for the armed services.

At the same time, as able women are involved in more responsibility in politics, business, education, and the other professions, those who reach the top echelons will undoubtedly feel the same pressures men have felt, and be subject to the same ills, as Caroline Bird has said.

Of course, nobody is saying that the traditional household, with the husband at work, and the wife as housekeeper, wife, mother, and family representative in the community, will totally disappear. The New Feminists have emphasized that if women continue to assume this role it should be from choice, rather than from tradition or a man's insistence.

The women who have achieved self-respect and confidence in their abilities have come too long a way toward equality to stop where they are. The problems and challenges of the technological age are too great for the concerned, well-educated, ambitious woman to be content to sit on the sidelines with her knitting while men make the decisions that count.

Women must rebel

SHIRLEY CHISHOLM

In 1894, Susan B. Anthony, who for more than six decades gave all of her energy to the cause of equality for women, wrote, "It is the disheartening part of all my life work—that so few women will work for the emancipation of their own half of the race."

In this generation Congresswoman Shirley Chisholm asks, "Will women dare in sufficient numbers to transform their own attitudes toward themselves and thus change the basic attitudes of males and the general society?"

Said Susan B. Anthony: "Cautious, careful people, always casting about to preserve their reputation and social standing, never can bring about a reform."

Says Shirley Chisholm: "Women will have to brave the social sanctions in great numbers in order to free themselves from the sexual, psychological, and emotional stereotyping that plagues us. . . . It is not feminine egoism to say that the future of mankind may well be ours to determine."

Shirley Chisholm was elected in 1968 as United States Representative from the Twelfth Congressional District in Brooklyn, New York. She campaigned under the slogan "Unbought and unbossed." She has served in the New York State Assembly and was formerly a public school teacher.

Do women dare take an active part in society and, in particular, do they dare take a part in the present social revolution? For myself, I find the question as much of an insult as I would the question, "Are you, as a black person, willing to fight for your rights?"

America has been sufficiently sensitized to the answer to the latter question to make the question itself seem asinine and superfluous. America is not yet sufficiently aware that such a question applied to women is equally asinine and superfluous.

I am both black and a woman. That is a good vantage point from which to view at least two elements of what is becoming a social revolution: the American Black Revolution and the Women's Liberation Movement. But it is also a horrible disadvantage. It is a disadvantage because America, as a nation, is both racist and antifeminist. Racism and antifeminism are two of the prime traditions of this country.

For any individual, challenging social traditions is a giant step —a giant step because there are no social traditions which do not have corresponding social sanctions, the sole purpose of which are to protect the sanctity of the traditions.

Thus when we ask, "Do women dare?" we are not asking, "Are women capable of a break with tradition?" so much as we are asking, "Are women capable of bearing with the sanctions that will be placed upon them?"

Coupling this with the hypothesis, presented by some social thinkers and philosophers, that in any given society the most active groups are those nearest to the particular freedom they desire, it does not surprise me that those women most active and vocal on the issue of freedom for women are those who are young, white, and middle class; nor is it too surprising that there are not more from that group involved in the women's liberation movement.

There certainly are reasons why more women are not involved. This country, as I said, is both racist and antifeminist. Few, if any, Americans are free of the psychological wounds imposed by racism and antifeminism.

A few months ago while testifying before the Office of Federal Contract Compliance, I noted that antifeminism, like every

form of discrimination, is destructive both to those who perpe-
trate it and to their victims; that males with their antifeminism
maim both themselves and their women.

In *Soul on Ice* Eldridge Cleaver pointed out how America's
racial and sexual stereotypes were supposed to work. Whether
his insight is correct or not, it bears close examination.

Cleaver, in the passage "The Primeval Mitosis," describes in
detail the four major roles. There is the white female who is
considered to be "Ultra-Feminine" because ". . . she is required to possess and project an image that is in sharp contrast
. . ." to the white male's image as the "Omnipotent Adminis-
trator . . . all brain and no body."

He goes on to identify the black female as "Subfeminine" or
"Amazon" by virtue of her assignment to the lowly household
chores and those corresponding jobs of tedious nature. He sums
up the role of the black male as the "Supermasculine Menial
. . . all body and no brain" because he was expected to supply
society with its source of brute power.

What the roles and the strange interplay between them have
meant to America, Cleaver goes on to point out quite well.

What he does not say, and what I think must be said, is that
because of the bizarre aspects of the roles and the influence that
nontraditional contact between them has on the general society,
blacks and whites—males and females—must operate almost independently of each other in order to escape from the quick-
sands of psychological slavery. Each—black male and black female; white female and white male—must escape first from his
own historical trap before he can be truly effective in helping to
free himself.

Therein lies one of the major reasons that there are not more
women involved in the women's liberation movement. Women
cannot, for the most part, operate independently of men because they often do not have sufficient economic freedom.

In 1966, the median earnings of women who worked full time
for the whole year was far lower than the median income of
males who worked full time for the whole year. In fact, white
women workers made less than black male workers and, of
course, black women workers made the least of all.

Whether it is intentional or not, women are paid less than men for the same work, no matter what their chosen field. Whether it is intentional or not, employment for women is regulated still more in terms of the jobs that are available to them. This is almost as true for white women as it is for black women.

Whether it is intentional or not, when it becomes time for a young high school girl to think about preparing for her career, her counselors, whether they are male or female, will think first of her "natural" career—housewife and mother—and begin to program her for a field with which marriage and children will not unduly interfere.

That is exactly the same as the situation of the young black or Puerto Rican whom the racist counselor advises to prepare for service-oriented occupations because he does not even think of them entering the professions.

The response of the average young lady is precisely the same as the response of the average young black or Puerto Rican— tacit agreement—because the odds do seem to be stacked against her.

This is not happening as much as it once did to young minority-group males. It is not happening because they have been radicalized, and the country is becoming sensitized to its racist attitudes and the damage that it does.

Women must rebel; they must react to the traditional stereotyped education mapped out for them by society. Their education and training is programmed and planned for them from the moment the doctor says, "Mr. Jones, it's a beautiful baby girl!" and Mr. Jones begins deleting mentally the things she might have been and adds the things that society says she *must* be.

That young woman (for society begins to see her as a stereotype the moment that her sex is determined) will be wrapped in a pink blanket (pink because that is the color of her caste) and the unequal segregation of the sexes will have begun.

Small wonder that the young girl sitting across the desk from her counselor will not be able to say *No* to educational, economic, and social slavery. Small wonder because she has been a psychological slave and programmed as such since the moment of her birth!

On May 20, 1969, I introduced legislation concerning the equal employment opportunities of women. At that time I pointed out that there were three and one-half million more women than men in America but women held only 2 per cent of the managerial positions; that no women sit on the AFL-CIO Council or the Supreme Court; that only two women have ever held Cabinet rank and that there were at that time only two women of Ambassadorial rank in the Diplomatic Corps. I stated then as I do now that this situation is outrageous.

In my speech on the Floor that day I said:

> It is true that part of the problem has been that women
> have not been aggressive in demanding their rights.
> This was also true of the black population for many
> years. They submitted to oppression and even
> cooperated with it. Women have done the same thing.
> But now there is an awareness of this situation,
> particularly among the younger segment of the
> population.
>
> As in the field of equal rights for blacks, Spanish-
> Americans, the Indians, and other groups, laws will
> not change such deep-seated problems overnight. But
> they can be used to provide protection for those who
> are most abused, and begin the process of evolutionary
> change by compelling the insensitive majority to
> re-examine its unconscious attitudes.

The law cannot do it for us, we must do it ourselves. Women in this country must become revolutionaries. We must refuse to accept the old traditional roles and stereotypes.

We must reject the Greek philosopher's thought, "It is thy place woman, to hold thy peace and keep within doors." We must reject the thought of St. Paul who said, "Let the woman learn in silence." And we must reject the Nietzschean thought "When a woman inclines to learning, there is something wrong with her sex apparatus."

But more than merely rejecting, we must replace those thoughts and the concept they symbolize with positive values based on female experience.

A few short years ago if you called most Negroes black it was tantamount to calling them niggers. But now black is beautiful and black is proud. There are relatively few people, white or black, who do not recognize what has happened.

Black people have freed themselves from the dead weight of the albatross of blackness that once hung around their neck. They have done it by picking it up in their arms and holding it out with pride for all the world to see. They have done it by embracing it—not in the dark of the moon but in the searing light of the white sun. They have said *Yes* to it and found that the skin that was once seen as symbolizing their shame is in reality their badge of honor.

Women must come to realize that the superficial symbols that surround us are negative only when we ourselves perceive and accept them as negative. We must begin to replace the old negative thoughts about our femininity with positive thoughts and positive actions, affirming it and more.

But we must also remember that will be breaking with tradition, and we must prepare ourselves—educationally, economically, and psychologically—in order that we will be able to accept and bear the sanctions society will immediately impose upon us.

I am a politician. I detest the word because of the connotations that cling like slime to it, but for want of a better term I must use it. I have been in politics for twenty years and in that time I have learned a few things about the role of women in politics.

The major thing I have learned is that women are the backbone of America's political organizations. They are the letter writers, the envelope stuffers, the telephone answerers; they are the campaign workers and organizers. They are the speech writers and the largest number of potential voters.

Yet they are but rarely the standard bearers or elected officials. Perhaps it is in America, more than any other country, that the inherent truth of the old bromide "The power behind the throne is a woman" is most readily apparent.

Let me remind you once again of the relatively few women standard bearers on the American political scene. There are only ten United States Representatives. There is only one Senator and there are no Cabinet members who are women. There are no women on the Supreme Court and only a small percentage of female judges at the Federal Court level who might be candidates.

It is true that at the state level the picture is somewhat brighter, just as it is true that the North presents a surface that is somewhat more appealing to the black American when compared with the South.

Secondly, I have learned that the attitude held by the high school counselors I mentioned earlier is a general attitude held by political bosses. A few years ago a politician remarked to me about a potential young female candidate, "Why invest all the time and effort to build up the gal into a household name when she's pretty sure to drop out of the game to have a couple of kids at just about the time we're ready to run her for mayor?"

I have pointed out time and time again that the harshest discrimination I have encountered in the political arena is antifeminism, from both males and brain-washed "Uncle Tom" females.

When I first announced that I was running for the United States Congress last year, both men and women advised me, as they had when I ran for the New York State Assembly, to go back to teaching, a woman's vocation, and leave politics to the men.

One of the major reasons I will not leave the American political scene—voluntarily, that is—is because the number of women in politics is declining.

There are at least two million more women than men of voting age, but the fact is that while we get out the vote we often do not get out to vote. In 1964, for example, 72 per cent of registered males voted while only 67 per cent of registered females voted. We seem to be a political minority by choice.

I believe that women have a special contribution to make to

help bring order out of chaos because they have special qualities of leadership which are greatly needed today. These qualities are the patience, tolerance, and perseverance which have developed in many women because of suppression. If we can add to these qualities a reservoir of information about techniques of community action we can indeed become effective harbingers of change. Women must participate more in the legislative process because even with the contributions that I have just mentioned, the single greatest contribution that women could bring to American politics would be a spirit of moral purpose.

But unfortunately women's participation in politics is declining. And politics is not the only place that we are losing past gains. Columnist Clayton Fritchey in a column *Women In Office* noted that

> Although more women are working, their salaries
> keep falling behind men's. Some occupations are [still]
> closed by law to women. Key property laws favor
> men. In 1940, women held 45 per cent of all professional
> and technical positions as against 37 per cent today.

The decline is a general one. But it is because it is a decline that I believe the true question is not whether or not women dare. Women have always dared! The question which now faces us is, "Will women dare in numbers sufficient to have an effect on their own attitudes toward themselves and thus change the basic attitudes of males and the general society?"

Women will have to brave the social sanctions in great numbers in order to free themselves from the sexual, psychological, and emotional stereotyping that plagues us.

It is not feminine egoism to say that the future of mankind may very well be ours to determine. It is simply a plain fact. The softness, warmth, and gentleness that are often used to stereotype us are positive human values—values that are becoming more and more important as the general values of the whole of mankind slip more and more out of kilter.

The strength that marked Christ, Gandhi, and Martin

Luther King was a strength born not of violence but of gentleness, understanding, and genuine human compassion.

We must move outside the walls of our stereotypes but we must retain the values on which they were built.

No, I am not saying that we are inherently those things that the stereotypes impute that we are; but I am saying that because of the long-enforced roles we have had to play, we should know by now that the values are good ones to hold, and I am saying that by now we should have developed the capacity to not only hold them but to also dispense them to those around us.

This is the reason that we must free ourselves. This is the reason that we must become revolutionaries in the fashion of Christ, Gandhi, King, and the hundreds of other men and women who held those as the highest of human values.

There is another reason. In working toward our own freedom we can only allow our men to work toward their freedom from the traps of their stereotypes.

We are challenged now as we never were before. The past twenty years show a decline for women in employment and government, there has been little change in the preparation of young women for certain professions. It is clear that evolution is not necessarily a process of positive forward motion. Susan B. Anthony, Carrie Nation, and Sojourner Truth were not evolutionaries. They were revolutionaries, as are many of the young women of today. More women and more men must join their ranks.

New goals and new priorities, not only for this country, but for all of mankind, must be set. Formal education will not help us do that; we must therefore depend on informal learning.

We can do that by confronting people with their own humanity and their own inhumanity—confronting them wherever we meet them: in the church, in the classroom, on the floors of Congress and the state legislatures, in bars and on the streets. We must reject not only the stereotypes that others hold of us but also the stereotypes that we hold of ourselves and others.

In a recent speech to an audience that was predominantly white and all female I suggested the following if they wanted to create change:

You must start in your own homes, your own schools
and your own churches. . . . I don't want you to go
home and talk about integrated schools, churches, or
marriages when the kind of integration you are talking
about is black with white.

I ask you to work for—fight for—the integration of
male and female, human and human. Frantz Fanon
pointed out in *Black Skins—White Masks* that the
anti-Semite was eventually the antifeminist. And even
further, I want to indicate that all discrimination is
eventually the same thing—antihumanism.

That is my charge to you whether you are male
or female.

Women: a bibliography

LUCINDA CISLER

This condensation of Women: A Bibliography *by Lucinda Cisler is selected from among more than 600 entries that appear in the uncut version. The latest revised edition of the full bibliography may be ordered from the author and publisher, Lucinda Cisler, 102 W. 80th St., New York, New York 10024, for 30¢.*

Lucinda Cisler is an architect and city planner; she is active in New York women's liberation. She is on the national board of the National Organization for Women, the National Association for Repeal of Abortion Laws, and Zero Population Growth, and is president of New Yorkers for Abortion Law Repeal. Her article "Unfinished Business: Birth Control and Women's Liberation" appears in Sisterhood Is Powerful, Robin Morgan, ed. New York: Random, 1970.

Condensed from the sixth edition (revised July 1970)
p denotes availability in a paperback edition as of early 1970
a denotes a work deserving special attention
Copyright 1970, 1969, 1968 by Lucinda Cisler; all rights reserved; reprinted by permission

GENERAL WORKS

Beard, Mary, *On Understanding Women*. London: Longmans, Green, 1931.

p a deBeauvoir, Simone, *The Second Sex*. New York: Knopf, 1953, and New York: Bantam, 1968. Classic, and a must, if somewhat too "European" in places for American women to empathize with completely.

Bennett, Margaret (pseud.), *The Feminine Mistake, or, Alice in Womanland*. Englewood Cliffs, N.J.: Prentice-Hall, 1967. Stereotypes of women neatly satirized.

p a Bird, Caroline, *Born Female: The High Cost of Keeping Women Down*. New York: McKay, 1968. Very good, especially for all the up-to-date facts on women's economic and employment position.

p a Brown, Helen Gurley, *Sex and the Single Girl*. New York: Geis, 1962. The Game and how to play it.

Cassara, Beverly Benner, ed., *American Women: The Changing Image*. Boston: Beacon, 1962. Articles by Mead, Buck, Gilbreth, and others. Sponsored by Alliance of Unitarian Women.

p Citizens' Advisory Council on the Status of Women, *American Women 1968*. U.S. Dept. of Labor, 1968. Four Task Force reports: labor standards, health and welfare, social insurance and taxes, family law and policy. (Free, from U.S. Dept. of Labor, Rm. 2131, Washington, D.C. 20210.) A formidable job; abortion law repeal, day care, major tax reforms—some of the resolutions from this largely female group.

p Farber, Seymour, and Roger H. L. Wilson, *The Potential of Woman*. New York: McGraw-Hill, 1963. Essays by E. Maccoby, *et al.*

p a Friedan, Betty, *The Feminine Mystique*. New York: Dell, 1963. Her perceptive analyses must be read, especially those on the media and popularized Freud and anthropology—*whatever* one's opinions may be about the solutions she then proposed.

Gilman, Charlotte Perkins, *The Manmade World: Our Andro-centric Culture.* 1911.

p a Herschberger, Ruth, *Adam's Rib.* Pellegrini & Cudahy, 1948; New York: Harper & Row, 1970. Especially perceptive on semantics of sexual terminology and biology; good, and ahead of its time all round.

Hunt, Morton, *Her Infinite Variety: The American Woman as Lover, Rival, and Mate.* New York: Harper & Row, 1962. Popular, rather pro-woman, commentary.

Mencken, H. L., *In Defense of Women.* New York: Knopf, 1922.

a Merriam, Eve, *After Nora Slammed the Door.* Incisive critique —with much irony—on the general topic.

a Mill, John Stuart, *On the Subjection of Woman.* 1869. Oxford Press edition (with *On Liberty* and *Representative Government*). Vital early theorizing by a male feminist.

a deRham, Edith, *The Love Fraud.* New York: Clarkson Potter, 1965. Self-abnegation is not the answer.

p a Solanas, Valarie, *SCUM Manifesto.* Olympia, 1968. A polar expression.

p a Wollstonecraft, Mary, *A Vindication of the Rights of Women.* 1792. Fiery eighteenth-century classic by a woman who lived what she preached.

a Woolf, Virginia, *A Room of One's Own.* New York: Harcourt, Brace, 1929. Among many other things, an eloquent plea for women's economic independence as a prerequisite to real accomplishment.

PERIODICALS (*Entire Issues of Interest*)

a "Sex and the Contemporary American Scene." Edward Sagarin, ed. Special issue of *The Annals of the American Academy of Political and Social Science,* vol. 376, March 1968. Entire issue worthwhile, but see especially "Sexual Patterns in Three Ethnic Subcultures of an American Underclass" (Rosenberg and Bensman, especially men's attitudes toward women and the words they use in speaking of sex; blacks, Puerto Ricans, and Appalachian/Chicago-

ans); "Attitudes Toward Sex in American 'High Culture' "
(Boyers, incisive literary and social criticism); "Prostitution in the United States" (Esselstyn, curiously blank and
obtuse); "Abortion" (Schur); "Sex Behavior and the American Class Structure; a Mosaic" (Ferdinand).

a "The Sexual Renaissance in America." Special issue of *Journal
of Social Issues*, XXII:2, April 1966. All articles worthwhile; see especially Broderick, Vincent, Bernard, Rainwater, Sherwin.

p a "The Woman in America." *Daedalus*, Spring 1964. Published
as a paperback, Robert Jay Lifton, ed., Boston: Beacon,
1965. See especially Rossi, Degler, but also Riesman, Erik-
son, Lifton, McClelland.

HISTORICAL STUDIES

a Anthony, Susan B., Elizabeth Cady Stanton, and I. H. Harper,
History of Women's Suffrage. The famous history written
by suffrage leaders.

p a Aries, Philippe, *Centuries of Childhood: A Social History of
Family Life*. New York: Knopf, 1962. Complex and thor-
ough; e.g., shows our idea of childhood to be a modern
concept.

Banks, J. A. and Olive, *Feminism and Family Planning in Victorian England*. New York: Schocken, 1964. Includes relevant bibliography for Great Britain, 1792-1880.

p a Beard, Mary R., *Woman as Force in History*. New York: Collier, 1946. The historian traces women's legal status.

Brittain, Vera, *Lady into Woman: A History of Women from
Victoria to Elizabeth II*. New York: Macmillan, 1953.
History of the British women's movement, by a participant.

p Degler, Carl N., *Out of Our Past*. New York: Harper & Row,
1958. Good American history; see passages on women and
the women's movement.

Dexter, Elizabeth A., *Career Women of America, 1776-1840*.
Francestown, N.H.: Marshall Jones, 1950.

Diner, Helen, *Mothers and Amazons: The First Feminine History of Culture*. New York: Julian, 1965. Early history.

a Ditzion, Sidney H., *Marriage, Morals, and Sex in America—A History of Ideas.* 1953. Extensive bibliographic essay, especially on interrelation between social and sexual reform movements and women's movement.

p a Flexner, Eleanor, *A Century of Struggle.* Cambridge, Mass.: Harvard, 1959. Exhaustive description of the suffrage and rights movements through 1920.

Fryer, Peter, *The Birth Controllers.* London: Secker and Warburg, 1965. A history of the movement, especially in England.

Grimké, Angelina, *Appeal to the Christian Women of the South.* By the nineteenth-century feminist abolitionist.

Grimké, Sarah, *Letters on Equality of the Sexes.*

Himmelfarb, Gertrude, *Victorian Minds.* London: Weidenfeld-Nicholson, 1968. Treats marriage, sexual ideas, Mill, etc.

a Irwin, Inez Haynes, *Angels and Amazons: 100 Years of American Women.* 1934.

———, *Up Hill with Banners Flying: The Story of the Woman's Party.* Penobscot, Me.: Traversity, 1964. Official, first-hand, post-1912 history. ($6.00 from National Woman's Party, 144 Constitution Ave., Washington, D.C. 20002.)

a Kraditor, Aileen S., *Ideas of the Woman Suffrage Movement, 1890-1920.* New York: Columbia, 1965. Key intellectual history of the movement, especially of the split between older suffragists and younger socialists.

———, ed., *Up from the Pedestal: Selected Documents from the History of American Feminism.* Chicago: Quadrangle, 1968.

Leonard, Drinker, and Holden, *The American Woman in Colonial and Revolutionary Times, 1565-1800: A Syllabus with Bibliography.* Philadelphia: U. of Pennsylvania, 1962.

Lutz, Alma, *Crusade for Freedom: Women in the Antislavery Movement.* Boston: Beacon, 1968. Account of the first fifty-years of the drive for abolition and for "woman's voice in national affairs." This historian is the biographer of several early feminists.

p a Marcus, Steven, *The Other Victorians: A Study of Sexuality and Pornography in Mid-nineteenth Century England.*

New York: Basic, 1966. Especially revealing analysis of pornographers' image of women, in social-class terms.

a Newcomer, Mabel, *A Century of Higher Education for Women.* 1959. Informative account—pointing up the present lack of progress on many fronts and regression on others.

O'Neill, William L., *Everyone Was Brave: The Rise and Fall of Feminism in America.* Chicago: Quadrangle, 1969. The "Sexual Revolution," marriage, and the family as obstacles to emancipation after suffrage was won. Beware his definition of "social feminism."

Pankhurst, Sylvia, *The Suffrage Movement: An Intimate Account of Persons and Ideals.* London: Longmans, Green, 1931.

Parker, Theodore, Essays on Women. Famous nineteenth-century transcendentalist and abolitionist, and an early male feminist.

p Putnam, Emily James, *The Lady, Studies of Certain Significant Phases of Her History.* Sturgis & Walton, 1910.

p Riegel, Robert E., *American Feminists.* Lawrence, Kans.: U. of Kansas, 1968. Historical.

p Rogers, Katharine M., *The Troublesome Helpmate: A History of Misogyny in Literature.* Seattle: U. of Washington, 1966.

p Sinclair, Andrew, *The Emancipation of the American Woman.* New York: Harper & Row, 1965. Lively, readable account of the rights movement, with notes on the situation in 1965. (Published in hard cover as *The Better Half.*)

Stevens, Doris, *Jailed for Freedom.* Includes account of suffragists in Occoquam prison. Stevens was there.

a Taylor, Gordon Rattray, *Sex in History.* New York: Vanguard, 1954. Interesting characterizations of historical periods as either "matristic" or "patristic."

Weld, Theodore, Angelina Grimké, and Sarah Grimké, *Letters of . . . , 1822-1844.*

a Woodward, Helen, *The Lady Persuaders.* New York: Astor-Honor, 1960. Over one hundred·years of women's magazines; their influence.

ECONOMICS, WORK, LAW

Bagdikian, Ben H., "Who is Sabotaging Day Care for Our Children?" *Ladies' Home Journal*, November 1966, pp. 86ff. Good indignant reportage, though not especially feminist; Congress sneers at "federalized baby-sitting" because they're scared Mama will leave home.

Beecher, Catherine E., *A Treatise on Domestic Economy*. 1842. Early and neglected advocate of household efficiency and mechanization, through planning and technology.

Benjamin, Lois, *So You Want to Be a Working Mother!* New York: McGraw-Hill, 1966. She's all for it and helps with very practical—though individualistic—"solutions."

a   Dichter, Ernest, *The Strategy of Desire*. Seemingly sexy title not a complete misnomer: daddy of motivational research explains his work; has an interesting rationale for "expanding our horizons" by selling us what we think we don't need.

p   Engels, Friedrich, *The Origins of Family, Private Property, and the State*. 1884. The family as a vehicle for perpetuating the economic *status quo*.

Fava, Sylvia, "The Status of Women in Professional Sociology." *American Sociological Review*, XXV, April 1960, pp. 271-276.

Fenberg, Matilda, "Blame Coke and Blackstone." *Women Lawyers Journal*, 34:2, Spring 1948, p. 7. History of women's legal status.

Flexner, Eleanor, *Woman's Work in America*.

p a   Gilman, Charlotte Perkins, *Women and Economics*. 1898. Treats collective solutions for "housework." See also her other writings on children, the home, human work, etc.

Ginsberg, Eli, and Marie Yohalem, *Educated American Women: Self-portraits*. New York: Columbia, 1966.

Hartman, Sylvia, "Should Wives Work?" *McCall's*, February 1969, pp. 57ff. A feminist's down-to-earth exposition of the idea that men mostly just don't *want* to do any of the dirty work of "homemaking": it's just unfair, and all the rationales are mere embroidery.

p   Hatterer, Lawrence J., M.D., *The Artist in Society: Problems and Treatment of the Creative Personality.* New York: Grove, 1966. Chapter on "The Woman Artist": guilts, conflicts, husband's influence.

Henry, Alice, *Women and the Labor Movement.* 1923.

a   Kanowitz, Leo, *Women and the Law: The Unfinished Revolution.* Albuquerque: U. of New Mexico, 1969. Contains articles on employment, rape, abortion, prostitution, divorce, the rights of single and married women, etc. Draws female/black parallel.

Marmor, Judd, "Women in Medicine: Importance of the Formative Years." *Journal of the American Medical Women's Association,* 23:7, July 1968.

p   Mattfield, Jacquelyn A., and Carol G. Van Aken, eds., *Women and the Scientific Professions.* Cambridge, Mass.: MIT, 1965. MIT symposium. See especially Rossi's piece.

Moore, Bernice Milburn, and Wayne H. Holtzman, *Tomorrow's Parents.* Austin: U. of Texas, 1965. Examines relative happiness of working mothers' and housewives' adolescent children; interesting findings; little difference.

a   Murray, Pauli, and Mary Eastwood, "Jane Crow and the Law: Sex Discrimination and Title VII." *George Washington Law Review,* 34:2, 1965, p. 232. A review of women's legal status, especially in employment.

Myrdal, Alva, and Viola Klein, *Women's Two Roles: Home and Work.* London: Routledge and Kegan Paul, 1956.

a   Nye, F. Ivan, and Lois Wladis Hoffman, eds., *The Employed Mother in America.* New York: Rand-McNally, 1963. Compendium of research findings, most disproving the working-mothers-are-ogres theory.

Pressman, Sonia, "Discrimination in Employment Because of Sex." Washington, D.C.: Equal Employment Opportunities Commission, 1969. Two speeches and a 12-page bibliography on employment; by an EEOC lawyer. (Available from the EEOC Public Affairs Office, Rm. 1232, 1800 G St., NW, Washington, D.C. 20506.)

Rossi, Alice S., "Women in Science: Why So Few?" *Science,* 148:3674, May 28, 1965, pp. 1196-1202.

Schreiner, Olive, *Women and Labour*. London: Fisher Unwin, 1911.

Simon, Rita J., Shirley Clark, and Larry L. Tifft, "Of Nepotism, Marriage, and the Pursuit of an Academic Career." *Sociology of Education*, 39:4, Fall 1966.

p U.S. Dept. of Labor, Women's Bureau, *The Fuller Utilization of the Woman Physician*. 1968.

p a ———, *Handbook on Women Workers*. Latest edition. Many facts and statistics.

p a ———, *Know Your Rights*. Summary of women's legal rights in the U.S. (Free.)

p a ———, *Leaflet #10*. Send for this free list of Bureau publications. Especially good on economics, law, education.

p ———, *Recommendations of the Four Task Forces of the Citizen's Advisory Council on the Status of Women*. Family law and policy, labor standards, health and welfare, social insurance and taxes.

White, James J., "Women in the Law." *Michigan Law Review*, vol. 65, April 1967, p. 1051. Placement officers, deans, employers, students, on discrimination in the legal profession.

SOCIOLOGY AND SOCIAL COMMENTARY

Berger, Bennett, *Working Class Suburb*. Berkeley and Los Angeles: U. of California, 1960. California; see passages on women's lives.

p Bernard, Jessie, *Academic Woman*. University Park, Pa.: Pennsylvania State University, 1964. Women as scholars, college teachers.

Blake, Judith, *Family Structure in Jamaica: The Social Context of Reproduction*. 1961.

a Carson, Josephine, *Silent Voices*. New York, 1969. Perceptive interviews with Southern black women from a broad variety of backgrounds. Good insights into the civil rights movement from black women's point of view.

p a Dollard, John. *Caste and Class in a Southern Town*. New Haven: Yale University Press, 1937. Especially Chapter 7, "The Sexual Gain."

Feldman, Harold, *Development of the Husband-Wife Relationship*. Ithaca: Cornell, 1965.

Folsom, Joseph Kirk, *The Family and the Democratic Society*. New York, 1943.

Gans, Herbert J., *The Levittowners*. New York: Pantheon, 1967. Incredibly passive attitude toward quality of lower-middle-class suburban life, especially toward the woman's role.

p   ———, *The Urban Villagers*. New York: Free Press, 1962. Boston Italian-American working-class neighborhood; see especially treatment of the highly segregated sex roles.

p   Goodman, Percival, and Paul Goodman, *Communitas*. New York: Random, 1944. Famous modern utopia, with three variations. One is a good satire on the "society of total consumption."

a   Hacker, Helen. "Women as a Minority Group." *Social Forces*, XXX, October 1951, pp. 60-69. Also: S-108 in the Bobbs-Merrill Reprint Series in the Social Sciences (25¢, 4300 West 62 St., Indianapolis, Indiana 46206). Social distance, marginality, caste/class, etc., treated provocatively.

Henriques, Fernando, *Love in Action: The Sociology of Sex*. New York: Dutton, 1960.

p   Henry, Jules, *Culture Against Man*. New York: Random.

p   Hernton, Calvin C., *Sex and Racism in America*. New York: Grove, 1964. A black man's frank analysis of interracial sex attitudes, but very condescending to women, especially black women.

Hollingworth, Leta S., "Social Devices for Compelling Women to Bear and Rear Children." *American Journal of Sociology*, XXII, July 1916, pp. 28-29. Notice the date.

p   Jacobs, Jane. *The Death and Life of Great American Cities*. New York: Random, 1961. See especially urbanistic implications for safety in the city and for raising children there.

Kennedy, Robert Woods, *The House and the Art of its Design*. New York: Reinhold, 1953. See chapters on the interaction of family and individual functioning and physical environment.

p   Kira, Alexander, *The Bathroom: Criteria for Design.* Ithaca: Cornell, 1966, and New York: Bantam, 1967. See his historical and psychological comments on the sexual meanings of bathroom functions and men's and women's attitudes toward them.

p a Komarovsky, Mirra, *Blue-Collar Marriage.* New York: Random, 1964.

    ———, *Women in the Modern World.* Boston, 1953. Cultural stresses on educated women are given special attention.

    Lynes, Russell, *The Domesticated Americans.* New York: Harper & Row, 1963, 1957. Popular, informative work on the evolution of the American house; always set in the social context of culture and family structure.

p   Marx, Karl, Engels, Lenin, and Stalin, *The Woman Question.* Little New World Paperback. Selections from their writings on women, the family, evolution of morals.

p   May Edgar, *The Wasted Americans.* New York: Signet, 1964. On poverty; especially chapter on poor women's desire for birth control.

p   McLuhan, H. Marshall, *The Mechanical Bride.* Boston: Beacon, 1964. Media manipulation.

p a Myrdal, Gunnar, *An American Dilemma.* New York: Harper, 1944, 1941. 2 volumes. A classic, with Appendix 5, "A Parallel to the Negro Problem" (pp. 1073-1078), devoted to the analogy between women and blacks.

    O'Neill, William, *Divorce in the Progressive Era.* New Haven: Yale, 1967. Divorce as savior of the family as an institution. See especially introduction and chapters on "The New Morality."

    Pollak, Otto, *The Criminality of Women.* Philadelphia: U. of Pennsylvania, 1950. Social conditions fostering crime among women; its hidden qualities, but great extent. Large bibliography included.

    Potter, David, *American Women and American Character.* Stetson U., 1962. See also this historian's *People of Plenty* for the effect of abundance on our culture.

p a Rainwater, Lee, Richard P. Coleman, and Gerald Handel, *Workingman's Wife: Her Personality, World, and Life*

Style. New York: Oceana, 1959. Bleak and revealing portrait of blue-collar woman's concepts of herself, her man, her world. Originally a market-research study, but actually much more.

deRham, Edith, *How Could She Do That?* New York: Clarkson Potter, 1969. On female criminality.

p   Schur, Edwin, *The Family and the Sexual Revolution.* Bloomington, Ind.: Indiana U., 1964. See especially Bettelheim, "The Case of the Kibbutz."

Sexton, Patricia Cayo. *The Feminized Male.* New York: Random, 1969. Wavering, ambivalent, ambiguous.

p a Skinner, B. F., *Walden Two.* New York: Macmillan, 1949. A utopia by the behaviorist psychologist. See child-rearing and relations between the sexes. Many of his arguments are hard to refute.

p a Taves, Isabella, *Women Alone.* New York: Funk & Wagnalls, 1968. Especially for the divorcee and the widow, but illuminates much for all women.

Thomas, William Isaac, *Sex and Society.* Chicago: U. of Chicago, 1906. The pioneering sociologist, on social determinism and individual psychology. See Viola Klein (section on PSYCHOLOGY AND PSYCHIATRY) for chapter on Thomas.

Wieth-Knudsen, K. A., *Feminism, A Sociological Study of the Woman Question From Ancient Times to the Present Day.* London: Constable, 1928. Translated from the Danish.

a   White, Lynn, *Educating Our Daughters.* 1950. Former president of Mills (who is, appropriately, an historian of the middle ages) describes the perfect "mystique" education for young women.

p a Wylie, Philip, *Generation of Vipers.* New York: Rinehart, 1942. Everything is Mom's fault; this best-seller of the '40's had tremendous popular impact.

ANTHROPOLOGY, RELIGION, PHILOSOPHY, WOMEN IN OTHER COUNTRIES

p   Bettelheim, Bruno, *Symbolic Wounds.* New York: Collier, 1962.

p   Briffault, Robert, *The Mothers: The Matriarchal Theory of Social Origins*. 1927 and abridged in Universal paperback edition. Anthropological study of women's roles.

Callahan, Sidney, *The Illusion of Eve*. New York: Sheed and Ward, 1965. A modern Catholic woman's view.

a   Dahlström, Edmund, ed., *The Changing Roles of Men and Women*. London: Duckworth, 1967. Important collection; includes a summary, in translation, of a major Scandinavian research work on the effects of sex roles, *Kvinnors Liv och Arbete* (1962).

Daly, Mary, *The Church and the Second Sex*. New York: Harper & Row, 1968. By a feminist Catholic theologian.

p a Fanon, Frantz, *The Wretched of the Earth*. New York: Grove, 1965. Colonial analogy useful for women.

p   Hall, Edward T., *The Silent Language*. New York: Premier, 1963. Nonverbal communication; see passages on inter-sex interactions.

p a Hays, H. R., *The Dangerous Sex: The Myth of Feminine Evil*. London: Putnam, 1964, and New York: Pocket, 1965. Exciting and literate historical and cross-cultural account of man's fear of women—especially of her genitals—and of how he has institutionalized his fear.

p a Leijon, Anna-Greta, *Swedish Women—Swedish Men*. Swedish Institute for Cultural Relations with Foreign Countries (Box 3306, Stockholm 3). A lively account of institutionalized and informal efforts, successes—and failures—to alter Swedish sex-role stereotypes. Many good pictures of boys and men sharing all kinds of work with girls and women.

p   Lewis, Oscar, *The Children of Sanchez*. New York: Vintage, 1961. See this and *La Vida* for revealing portraits of oppressed Latin women.

p   ———, *La Vida*. New York: Vintage, 1965.

a   Linnér, Birgitta, *Sex and Society in Sweden*. New York: Pantheon, 1967. Changing sex-roles.

a   Ludovici, L. J., *The Final Inequality*. New York: Norton, 1965. Especially good for history of religious misogyny.

Mead, Margaret, *And Keep Your Powder Dry*. New York:

Morrow, 1943. See especially competitiveness between the sexes.

p a ———, *Male and Female*. New York: Morrow, 1949, and New York: Mentor, 1955. Subtly persuasive, but finally lethal.

p a ———, *Sex and Temperament in Three Primitive Societies*. New York: Peter Smith, 1935. Culture determines the meaning of "gender."

Patai, Raphael, ed., *Women in the Modern World*. New York: Free Press, 1967. Cross-cultural comparisons.

p Sandlund, Maj-Britt, *Status of Women in Sweden*. Report to the United Nations, 1968. (Single copies available from the Swedish Embassy, Washington, D.C.)

p Tiger, Lionel, *Men in Groups*. New York: Random, 1969. Pathetic. Antidote: Hays' *The Dangerous Sex*.

PSYCHOLOGY AND PSYCHIATRY

a Bernard, Jessie, *The Sex Game*. Englewood Cliffs, N.J.: Prentice-Hall, 1968. On inter-sex communications, both verbal and nonverbal. Rambling and disappointingly ambivalent about feminism.

p Brenton, Myron, *The American Male*. New York: Coward, 1966. Effect on both sexes of doubts and rigidities about masculinity and femininity.

a Deutsch, Helene, *The Psychology of Women*. New York: Grune and Stratton, 1944. 2 volumes. To be adult, a woman must be narcissistic, masochistic, and passive.

a Flugel, J. C., *Men and Their Motives*. London, 1934. Psychology of birth control.

p a Freud, Sigmund, "Femininity." In *New Introductory Lectures on Psychoanalysis*. Trans. by James Strachey. New York: Norton, 1965.

Horney, Karen, *Feminine Psychology*. New York: Norton, 1967.

p a ———, *New Ways in Psychoanalysis*. New York: Norton, 1939. Her chapter "Feminine Psychology" gives a good rejoinder to the penis-envy theory.

Kirkpatrick, Clifford, "Inconsistency in Attitudinal Behaviour with Special Reference to Attitudes Toward Feminism." *Journal of Applied Psychology*, 1936, p. 20.

a Klein, Viola, *The Feminine Character: History of an Ideology*. New York: International Universities, 1948, 1946. The early biological and social sciences as tools for approach to defining "feminine character."

a Legman, Gershon, *The Rationale of the Dirty Joke: An Analysis of Sexual Humor*. New York: Grove, 1968. The dynamics of ambivalence as expressed in humor.

p a Lundberg, Ferdinand, and Marynia F. Farnham, *Modern Woman: The Lost Sex*. New York: Harper, 1947. Rabidly antifeminist and psychoanalytic, but it has good appendices and a good bibliography of feminist literature and individuals' thoughts. ·

a Maccoby, Eleanor, ed., *The Development of Sex Differences*. Stanford: Stanford U., 1966. Extensive bibliography; a review of the literature. Shows how badly new research is needed—new questions, new answers, new research people.

a Maslow, Abraham H., "Self-Actualizing People: A Study of Psychological Health." In *Self: Explorations in Personal Growth*, Clark E. Moustakas, ed., New York: Harper, 1956. A fruitful ideal; see observations on healthy people's perceptions of gender.

a ———, "Self-Esteem (Dominance Feeling) and Sexuality in Women." *Journal of Social Psychology*, 16, 1942, pp. 259-294. Also in deMartino (see section on REPRODUCTION AND ITS CONTROL). He stresses that these women are functioning in an abnormal, unhealthy culture.

a Money, John, ed., *Sex Research, New Developments*. New York: Holt, Rinehart, and Winston, 1965. By a leading researcher in gender-learning.

Rheingold, J. C., *The Fear of Being a Woman: A Theory of Maternal Destructiveness*. New York: Grune and Stratton, 1964.

p Ruitenbeek, Hendrik M., *The Male Myth*. New York: Dell, 1967.

Salzman, Leon, M.D., "Psychology of the Female: A New

Look." *Archives of General Psychiatry*, 17, August 1967, pp. 195-203. Distinguishes socially formed sex roles from sexuality; attacks penis-envy theory.

p a Sampson, Ronald V., *The Psychology of Power*. New York: Pantheon, 1965. Traces pattern of dominance-and-submission from its roots in the family—between men and women —to its violent international culmination: war. Uses literary history to make many points: J. S. Mill, Elizabeth Barrett Browning, etc.

p Sanford, Nevitt, ed., *The American College*. New York: Wiley, 1962. See the sections on the personality development of women as they pass through college; based on the Mellon studies at Vassar in the mid- and late '50's. (Paper edition abridged.)

a Sherman, Julia A., "Problem of Sex Differences in Space Perception and Aspects of Intellectual Functioning." *Psychological Review*. 74:4, July 1967, pp. 290-299. The apparent "inferiority" of women in analytical reasoning and in mathematics is explained in a critique of the literature and especially of Maccoby.

p Stern, Karl, *The Flight from Woman*. New York: Noonday, 1965. Polarity of sexes as reflected in the conflict between scientific/rational and intuitive/poetic knowledge. Assumes this IS a dichotomy and that it is sex-linked and inherent.

a Stoller, Robert J., M.D., *Sex and Gender: On the Development of Masculinity and Femininity*. New York: *Science*, 1968. Important research study of the contribution of sex to "gender identity" and of cross-sex aberrations.

Terman, Lewis, and C. C. Miles, *Sex and Personality: Studies in Masculinity and Femininity*. New York: McGraw-Hill, 1936. See Viola Klein, *The Feminine Character*, for chapter on this early work in psychometry.

Thompson, Helen Bradford, *The Mental Traits of Sex*. Chicago: U. of Chicago, 1903. See chapter in Viola Klein, *The Feminine Character*, on this early work in experimental psychology.

a Van Den Berg, J. H., *The Changing Nature of Man*. New York: Norton, 1961. Constantly changing individual psy-

chology of men and women, parents and children, as social settings alter them through time.

SEX AND SEXUALITY

Bergler, Edmund, and William S. Kroger, *Kinsey's Myth of Female Sexuality: The Medical Facts*. New York: Grune and Stratton, 1954. They were incensed when Kinsey reported that some women say they have multiple orgasms; Bergler and Kroger knew this meant these women were frigid!

p Bonaparte, Marie, *Female Sexuality*. New York: International Universities, 1953, and New York: Grove, 1965. Psychoanalytic; one chapter heading: "The Essential Masochism of Women."

p a Brecher, Ruth and Edward, *An Analysis of Human Sexual Response*. Boston: Little, Brown, 1966. A must. On Masters and Johnson, but very readable, unlike the original. Also includes other excellent essays, especially a 50-page history of the idea of female orgasm.

p Chartham, Robert, *Husband and Lover*. New American Library. "Sex manual": interesting and sensible despite title.

p ———, *Mainly for Wives: The Art of Sex for Women*. New American Library, 1969. His other book tells more; this one—like many of its kind—warns the woman always to be a little less active than her man.

p a Ejlersen, Mette, *"I Accuse."* London: Universal-Tandem, 1969, and New York: Award, 1969. Translated from the Danish by Marianne Kold Madsen. Outspoken Scandinavian best-seller in which a *woman* describes female sexuality and dissects male myths about it.

p a Ellis, Albert, *The American Sexual Tragedy*. New York: Twayne, 1954 (revised 1962). Includes good analyses of cultural myths about women and their behavior, especially as presented in the media.

a Etzioni, Amitai. "Sex Control, Science, and Society." *Science*, September 13, 1968, pp. 1107-1112. Speculates on social results of ability to choose babies' sex, and on the ethics of research to these kinds of ends. Depressing.

Gittelson, Natalie, "The Erotic Life of the American Wife." *Harper's Bazaar*, July 1969. Lengthy and querulous; misunderstands and puts down the women's liberation movement.

p   Gray, Madeline, *The Normal Woman*. New York: Scribner's, 1967. Author shows a dubious attitude, but includes much valuable information on the history of the medical treatment (and mistreatment) of women. Execrable bibliography.

p a Greene, Gael, *Sex and the College Girl*. 1965. Don't be misled by the Helen-Gurley-Brown-like title; the very perceptive result of conversations with many U.S. college women. See especially chapters on contraception and abortion.

Hall, Mary Harrington, "A Conversation with Masters and Johnson." *Psychology Today*, vol. 3, #2, July 1969, pp. 50-58. Good clarification of Masters and Johnson and of their work.

p   Hegeler, Inge and Sten, *An ABZ of Love*. Sensible Scandinavian view of sexuality and love.

Himelhoch, Jerome, and Sylvia F. Fava, eds., *Sexual Behavior in American Society*. New York: Norton, 1955. Critiques of Kinsey studies.

p a Kinsey, Alfred C., Wardell B. Pomeroy, Clyde E. Martin, and Paul H. Gebhard, *Sexual Behavior in the Human Female*. Philadelphia: Saunders, 1953. Still of great interest, despite the almost purely quantitative approach to sex.

p a Kronhausen, Phyllis and Eberhard, *The Sexually Responsive Female*. New York: Ballantine. Dubious title and too many "case histories," but it does present women as interested, active, and competent.

p a deMartino, Manfred F., ed., *Sexual Behavior and Personality Characteristics*. New York: Citadel, 1963, and New York: Grove, 1966. A collection of articles edited by a Maslowian; includes an excellent section "Effect of Self-Esteem . . . on Sexual Behavior," and Albert Ellis' "Is the Vaginal Orgasm a Myth?"

a Masters, William H., M.D., and Virginia Johnson, *Human Sexual Response*. Boston: Little, Brown, 1966. Language so medical you may forget why you started reading; try the Brechers' paperback first—or instead. A milestone, nevertheless.

p a Montagu, Ashley, *The Natural Superiority of Women*, rev. ed. New York: Collier-Macmillan, 1968. Especially see parts describing women's constitutional strength.

p a Robinson, Marie N., M.D., *The Power of Sexual Surrender*. Garden City, N.Y.: Doubleday, 1959. Handbook for the Compleat Slave, a la Deutsch.

p Stearn, Jess, *The Grapevine*. New York: Macfadden, 1965. Popular book on lesbianism; many insights into question of women's role generally.

p a Thurber, James, and E. B. White, *Is Sex Necessary?* (1929) New York: Dell, 1964. Many good things for feminists in this classic put-on of ponderous psychoanalytic sex books.

p Young, Wayland, *Eros Denied: Sex in Western Society*. New York: Grove.

REPRODUCTION AND ITS CONTROL

Association for the Study of Abortion (ASA), 120 West 57 Street, New York, New York 10019. Bibliography/reprint list. Over three dozen reprints available at 10¢ apiece (see below for especially good ones). Also ask for their current newsletter.

Bates, Jerome E., and Edward S. Zawadzki, M.D., *Criminal Abortion: A Study in Medical Sociology*. Springfield, Ill.: Thomas, 1964. Terrible attitude; but good facts and a 32-page bibliography.

p California Conference on Abortion (Santa Barbara, February 10-11, 1968). *Abortion Law Reform*. Ninety pages of speeches and symposia on means of changing the law. See speeches by Hardin, Studhalter, Ash, Phelan. ($2.00 from CCA, Box 526, Ross, California 94957.)

Cisler, Lucinda, "Abortion Law Repeal (sort of): a Warning to Women." 1970. A feminist analysis of recent near-

repeal legislation and court decisions, and of why women—
and men—must work for true repeal. 15¢ from New
Yorkers for Abortion Law Repeal, P.O. Box 240, New
York, New York 10024.

p a Day, Lincoln H., and Alice Taylor Day, *Too Many Americans: Tomorrow's Issue.* Boston: Houghton Mifflin, 1964.
Stabilizing our population. See parts on the relation between
attitudes toward this issue and toward "women's role."

p Dick-Read, Grantly, M.D., *Childbirth Without Fear: The
Principles and Practices of Natural Childbirth.* (1944) New
York: Dell, 1962. By famous proponent of the method;
good also for its history of attitudes toward labor pains
and birth.

p a Doctor X., *Doctor X, The Abortionist.* As told to Lucy Freeman. Garden City, N.Y.: Doubleday, 1962. Autobiography
of a still-active East Coast abortion specialist, an M.D.
Notice his attitudes to the women who come to him.

Farber, Seymour, and Roger H. L. Wilson, eds., *The Challenge to Women.* New York: Basic, 1966. Focuses on relation between women's roles and family-size preferences.
Good essays by Merriam, Komarovsky, Ethel Albert,
Dorothy Lee.

p a Gebhard, Paul H., Wardell B. Pomeroy, Clyde Martin, and
Cornelia Christenson, *Pregnancy, Birth and Abortion.*
New York: Hoeber (Harper), 1958. A Kinsey Institute
report; many tables.

Graham, Harvey. *Eternal Eve: The History of Gynecology
and Obstetrics.* Garden City, N.Y.: Doubleday, 1951.

a Hardin, Garrett, "Abortion—or Compulsory Pregnancy?"
Journal of Marriage and the Family. XXX: 2, May 1968.
Eloquent reverse phrasing of the usual question, likening
forced childbearing to rape and showing women's absolute
right to decision. (Reprint: 10¢ from ASA.)

a ———, "The History and Future of Birth Control." *Perspec-
tives in Biology and Medicine.* 10:1, Autumn 1966. More
of Hardin's always-provocative thoughts on contraception
and abortion.

p a Havemann, Ernest K., *Birth Control: A Special Time-Life Re-*

port. New York: Time-Life, 1967. Excellent text and pictures on genetics, embryology; useful facts, doubtful attitudes.

Himes, Norman A., *A Medical History of Contraception.* Baltimore, 1936, and (revised) New York: Gamut, 1963. Exhaustive and fascinating account, from 1850 B.C. to 1962 A.D.

p   International Conference on Abortion, Proceedings (Fall 1967), *The Terrible Choice: The Abortion Dilemma.* New York: Bantam, 1968. A terrible, maudlin, and inaccurate book, funded by Kennedy Foundation money and heavily biased against the voices and rights of women. Even the meager bibliography is bigoted—a sign of fear.

p   Karmel, Marjorie, *Thank You, Dr. Lamaze.* Philadelphia: Lippincott, 1959. A woman's account of the Lamaze method of "prepared childbirth."

p a   Lader, Lawrence, *Abortion.* Indianapolis: Bobbs-Merrill, 1966, and Boston: Beacon. Best general work to date; readable.

Lasagna, Louis, M.D., *Life, Death, and the Doctor.* New York: Knopf, 1968. Especially sections on the pill, the loop, and abortion.

a   Lee, Nancy Howell, *The Search for an Abortionist.* Chicago: U. of Chicago, 1969. Paths of communication in the search; based on a Harvard dissertation.

Moskin, J. Robert, "The New Contraceptive Society." *Look.* February 4, 1969, pp. 50-53. Very good summary of the findings of Hans Zetterberg's new study *On Sexual Life in Sweden.* Changed attitudes to sex, marriage, sex roles, etc.

p   National Observer, *The Pill and Its Impact.* National Observer Newsbook, 1966. Many subtle observations, especially on pill's effect on power relations between the sexes.

p a   Neubardt, Selig, M.D., *A Concept of Contraception.* New York: Trident, 1967. (Reprinted as *Contraception*). Very sensible and down-to-earth explanation of why different methods—abortion included—suit different people; good psychological insights.

a   Osofsky, Howard, M.D., *The Pregnant Teenager.* Springfield, Ill.: Thomas, 1968. By a Feminist Ob-Gyn.

p a Petersen, William, *The Politics of Population.* Garden City, N.Y.: Doubleday, 1964. Especially "59 Million Babies"; "Malthusian Theory: a Commentary and Critique"; "Marx versus Malthus: the Symbols and the Men"; "Notes on the Socialist Position on Birth Control."

p a Phelan, Lana Clarke, and Patricia T. Maginnis, *The Abortion Handbook for Responsible Women.* Contact Books, 1969. ($3.00 from Contact Books, Inc., 6340 Coldwater Canyon, North Hollywood, California.) By two of the most active women in the abortion movement: our problem as it really is, and how to survive it in a "retarded culture." Among the chapter headings: "Qualifying for Rape: Plain Old Rape, Miscegenous Rape, Incest"; "How to Avoid a Neurotic Physician"; "Instant Psychoses for Pregnant Women"; "Expert Manic-Depression Takes Practice."

p a Rainwater, Lee, and Karol Weinstein, *And the Poor Get Children.* Chicago: Quadrangle, 1960. Working- and lower-class contraceptive and sexual attitudes and practices, in relation to various modes of marital power structures.

a ———, *et al., Family Design: Marital Sexuality, Family Size, and Contraception.* Chicago: Aldine, 1965. Similar to earlier book, but compares middle- and lower-class couples. Many subtle insights into sex/power relations. Omits abortion!

a Rossi, Alice, "Abortion and Social Change." *Dissent.* July-August 1969, pp. 338-346. See especially her thoughts on the politics of repeal vs. "reform."

a Schenk, Roy U., "Let's Think About Abortion." *The Catholic World*, 207:1237, April 1968. Shows how capacity of any cell of an organism to become another such organism ("totipotence") destroys the fetuses-are-unique argument. (10¢ from ASA.)

p Vincent, Clark, *Unmarried Mothers*, New York: Free Press, 1961. Studies premarital sex and unwed mothers of all social classes.

CLOTHES

p Bender, Marylin, *The Beautiful People.* New York: Coward, 1967. Interesting in the way it puts the fashion mania into a broader social context than is usual. Good implicit material on women.

a Hawes, Elizabeth, *Fashion Is Spinach*. New York: Random, 1938. Sense about clothes, from a woman designer.

a ———, *It's Still Spinach*. Boston: Little, Brown, 1954. More good sense, and a plea for greater freedom in dress.

Riegel, R., "Women's Clothes and Women's Rights." *American Quarterly*, Autumn 1963.

Rudofsky, Bernard, *Are Clothes Modern? An Essay on Contemporary Apparel*. Chicago: Theobald, 1947. An architect's argument for more rational clothing. See especially section on bound feet and other sadistic customs.

Veblen, Thorstein, "The Economic Theory of Women's Dress." *Popular Science Monthly*, XLVI, November 1894.

BIOGRAPHY AND AUTOBIOGRAPHY

Anderson, Mary, *Woman At Work*. Minneapolis: U. of Minnesota, 1951. Autobiography of Women's Bureau head and story of the Bureau.

p deBeauvoir, Simone, *Memoirs of a Dutiful Daughter*.

Besant, Annie, *An Autobiography*. London: Fisher Unwin, 1893. The theosophist and birth-control pioneer.

Dell, Floyd, *Women As World Builders: Studies In Modern Feminism*. Chicago, 1913. Biographies of Pankhurst, Gilman, Jane Addams, Olive Schreiner, Isadora Duncan, Beatrice Webb, Emma Goldman, Margaret D. Robins, Ellen Key, Dora Marsden.

p Drinnon, Richard, *Rebel in Paradise: A Biography of Emma Goldman*. Chicago: U. of Chicago, 1961. (Also in paperback—Boston: Beacon Press, 1970.)

Duncan, Isadora, *My Life*. New York: Award, 1966. The pioneering American dancer's life in America, Europe, early Soviet Russia.

Fauset, Arthur, *Sojourner Truth, God's Faithful Pilgrim*. 1938. The powerful woman abolitionist who had been a slave.

Gilman, Charlotte Perkins, *The Living of Charlotte Perkins Gilman*. 1935.

Goldman, Emma, *Living My Life*. 2 volumes.

Hays, Elinor Rice, *Morning Star, A Biography of Lucy Stone*. New York, 1961.

Ibarruri, Dolores, *They Will Not Pass: The Autobiography of La Pasionaria*. International Pubs., 1966. Spanish Civil War leader known across Europe for her eloquence.

p   deJesus, Carolina Maria, *Child of the Dark*. New York: Signet. Autobiography of an amazing São Paulo *favela* woman and her courage.

Lader, Lawrence, *The Margaret Sanger Story, and the Fight for Birth Control*. Garden City, N.Y.: Doubleday, 1955. Moving and little-known story of a key figure in women's liberation.

Lerner, Gerda, *The Grimké Sisters from South Carolina: Rebels Against Slavery*. Houghton Mifflin, 1967. Excellent study of early abolitionist/suffragist sisters.

Lutz, Alma, *Created Equal*. 1940. Elizabeth Cady Stanton.

———, Emma Willard, *Pioneer Educator of American Women*. 1964.

———, *Susan B. Anthony*. Boston: Beacon, 1959.

Marder, Herbert, *Feminism and Art: A Study of Virginia Woolf*. Chicago: U. of Chicago, 1968.

p   McCarthy, Mary, *Memories of a Catholic Girlhood*. New York: Harcourt, Brace & World, 1957.

Pankhurst, Emmeline, *My Own Story*. London: Eveleigh Nash, 1914. One of a family of leading British feminists.

Richardson, Dorothy, *Pilgrimage*. London: Dent, 1967. 4 volumes. Novelist's feminist autobiography.

Sanger, Margaret, *An Autobiography*. 1939. Story of the great feminist birth-control crusader.

Wardle, Ralph, *Mary Wollstonecraft: A Critical Biography*. Lawrence, Kans.: U. of Kansas, 1951.

LITERATURE AND LITERARY CRITICISM

Aldridge, John W., *In Search of Heresy: American Literature in an Age of Conformity*. Port Washington, N.Y.: Kennikat, 1956. One section mourns the lack of realistic women in American fiction.

p   Aristophanes, *Lysistrata*. Dudley Fitts translation.

p   deBeauvoir, Simone, *The Mandarins*.

Brophy, Brigid, *Don't Never Forget: Collected Views and Reviews*. New York: Holt, 1966. Tart literary essays; see especially her observations on women writers and women in fiction.

p   Colebrook, Joan, *The Cross of Lassitude*. New York: Knopf, 1967. Insightful look at some young "delinquent" women, in prison and out.

p   *Dickinson*, Emily. Collected works.

p   Dryer, Bernard V., *The Torch Bearers*. New York: Simon & Schuster, 1967. Rococo novel about contraception, Castro, abortion, Catholicism, Nazism; but its facts are straight.

Ellmann, Mary, *Thinking About Women*. New York: Harcourt, Brace & World, 1968. Feminist literary criticism. Subtle, incisive, and devastatingly funny. See how she dissects Mailer *et al*.

Farrar, Rowena, *A Wondrous Moment Then*. New York: Holt, Rinehart & Winston, 1968. Novel of World War I Nashville, the women's lives, how the war changed them, and the fight for ratification of the women's suffrage amendment.

p   Fiedler, Leslie, *Love and Death in the American Novel*. Revised ed., New York: Dell, 1967. One thing he considers is the dearth of live women in American literature, and some reasons for the lack.

p   Ibsen, Henrik, *A Doll's House*. The nineteenth-century wife withdraws consent to oppression.

p   Kaufmann, Sue, *Diary of a Mad Housewife*. New York: Random, 1967. Includes excruciating descriptions of a woman's attempts at salvation through creative housewifery.

p   Lessing, Doris, *The Golden Notebook*. New York: Ballantine, 1968. Autobiographical; a woman alone with her child in postwar London. Her experiences with the Left; her attempts at independence.

p   Lewis, Sinclair, *Main Street*. Carol Kennicott: classic portrait
       of a midwestern woman of the 'twenties.

p   Mailer, Norman. "The Time of Her Time." In *Advertise-
       ments for Myself*. Mailer's most charming evocation of
       his myth of "good" (sado-masochistic) sex.

p   McCarthy, Mary, "The Man in the Brooks Brothers Shirt."
       In *The Company She Keeps*. New York: Dell, 1955.
       Portrayal of impervious male vanity.

p   Merriam, Eve, *The Double Bed from the Feminine Side*,
       New York: Marzani and Munsell, 1958. Poems.

p   Millay, Edna St. Vincent, Collected poetry.

p   Nabokov, Vladimir, *Lolita*. Medallion, 1959. A *real* child-
       woman: the common fantasy brought to its logical con-
       clusion.

p   Olsen, Tillie, *Tell Me a Riddle*. Short stories.

       O'Neill, Eugene, *Abortion* (A Play in One Act). In *Lost
       Plays of Eugene O'Neill*. New York: New Fathoms,
       1950, pp. 11-34.

p   Paley, Grace, *The Little Disturbances of Man*. New York:
       Viking, 1968. Shrewd and funny portrayals of men and
       women together.

p   Parker, Dorothy. Collected short stories and poetry.

       Riley, Madeleine, *Brought to Bed*. New York: Barnes, 1968.
       Lively commentary on childbirth, sex preferences, ob-
       stetrics, infanticide, abortion, etc. as seen by English
       novelists since the 18th century.

p   Rimmer, Robert, *Proposition 31*. 1968. Deals with *some*
       aspects of group or "corporate" marriage.

p   Sartre, Jean-Paul, *Saint Genet*. Pathology of oppression.
       Frequent analogies with women, and references to
       Beauvoir.

p   Sophocles, *Elektra*.

       Stead, Christina, *The Man Who Loved Children*. New York:
       Holt, Rinehart & Winston, 1965. Excruciating portrait of a
       family in pre-war Washington: the bullying child-father
       is a negative archetype, the mother one awful extreme to
       which a woman can be brought.

Thomson, P. *The Victorian Heroine, A Changing Ideal, 1837-1873.* New York: Oxford U., 1956.

Tolstoy, Leo, *Anna Karenina.*

p   Wertenbaker, Lael Tucker, *The Afternoon Women.* 1966. Novel on abortion, perhaps based partly on the life of the late, famous Dr. Robert Spencer, of Ashland, Pennsylvania.

WOMEN AND SOCIALISM

Balabanoff, Angelina, *Impressions of Lenin.* Trans. by Isotta Cesari. Ann Arbor: U. of Michigan, 1964.

Bebel, August. *Women and Socialism.* 1891.

p   *Chinese Women in the Great Leap Forward.* Peking: Foreign Language Press, 1960. (Available from China Press and Periodicals, 2929 24 Street, San Francisco, California 94110.)

Flynn, Elizabeth Gurley, *Women's Place in the Fight for a Better World.* New Century, 1947.

Herreshoff, David, *American Disciples of Marx: From the Age of Jackson to the Progressive Era.* Detroit: Wayne State U., 1967.

Landy, Avrom, *Marxism and the Woman Question.* Toronto: Progress Publishing, 1943.

Lenin, V. I., *The Emancipation of Women.*

Schlesinger, Rudolf, *Changing Attitudes in Soviet Russia: The Family.* Humanities, 1949. Reports and feminist papers from just post-1917 and later.

Shaw, George Bernard, *The Intelligent Woman's Guide to Socialism.* A Fabian view.

Zetkin, Klara, *Lenin on the Woman Question.* International Publishers.

SOME WRITINGS OF AND ABOUT
TODAY'S WOMEN'S MOVEMENT

Aphra. A feminist literary journal. ($1.00 a copy or $3.50 for 4-issue subscription, from *Aphra*, Box 322, Springtown, Pennsylvania 18081). Issue 1. Includes Myrna Lamb's play on abortion, "But What Have You Done for Me Lately?"

Baumgold, Julie, "You've Come a Long Way, Baby." *New York.* June 9, 1969, pp. 26-32. A pitiful caricature of the movement and of the spring 1969 Boston regional women's liberation conference.

Bem, Sandra L. and Daryl J., "Case Study of a Nonconscious Ideology: Training the Woman to Know Her Place." In D. J. Bem, ed., *Beliefs, Attitudes, and Human Affairs.* Belmont, California; Brooks/Cole, 1970.

Benston, Margaret, "The Political Economy of Women's Liberation." *Monthly Review.* September 1969.

Brown, Judith, and Beverly Jones, *Toward a Female Liberation Movement.* 40 pages. The classic "Florida Paper." 25¢ from New England Free Press. (q.v.)

Cade, Toni, ed., *Anthology on Black Women.* New York: New American Library, 1970.

Cisler, Lucinda. "Unfinished Business: Birth Control and Women's Liberation." Winter 1970. (25¢ or 10 for $2 from Lucinda Cisler, 102 West 80 Street, New York, New York 10024.)

Firestone, Shulamith, *The Dialectic of Sex: The Case for Feminist Revolution.* New York: Morrow, 1970.

Freeman, Jo, "The New Feminists." *Nation,* 208:8, February 24, 1969, pp. 241-244.

Gornick, Vivian, and Barbara K. Moran, eds., *Fifty-One Percent: The Case for Women's Liberation.* New York: Basic, 1971.

Hayden, Casey, *et al.,* "Sex and Caste." *Liberation.* Part I, April 1966, II, December 1966. An early exchange about women and contemporary radical movements.

Hinckle, Warren and Marianne, "A History of the Rise of the Unusual Movement for Women Power in the United States 1961-1968." *Ramparts,* February 1968, pp. 22-31. All parts of the women's movement gave this patronizing, aren't-they-cute? article the reception it deserved. Still, here it is . . . in the know-your-enemy category.

"Is a Women's Revolution Really Possible? Yes (Leslie Aldridge Westoff); No (John Gagnon and William Simon)." *McCall's,* October 1969, pp. 76ff. Somebody at McCall's must

must have switched the "yes" and "no" headlines on these articles: "no" = "yes."

A Journal of Female Liberation. ("No More Fun and Games.") Theoretical and literary writings. $1.00, from Female Liberation, 371 Somerville Ave., Somerville, Massachusetts 02143.)

League for Socialist Action (Canada), *The Status of Women in Canada.* (15¢ from Vanguard Books, 1208 Granville St., Vancouver, B.C., Canada.)

Limpus, Laurel, "Liberation of Women: Sexual Repression and the Family." *This Magazine Is About Schools,* Spring 1969.

Millett, Kate, "Sexual Politics in Miller, Mailer, and Genet." *New American Review,* #7, August 1969. First chapter of *Sexual Politics* (New York: Doubleday, 1970); analyzes sexual-intercourse passages in the works of three authors.

Mitchell, Juliet, "The Longest Revolution." *New Left Review,* 40, November-December 1966. Study showing that the role of women has never been dealt with properly throughout the history of socialist movements. (Reprint: 20¢+ from NEFP.)

p   Morgan, Robin, ed., *Sisterhood Is Powerful.* New York: Random, 1970. Extensive compendium of writings by women's liberation people: psychology, education, sexuality, birth control, etc.

Murray, Pauli, "The Negro Woman in the Quest for Equality." *The Acorn* (Lambda Kappa Mu Sorority), June 1964.

National Organization for Women (NOW). (Membership and other information from NOW National Office, Room 503, 1525 E. 33rd St., Chicago, Ill. 60615.)

New England Free Press, 791 Tremont Street, Boston, Massachusetts 02118. Source for many pieces of women's movement literature; write for their complete current literature list.

Notes (from the Second Year): Radical Feminism. May 1970. 128 pages. Includes manifestoes of Redstockings, New York Radical Feminists, and The Feminists, and articles by Ti-Grace Atkinson, Firestone, Anne Koedt ("The Myth of the Vaginal Orgasm"), Millett, Willis, et al. $1.50 from

Notes, P.O. Box AA, Old Chelsea Station, New York, New York 10013.

"On the Liberation of Women." Special issue of *Motive*, XXIX:6 and 7, March-April 1969. Superb graphics and poetry. Articles by Cynthia Ozick, Marlene Dixon, Susan Sutheim, Marilyn Salzman Webb, Del Martin and Phyllis Lyon, Linda Seese, Andy Hawley, WITCH, Naomi Weisstein, *et al.* It was so good that *Motive* nearly got shut down. ($1.00, or 10 for $8.00, from *Motive*, P.O. Box 871, Nashville, Tennessee 37202.)

p   Reed, Evelyn, *Problems of Women's Liberation: A Marxist Approach*. New York: Pathfinder, 1969. A 63-page collection of articles. ($1.00 from Pathfinder Press, 873 Broadway, New York, New York 10003.)

Steinem, Gloria, "After Black Power, Women's Liberation." *New York*. April 7, 1969, pp. 8-10. Catches quite well the nuances of WL generally and of New York City groups in particular.

Tanner, Leslie B., ed., *The Women's Liberation Movement*. New York: New American Library, 1971.

Weisstein, Naomi, "Kinder, Küche, Kirche as Scientific Law: Psychology Constructs the Female." *Motive*, March-April 1969 (q.v.). A different, condensed version appears in *Psychology Today*, October 1969, pp. 20ff., under the title "Woman as Nigger."

Willis, Ellen, "Up from Radicalism: a Feminist Journal." In US #2, October 1969, pp. 102-122.

————, "Whatever Happened to Women? Nothing. That's the Trouble." *Mademoiselle*. September 1969.

Women: A Journal of Liberation. (4-issue subscription—one year—$5.00 from *Women*, 3011 Guilford Avenue, Baltimore, Maryland 21218.)

Women's Equity Action League (WEAL). (Membership and other information from Nancy Dowding, President, 22414 Fairlawn Circle, Fairview Park, Ohio 44126.)